CCCC

Bibliography of Composition and Rhetoric

1987

Erika Lindemann
Managing Editor

Sandra Monroe
Terri O'Quin
Associate Editors

Conference on College Composition and Communication

Southern Illinois University Press
Carbondale and Edwardsville

ISSN 1046–0675
ISBN 0-8093-1647-1
ISBN 0-8093-1648-x (pbk.)

The paper used in this publication meets the minimum requirements of American National Standard for Information Sciences—Permanence of Paper for Printed Library Materials, ANSI Z39.48-1984. ∞

Contents

Entries that discuss concepts or hypotheses, that explain how people learn, that describe fields or
general methodologies, that examine historical developments, that review previous explanations
of a subject, or that advance conclusions drawn from empirical evidence.

3   Teacher Education, Administration, and Social Roles   87

Entries that discuss the education of teachers, that examine administrative or personnel policies and procedures, that describe services supporting classroom instruction, or that treat relations between educational institutions and the larger society.

4   Curriculum   103

Entries that explain teaching methods, that describe courses or units of instruction, or that combine theory with practice in a specific subject area or skill.

5   Testing, Measurement, and Evaluation   152

Entries that examine ways to assess students' work, that describe statistical or analytical techniques to measure or evaluate teaching and learning, or that discuss appropriate criteria for and uses of tests, scales, or other instruments.

Preface

Erika Lindemann

The CCCC Bibliography of Composition and Rhetoric, published by the Conference on College Composition and Communication, offers teachers and researchers an annual classified listing of scholarship on written English and its teaching. This volume cites 1813 titles that, with few exceptions, were published during the 1987 calendar year. The bibliography lists each work only once, but it descriptively annotates all citations, cross-references them when appropriate, and indexes all authors and editors. A group of 166 contributing bibliographers, whose names appear on pages xi to xii, prepared the citations and annotations for all entries appearing in this volume. As the first volume in an annual series, *The CCCC Bibliography* continues work begun by *The Longman Bibliography of Composition and Rhetoric*, which appeared in two volumes annotating scholarship published from 1984 through 1986. However, *The Longman Bibliography* and *The CCCC Bibliography* differ in scope. Whereas *The Longman Bibliography* attempts a comprehensive listing of scholarship on written English and its teaching, kindergarten through graduate school, *The CCCC Bibliogra-phy* focuses on work of interest to teachers and researchers in colleges and universities.

SCOPE OF THE BIBLIOGRAPHY

The CCCC Bibliography includes works that treat written communication (whether the writing people do is in English or some other language), the processes whereby human beings compose and understand written messages, and methods of teaching people to communicate effectively in writing. The bibliography lists entries in five major categories (see the Contents for a fuller description of these categories):

Section 1. Bibliographies and Checklists
Section 2. Theory and Research
Section 3. Teacher Education, Administration, Social Roles
Section 4. Curriculum
Section 5. Testing, Measurement, and Evaluation

The bibliography makes few restrictions on the format, medium, or purpose of the works it includes, so long as the subject of the work falls into one of the five categories described in the preceding paragraph. It lists only published works: books, articles, monographs, published collections (of essays, conference presentations, or working papers), bibliographies and other reference works, films, microforms, videotapes, and sound recordings. It includes citations for unpublished doctoral dissertations appearing in *Dissertation Abstracts International*. It also includes review articles that discuss several works, define movements or trends, or survey an individual's contribution to the discipline. It excludes masters theses, textbooks, computer software, book reviews, and works written in a language other than English.

SOURCES

The CCCC Bibliography cites works from four major sources.

Periodicals. Journals publishing articles on composition and its teaching are one source. Each journal is identified by an abbreviation; an alphabetical list of Journal Abbreviations appears on page xiii. With few exceptions, the contributing bibliographers preparing entries for journal articles examined the material first hand.

Publishers. A second source of materials are commercial publishers and university presses. These publishers, whose participation in the bibliography project is voluntary, provided contributing bibliographers with written information necessary to preparing entries for this volume. By and large, contributing bibliographers were unable to examine these materials first hand.

This volume also includes scholarly essay collections, books that bring together essays, articles, or papers by several authors. The bibliography annotates these collections, but does not annotate each essay. Unless the annotation for a collection says otherwise, all authors contributing to the collection are listed in the Author Index.

Dissertation Abstracts International (DAI). *DAI* represents a third source of citations. Not all degree granting institutions list their unpublished doctoral dissertations in *DAI*, and as a rule, the contributing bibliographers have not examined these dissertations first hand. The citations in this volume serve only to direct readers to abstracts in *DAI*. Users will want to consult the *DAI* abstracts for additional information, including who supervised the degree candidate's work and which institution granted the degree.

Resources in Education (RIE). A fourth source of materials in *The CCCC Bibliography* is the Educational Resources Information Center (ERIC), a federally funded document retrieval system coordinated by sixteen clearinghouses.

ERIC indexes its materials in two reference works. Journal articles appear in *Cumulative Index to Journals in Education* (CIJE). *Resources in Education* (RIE), on the other hand, indexes documents in the ERIC microfiche collection, which is available in 2600 regional libraries or directly from ERIC. These documents, frequently published elsewhere, include government documents, research and project reports, bibliographies, and conference papers. Documents indexed in *RIE* receive a six-digit "ED" number (e.g., ERIC ED 269 701) and are cross-referenced under various subject headings or "descriptors."

Some documents may be listed in *RIE*, and available in ERIC, several years after they were written. For convenience and to ensure comprehensiveness, *The CCCC Bibliography* reports ERIC documents cited in *RIE* during the years covered in the current volume; that is, this volume cites ERIC documents listed in *RIE* in 1987, even though the works themselves may have an earlier "date of publication." Also as a convenience, each ERIC entry includes the six-digit "ED" number.

Contributing bibliographers working with ERIC materials have developed the following criteria for determining what documents to include in this volume:

Substantiveness. Substantive documents of general value to college composition teachers and researchers are included. Representative publications are curriculum guides, federal government final reports, and technical reports from various publication series, such as those published, for example, by the University of Illinois Center for the Study of Reading and the recently established Centers for the Study of Writing.

Relevance. Documents that seem to represent concerns of high interest to researchers are included. The topics of functional literacy, computer-assisted instruction, and revision, for example, represent concerns of greater relevance than the teaching of handwriting.

Inclusiveness. All papers on composition and rhetoric available in ERIC and delivered at the annual meetings of the Conference on College Composition and Communication (CCCC) and the National Council of Teachers of English (NCTE—Fall and Spring conventions) are included. Papers delivered at other regional and national meetings—for example, meetings of the American Educational Research Association (AERA), the International Reading Association (IRA), and the Modern Language Association (MLA)—are selected for inclusion on the basis of their substantiveness and relevance.

Reference value. Items for which the ERIC microfiche system might provide unique access are included. Representative of entries meeting this criterion would be books or collections of articles no longer available from their original publishers.

Alternate access. Many professional organizations regularly make copies of book and monograph publications available as ERIC microfiche. And many papers presented as reports or conference talks and available in ERIC are later published as monographs or as articles in journals. When such information is available, the entry in this volume will include ERIC ED numbers to indicate an alternate source of access to the document. However, users of this volume should keep in mind that, although a book in ERIC reflects the exact contents of the published work, an article in ERIC is a manuscript that may see substantial revision before it is published.

The following criteria determine which items cited in RIE are excluded from this volume:

Communication theory. ERIC documents broadly concerned with human communication or with language study in general, rather than with college composition and rhetoric, are routinely excluded.

Local interest. ERIC documents concerned with composition and rhetoric but judged to be primarily of local interest are excluded. For example, this volume omits annual evaluation reports of writing programs in local schools.

Availability. Publications of commercial publishers and other organizations that are listed in *RIE* and assigned an ERIC ED number but are not available through the ERIC microfiche system are omitted.

Users of *The CCCC Bibliography* may wish to supplement this resource by consulting *RIE* or various computer-assisted retrieval systems that access ERIC documents. Copies of most documents indexed in *RIE* can be purchased in paper or microform from the ERIC system. ERIC clearinghouses also make available free or inexpensive guides to special topics of interest to rhetoric and composition teachers and researchers. Order forms and current addresses for these clearinghouses appear at the back of each monthly issue of *RIE*.

A few entries in this volume show publication dates earlier than 1987. By and large, these materials have two sources. They represent articles published in 1987 but in journals showing 1986 volume and issue numbers, or materials accessioned by ERIC Clearinghouses in 1987 but originally published earlier.

Authors, publishers, and editors may send offprints of articles, copies of books and journals, or microforms to me for possible inclusion in *The CCCC Bibliography*; however, I will be unable to return these materials.

The items listed in the annual bibliography are not housed in any single location or owned by any single individual. *The CCCC Bibliography* lists and describes these materials but does not provide users of the bibliography any additional means of retrieving them. However, users of this volume will find librarians extremely helpful in finding copies of particular works to examine firsthand. Some materials may be available through interlibrary loan, OCLC and on-line catalogues, ERIC and other information retrieval systems, or in state and university libraries. To locate materials cited in this volume, ask your librarian to help you.

CONTRIBUTING BIBLIOGRAPHERS

The reliability and usefulness of *The CCCC Bibliography*'s annual volumes depend primarily on a large group of contributing bibliographers, listed on pages xi to xii. Contributing bibliographers accept responsibility for compiling accurate entries in their areas of expertise, for preparing brief, descriptive annotations for each entry, for determining where each entry will appear within one of the five sections of the bibliography, for cross-referencing entries when appropriate, and for submitting completed entries by a specified deadline.

To ensure consistency, contributing bibliographers receive a *Handbook for Contributing Bibliographers* to guide them in their work and fill out a printed form for each entry. Contributing bibliographers agree to serve a three-year term and, thereafter, may request reappointment for another two-year term. In return for their valuable service to the profession, they receive a copy of each annual volume they have helped to prepare. Graduate students, teachers, researchers, or other individuals who wish to become contributing bibliographers may write to me.

ANNOTATIONS

Annotations accompany all entries in this volume. They describe the document's contents and are intended to help users determine the document's usefulness. Annotations are brief: up to fifty words for books and up to twenty-five words for all other documents. Insofar as the English language allows, annotations are also meant to be descriptive, not evaluative. They explain what the work is about but leave readers free to judge for themselves the work's merits. Most annotations fall into one of three categories: they present the document's thesis, main

argument, or major research finding; they describe the work's major organizational divisions; or they indicate the purpose or scope of the work.

CROSS-REFERENCES

This volume lists the citation and annotation for each document only once, in one of the five major sections of the bibliography. Every entry, however, receives an "entry number" so that cross-references to other sections are possible. Cross-references are necessary because much scholarship in composition and rhetoric is interdisciplinary. Cross-references appear as a listing of entry numbers preceded by "See also," found at the end of each subsection of the bibliography.

ACKNOWLEDGMENTS

A publication of this scope depends on many people, especially those who offer advice, encouragement, and criticism during its planning and preparation. I am grateful to David Bartholomae, Jack Selzer, Andrea Lunsford, the CCCC Executive Committee, and other members of the profession whose confidence in this project have made it possible. The contributing bibliographers also deserve thanks for their significant efforts, work often made troublesome because deadlines were demanding and some materials difficult to locate. The Miami University Center for Writing and the Department of English at the University of North Carolina—Chapel Hill have offered generous and welcome financial support. For their invaluable editorial assistance, I am indebted to Sandra Monroe, Terri O'Quin, and Mary Beth Harding. Larry Mason provided important technical help in computer programming. Finally, my thanks to Kenney Withers of Southern Illinois University Press not only for his sound editorial advice but also for his extraordinary commitment to publishing works important to the profession.

Contributing Bibliographers

Jim Addison
Clara Alexander
Ken Autry
David Bartholomae
Walter Beale
Larry Beason
Richard Behm
Joye Pettigrew Berman
Virginia A. Book
Kate Boyes
Ann K. Brandt
Linda Brant
Jody Brown
Stuart C. Brown
Mary Louise Buley-Meissner
Barbara Cambridge
Iris Chapman
Gregory Clark
John Clifford
Joseph J. Colavito
Robin B. Cook
Susan Currier
Rick Cypert
Donald A. Daiker
Thomas E. Dasher

Kenneth W. Davis
Susan S. Davis
Paige Dayton
Bonnie Devet
Judith Dobler
William M. Dodd
Angela G. Dorenkamp
J. Daniel Eilola
Paul Eschholz
Marisa Esposito
Timothy J. Evans
Helen V. Fairbanks
Sara Farris
Linda Ferreira-Buckley
Sandra Squire Fluck
Janis Forman
William Forssburg
Tim R. Fountaine
Richard Fulkerson
Patricia Goubil Gambrell
Ellen F. Gardiner
Dennis Gendron
Joan I. Glazer
Gwendolyn Gong
Kay Gore

Mary Lou V. H. Greenfield
Julie A. Greer
C. W. Griffin
Marsha Groff
Nedra C. Grogan
Susan Guitar
Evonne Kay Halasek
Anne-Marie Hall
Jeanne W. Halpern
Kathy Haney
Jim Hanlon
Tori Haring-Smith
Myrna Harrienger
Elizabeth Harris
Jeanette Harris
Sarah E. Harrold
Patrick Hartwell
Janice Hays
John F. Heyda
Dixie Elise Hickman
Betsy Hilbert
Deborah H. Holdstein
Sylvia A. Holladay
C. Mark Hurlbert
Janie Hydrick

Zita Ingham
Jack Jobst
Kenneth Kantor
Patricia P. Kelly
Joyce Kinkead
James Kinney
Alexandra R. Krapels
Elizabeth Larsen
Janice M. Lauer
Steven Lynn
Sandra Macleod
Kate Mangelsdorf
James D. Marshall
Stefan E. Martin
Beryl C. Martinson
Rhoda Maxwell
Donald A. McAndrew
Ben W. McClelland
Lisa J. McClure
Ilona McGuiness
Geraldine McNenny
Stephen Merrill
Vincent P. Mikkelsen
Corinne L. Miller
Susan Miller
Lucy Morcock Milner
Walter S. Minot
Nancye Mitchell
Max Morenberg
Joseph M. Moxley
Neil Nakadate

William F. Naufftus
Virginia Nees-Hatlen
Marie Wilson Nelson
Terence Odlin
Rory J. Ong
Peggy Parris
Michael A. Pemberton
Elizabeth F. Penfield
Virginia G. Polanski
James Postema
John W. Presley
Bennett A. Rafoth
Paul W. Ranieri
Rebecca R. Rickly
Duane Roen
Lois M. Rosen
Christine Ross
Audrey J. Roth
Jacqueline Jones Royster
Sara Sanders
Dolores J. Sarafinski
Mary Sasse
Robert E. Sawyer
Judith Scheffler
Barbaranne Schuyler
Marian M. Sciachitano
Cynthia L. Selfe
Yolan Shetty
Barbara M. Sitko
Louise Z. Smith
Mark E. Smith

Steve Smith
Jeffrey D. Sommers
Freda F. Stohrer
James Strickland
Michael Strickland
Patricia Sullivan
Dan J. Tannacito
Josephine K. Tarvers
Vicki Taylor
Nathaniel Teich
John Trimbur
Myron Tuman
Elizabeth A. Vander Lei
Christine A. Vonder Haar
Billie J. Wahlstrom
Preston Lynn Waller
Barbara Weaver
Robert H. Weiss
Robert C. Wess
Karen West
Robert D. Whipple, Jr.
R. J. Willey
James D. Williams
Michael M. Williamson
David E. Wilson
Jeanne Wilson
W. Ross Winterowd
J. Randal Woodland
Arthur P. Young

Journal Abbreviations

A&E	Anthropology and Education Quarterly
ABCAB	The American Business Communication Association Bulletin
AdEd	Adult Education
AdLBEd	Adult Literacy and Basic Education
ALAN	The Alan Review
AmA	American Anthropologist
AmE	American Ethnologist
AmP	American Psychologist
ArEB	Arizona English Bulletin
AS	American Speech
ASBJ	American School Board Journal
ASch	The American Scholar
BADE	Bulletin of the Association of Departments of English
BRMMLA	Rocky Mountain Review of Language and Literature
CAC	Computer-Assisted Composition Journal
CalE	California English
CC	Computers and Composition
CCC	College Composition and Communication
CCR	Community College Review
CE	College English
CEAF	CEA Forum
CET	Carolina English Teacher
CHE	Chronicle of Higher Education
CI	Cognition and Instruction
CJCJ	Community, Technical, and Junior College Journal
Cognition	Cognition
CollT	College Teaching
ComEd	Communication Education
ComM	Communication Monographs
ComQ	Communication Quarterly
ComR	Communication Research
CPsy	Cognitive Psychology
CritI	Critical Inquiry
CurrR	Curriculum Review
Daedalus	Daedalus: Journal of the American Academy of Arts and Sciences
DAI	Dissertation Abstracts

	International	JEdR	Journal of Educational Research
DP	Developmental Psychology	JEPG	Journal of Experimental Psychology: General
DPr	Discourse Processes	JEPH	Journal of Experimental Psychology: Human Perception and Performance
EdM	Educational Measurement: Issues and Practice		
EEd	English Education	JEPL	Journal of Experimental Psychology: Learning, Memory, Cognition
EJ	The English Journal		
ELT	English Language Teaching Journal		
EngR	English Record	JFR	Journal of Folklore Research
EQ	English Quarterly	JGE	JGE: The Journal of General Education
ESP	English for Specific Purposes		
ET	English in Texas	JMEd	Journal of Medical Education
ETC	ETC: A Review of General Semantics	JML	Journal of Memory and Language
ExC	Exceptional Children	JNT	Journal of Narrative Technique
ExEx	Exercise Exchange	JPsy	Journal of Psychology
FEN	Freshman English News	JPsyR	Journal of Psycholinguistic Research
FLA	Foreign Language Annals		
FlaEJ	Florida English Journal	JQ	Journalism Quarterly
FS	Feminist Studies	JR	Journal of Reading
GCQ	Gifted Child Quarterly	JT	Journal of Thought
GR	Georgia Review	JTEd	Journal of Teacher Education
HCR	Human Communication Research	JTW	Journal of Teaching Writing
HT	History Teacher	JTWC	Journal of Technical Writing and Communication
IDJ	Information Design Journal		
IE	Indiana English	Lang&S	Language and Style
IlEB	Illinois English Bulletin	LangS	Language Sciences
Intell	Intelligence	LArts	Language Arts
IPM	Information Processing and Management	Leaflet	The Leaflet
		Learning	Learning
JAC	Journal of Advanced Composition	Ling	Linguistics
		LL	Language Learning
JAF	Journal of American Folklore	LSoc	Language in Society
JBC	Journal of Business Communication	MarylandEJ	Maryland English Journal
JBTC	Iowa Journal of Business and Technical Communication	MCQ	Management Communication Quarterly
JBW	Journal of Basic Writing	MEd	Medical Education
JCS	Journal of Curriculum Studies	NCET	North Carolina English Teacher
JCST	Journal of College Science Teaching	NYRB	The New York Review of Books
JDEd	Journal of Developmental Education	OralH	Oral History Review
		OrE	Oregon English
JEdM	Journal of Educational Measurement	P&L	Philosophy and Literature
		P&R	Philosophy and Rhetoric
JEdP	Journal of Educational	PCTEB	PCTE Bulletin
		PhiDK	Phi Delta Kappan

PMLA	Publication of the Modern Language Association	TECFORS	TECFORS
PR	Partisan Review	TESOLQ	Teachers of English to Speakers of Other Languages Quarterly
Praxis	Praxis	TETYC	Teaching English in the Two-Year College
Psychology	Psychology: A Quarterly Journal of Human Behavior	Thought	Thought
PT	Poetics Today	TWM	Teachers and Writers of Magazines
QJS	Quarterly Journal of Speech	TWT	Technical Writing Teacher
QRD	Quarterly Review of Doublespeak	UEJ	Utah English Journal
Raritan	Raritan	VEB	Virginia English Bulletin
Reader	Reader	VLang	Visible Language
Rhetorica	Rhetorica		
RR	Rhetoric Review	WAC	Writing across the Curriculum
RRQ	Reading Research Quarterly	WC	Written Communication
RSQ	Rhetoric Society Quarterly	WCJ	Writing Center Journal
RTE	Research in the Teaching of English	WD	Writers Digest
		WI	Writing Instructor
SAm	Scientific American	WiEJ	Wisconsin English Journal
SCETCJ	SCETC Journal	WJSC	Western Journal of Speech Communication
SCL	Studies in Canadian Literature		
SFS	Science Fiction Studies	WLN	Writing Lab Newsletter
SLATE	SLATE Newsletter	WLT	World Literature Today
SNNTS	Studies in the Novel	WLWE	World Literature Written in English
SSCJ	Southern Speech Communication Journal	WPA	Journal of the Council of Writing Program Administrators
Style	Style	WS	Women's Studies
SubStance	SubStance		

Abbreviations in Entries

ABC	Association for Business Communication
ABE	Adult Basic Education
ACT	American College Test
ADE	Association of Departments of English
AERA	American Educational Research Association
APA	American Psychological Association
CAI	Computer-Assisted Instruction
CCCC	Conference on College Composition and Communication
CEE	Conference on English Education
CSW	Center for the Study of Writing
EFL	English as a Foreign Language
ERIC	Educational Resources Information Center
ERIC/JC	ERIC Clearinghouse on Junior Colleges
ERIC/RC	ERIC Clearinghouse on Rural Education and Small Schools
ERIC/RCS	ERIC Clearinghouse on Reading and Communication Skills
ERIC/UE	ERIC Clearinghouse on Urban Education
ESL	English as a Second Language
ESP	English for Specific Purposes
EST	English for Science and Technology
ETS	Educational Testing Service
FIPSE	Fund for the Improvement of Postsecondary Education
GED	General Education Development
GPA	Grade Point Average
GRE	Graduate Record Examination
IRA	International Reading Association
LEP	Limited English Proficiency
LES	Limited English Speaking
L1	First Language
L2	Second Language
MLA	Modern Language Association
NAEP	National Assessment of Educational Progress
NCTE	National Council of Teachers of English
NEA	National Education Association
NIE	National Institute of Education
NIH	National Institute of Health

SAT	Scholastic Aptitude Test		of Other Languages
SCA	Speech Communication Association	TOEFL	Test of English as a Foreign Language
SLATE	Support for the Learning and Teaching of English	TSWE	Test of Standard Written English
TESOL	Teachers of English to Speakers	WPA	Council of Writing Program Administrators

CCCC

Bibliography of Composition and Rhetoric

1987

1
Bibliographies and Checklists

1 BIBLIOGRAPHIES AND CHECKLISTS

1. Bishop, Wendy. *Research, Theory, and Pedagogy of Peer Writing Groups: Annotated Bibliography*. Urbana, Ill.: ERIC/RCS, 1986. ERIC ED 276 035. 23 pages

   Describes sources useful for introducing students to the vocabulary of the composition community.

2. Bizzell, Patricia, and Bruce Herzberg. *The Bedford Bibliography for Teachers of Writing*. Boston: Bedford Books, 1987. 74 pages

   Provides 267 annotated entries for works in rhetoric, composition, teaching, and related fields. Includes a brief history of rhetoric and composition, an author index, a catalogue of Bedford books, and an almanac of college composition.

3. Boice, Robert. *Causes and Cures of Writing Blocks: An Annotated Bibliography*. Urbana, Ill.: ERIC/RCS, 1985. ERIC ED 277 046. 44 pages

   Includes 100 sources that discuss early views, contemporary cures, accounts by successful writers, and assessment measures.

4. Book, Virginia. "1986 Association of Teachers of Technical Writing Bibliography." *TWT* 14 (Fall 1987): 372–396.

   This annual bibliography covers such topics as bibliographies, books, reviews, the profession, theory and philosophy, research, pedagogy, and communication in the profession.

5. Coney, Mary B. "Contemporary Views of Audience: A Rhetorical Perspective." *TWT* 14 (Fall 1987): 319–336.

   This bibliographic review finds that the classical model on which audience analysis and adaptation are based is now being challenged by contemporary scholars.

6. Connor, Ulla. "Research Frontiers in Writing Analysis." *TESOLQ* 21 (December 1987): 677–691.

Reviews recent research in L1 and L2 "text analysis of written products." Maintains that both product- and process-centered research is needed for an "integrated theory of writing."

7. Harrold, Sarah Elberfield. "A Selective Annotated Bibliography of Research on Basic Writing: 1975–1986." *DAI* 47 (February 1987): 2927A.

   Includes an introductory essay that discusses developments in eight areas of the field and a bibliography of relevant books.

8. Katz, Steven B. "The Epistemic Trend in Rhetorical Theory: A Four-Dimensional Review." *TWT* 14 (Fall 1987): 355–371.

   This bibliographic review traces the epistemic trend through "the literature of four disciplines: new physics, reader-response criticism, the history of classical rhetoric, and composition theory."

9. Larson, Richard L. "Selected Bibliography of Scholarship on Composition and Rhetoric, 1986." *CCC* 38 (October 1987): 319–336.

   Eighty annotated entries are grouped into 12 categories of theory, research, and instruction.

10. Leger, Susan, and others. "Stylistics Annual Bibliography for 1986." *Style* 21 (Winter 1987): 491–572.

    Includes annotated entries of key articles and books in stylistics and related fields, each categorized according to different aspects of style.

11. Lindemann, Erika, ed. *Longman Bibliography of Composition and Rhetoric, Volume I: 1984–1985*. Longman Series in College Composition and Rhetoric. White Plains, N.Y.: Longman, 1987. 318 pages

    An annotated list of 3853 works grouped into six categories: bibliographies and checklists; rhetorical history, theory, and research; the education and professional environments of composition teachers; writing courses and teaching methods; text-books and instructional materials; and the assessment of writing and its teaching.

12. Luchte, Jeanne. "Computer Programs in the Writing Center: A Bibliographic Essay." *WCJ* 8 (Fall–Winter 1987): 11–19.

    Surveys software programs in four areas: prewriting, organizing, drafting, revising, and proofreading/editing.

13. Lutz, Jean, Susan Jarratt, Patricia Harkin, and Mary Beth Debs. "Practical Rhetoric—The Art of Composing." *TWT* 14 (Fall 1987): 300–313.

    This bibliographic survey finds that "scholars, researchers, and teachers are redefining 'practical rhetoric' as a socially-based, multidisciplinary, theoretically responsive art of composing."

14. Madigan, Chris. "Writing across the Curriculum Resources in Science and Mathematics: A Selected, Annotated Bibliography." *JCST* 16 (February 1987): 250–253.

    A list of resources, most written by teachers of science or mathematics, that describe writing assignments appropriate to science or mathematics courses.

15. Marek, Ann, Kenneth S. Goodman, and Pamela Babcock. *Annotated Miscue Analysis Bibliography*. Program in Language and Literacy Occasional Paper, no. 16. Tucson, Ariz.: University of Arizona, 1985. ERIC ED 275 998. 45 pages

    Describes material on miscue analysis available in journals, books, collections, and dissertations.

16. Marshall, James D., and Russel K. Durst. "Annotated Bibliography of Research in the Teaching of English." *RTE* 21 (May 1987): 202–221.

    Annotates works on writing, language, literature, and teacher education.

17. McDaniel, Ellen. "Bibliography of Text-Analysis and Writing-Instruction Software." *JAC* 7 (1987): 139–170.

An annotated list, based on correspondence and telephone contacts made in 1985 to 1986, of 54 software packages.

18. Mitton, Roger. "Computer-Readable Corpora of Spelling Errors." *TESOLQ* 21 (March 1987): 153–155.

Lists nine available computer-readable files of English spelling errors suitable for use in research.

19. Nightingale, Peggy. *Universities and Student Writing: Selected, Annotated Bibliography.* Tertiary Education Research Centre Occasional Paper, no. 27. Kensington, Australia: New South Wales University, 1986. ERIC ED 276 065. 51 pages

Offers college writing instructors an annotated bibliography of the process and development of students' writing ability, especially as related to the use of computers.

20. Pursell, Frances Josephson. *Books for Adult New Readers.* 3d ed. Cleveland, Ohio: Project Learn, 1986. ERIC ED 275 809. 331 pages

An annotated bibliography of recommended print materials for English-speaking adults reading at or below the seventh grade.

21. Queenan, Margaret. "Teachers as Researchers?" *EJ* 76 (April 1987): 88–90.

An informal annotated bibliography of reports by teacher researchers that have appeared since 1974.

22. Schwartz, Helen J., and Lillian S. Bridwell-Bowles. "A Selected Bibliography on Computers in Composition: An Update." *CCC* 38 (December 1987): 453–457.

Updates a 1984 bibliography. Includes 29 annotated entries as well as information about annual conferences, composition textbooks, and NCTE-sponsored professional groups.

23. Secor, Marie M. "Recent Research in Argumentation Theory." *TWT* 14 (Fall 1987): 337–354.

This bibliographic review surveys work by "argumentation scholars in speech communications and. . . by informal logicians in philosophy."

24. Suhor, Charles. "English and Language Arts: A Guided Tour through the State of the Art." *ArEB* 29 (Winter 1987): 15–19.

"Thumbnail portrait[s] of the state-of-the-art" for composition, reading, literature, and speaking and listening. Extensive reference list.

25. Suhor, Charles. "English and the Language Arts: A Guided Tour through the State of the Art." *PCTEB* 55 (April 1987): 23–30.

The director of ERIC provides "a quick overview" of recent work in English and language arts instruction. Includes a bibliography of recent important books and articles.

26. Tate, Gary, ed. *Teaching Composition: Twelve Bibliographical Essays.* Rev. ed. Fort Worth, Tex.: Texas Christian University Press (distributed by NCTE), 1987. 434 pages

Essays survey research on basic writing, rhetoric and literature, writing across the curriculum, computers and writing, rhetorical invention, cognitive patterns, and other topics.

27. Wagner, Carl G. "The Technical Writing Audience: A Recent Bibliography." *TWT* 14 (Spring 1987): 243–263.

Surveys materials on adapting texts to audiences, defining "audience," teaching audience analysis and adaptation, and considering the ethics of this approach.

28. Weaver, Barbara. "Annual Bibliography of Writing Textbooks." *WPA* 10 (Spring 1987): 59–78.

Annotated bibliography of selected developmental writing, freshman writing, advanced writing, and professional textbooks published in 1986 and 1987.

29. Weintraub, Sam, ed. *Summary of Investigations Relating to Reading, July 1, 1985 to June 20, 1986.* Newark, Del.: IRA, 1987. ERIC ED 284 175. 273 pages

    Abstracts approximately 800 reading research reports.

30. Zamel, Vivian. "Recent Research on Writing Pedagogy." *TESOLQ* 21 (December 1987): 697–715.

    Surveys 1980s research, both process studies and ethnographies, and argues that teachers must be researchers so that research can affect pedagogy.

31. Zappen, James P. "Historical Studies in the Rhetoric of Science and Technology." *TWT* 14 (Fall 1987): 285–298.

    This bibliographic review suggests that earlier studies (1950 to 1975) emphasize differences between classical rhetoric and modern science and technology while more recent studies emphasize similarities.

See also 311, 1274, 1398

2
Theory and Research

2.1 RHETORICAL THEORY, DISCOURSE THEORY, AND COMPOSING

32. Aderman, Betty, Susan Nitzke, Suzanne Pingree, and Jane Voichick. "Readers' Responses to Language Experience Approach Materials." *AdLBEd* 11 (1987): 13–22.

A nutrition pamphlet for a low-income audience tested better than the standard version because it was composed of content statements provided by low-income students of nutrition.

33. Allen, Nancy, Dianne Atkinson, Meg Morgan, Teresa Moore, and Craig Snow. "What Experienced Collaborators Say about Collaborative Writing." *JBTC* 1 (September 1987): 70–90.

Intensive interviews with 20 business and professional writers help to define and describe a typology of a specific type of interactive writing: shared document collaboration.

34. Allister, Mark. "Using Metaphor to 'Re-See': An Aid to Revision." *EngR* 38 (1987): 4–6.

Explores how the use of metaphor enables students to revise their work.

35. Amrhein, Paul Conrad. "Speech Act Comprehension: Processing the Underlying Structure of Pragmatic Information in Verbs of Committing." *DAI* 48 (November 1987): 1532B.

Proposes and tests a model for speakers' intentions conveyed by four verbs of committing. Finds that such verbs are an important source of pragmatic information.

36. Andersen, Laurie J. "A Sense of Audience or Conventional Wisdom?" *JAC* 7 (1987): 112–120.

Compares articles on AIDS from *Newsweek* and *Harpers*. Finds essentially the same general readership but differing expectations, which lead to a contrast in registers.

37. Anderson, Chris. "Teaching Students What Not to Say: Iser, Didion, and the Rhetoric of Gaps." *JAC* 7 (1987): 10–22.

   Applies Iser's concept of meaningful gaps in literature first to the modern artistic essay, then to advanced poetry.

38. Andrews, Patricia. "Gender Differences in Persuasive Communication and Attribution of Success and Failure." *HCR* 13 (Spring 1987): 372–385.

   Examines success and failure attribution, gender, and self-confidence in a persuasive task. Findings reveal gender differences in types of argument and gender-based assumptions about audience.

39. Armstrong, Cheryl. "The Poetic Dimensions of Revision." Paper presented at the CCCC Convention, New Orleans, March 1986. ERIC ED 278 024. 14 pages

   Discusses poets' working drafts and the nature of their revisions, which rely more on deletion than elaboration. Discusses the movement from expressive to transactional text.

40. Arnold, Carroll C. "Johnstone's 'Wedge' and Theory of Rhetoric." *P&R* 20 (1987): 118–128.

   Defines the "wedge" or appeal of rhetoric as a rhetoric-to-oneself, opening up reflection that compels a choice from competing preferences.

41. Asher, Deborah L. "Decision-Making Processes in Writing: Students and Teachers." *DAI* 48 (October 1987): 855A.

   A case study examining the "network of decisions through which a text is created" by comparing the composing processes of community college teachers and freshmen.

42. Athey, Joel Walter. "The Rhetoric of John Stuart Mill's *A System of Logic*." *DAI* 48 (August 1987): 395A.

   Argues that the work provides a strong example for the modern theory that rhetoric can function epistemologically.

43. Autrey, Kenneth M. "Aims, Topics, and Attitudes in Student Journals." *DAI* 47 (May 1987): 4077A.

   Examines 16 journals, 4 in detail as case studies, and finds them varied in aims, topics, and attitudes.

44. Bakhtin, M. M. *Speech Genres and Other Late Essays*. Translated by Vern W. McGee. University of Texas Press Slavic Series, no. 8. Edited by Michael Holmquist and Caryl Emerson. Austin, Tex.: University of Texas Press, 1986. 177 pages

   Includes six short works from Bakhtin's *Esthetics of Creative Discourse*, a fragment from a book on Goethe, an essay on the fundamental distinction between the human and natural sciences, an interview commenting on structuralism and semiotics, a selection from Bakhtin's notebooks, and an essay on speech genres.

45. Balgley, Kathleen Anne. "Language as a Way of Knowing: The Epistemic Nature of Composing in Writing." *DAI* 47 (January 1987): 2578A.

   Explores how "composing in writing" functions as a "mode of learning and a way of knowing."

46. Beale, Walter H. *A Pragmatic Theory of Rhetoric*. Carbondale, Ill.: Southern Illinois University Press, 1987. 208 pages

   Offers a coherent theoretical treatment of aims and modes of discourse. Develops a semiotic "grammar of motives" that relates the problem of meaning in discourse both to linguistic structure and ways of constructing reality.

47. Bear, Jean Munro. "Development Segments in Discourse: The Interaction of Topic and Cohesion with Implications for Native and Nonnative Speakers of English." *DAI* 47 (June 1987): 4373A.

   Analyzes the consequences of viewing topics and comments as organizing structures independent of sentences and paragraphs.

48. Beauvais, Paul J. "A Speech Act Theory of Metadiscourse." *DAI* 47 (June 1987): 4374A.

Reviews old and new theories of metadiscourse and offers an alternative theory.

49. Becker, Samuel L. "Constructing the World in Your Head." *ETC* 44 (Winter 1987): 373–381.

Discusses how "scripts" from the past affect the ways we attach words and meanings to experience. Covers selective perception, the principle of least effort, reference groups, and dogmatism.

50. Begres, Sherril Jean. "Theories of Metaphor." *DAI* 47 (June 1987): 4411A.

Concludes that metaphors are an essential type of expression used to communicate information that is beyond literal meaning.

51. Bennett, George E. "Conventions of Subordination: An Interpretive Analysis of Texts That Define the Professional Identity of Academic Librarians." *DAI* 48 (August 1987): 259A.

Finds that interpretive conventions reveal the subordinate academic and social standing of librarians.

52. Betancourt, Francisco, and Marianne Phinney. *Sources of Writing Block in Bilingual Writers*. Urbana, Ill.: ERIC/RCS, 1987. ERIC ED 281 361. 58 pages

Reports on a study of writing apprehension among three groups of Puerto Rican college students. Traditional composition instruction is one source.

53. Bineham, Jeffrey Linn. "Beyond Dualism: The Hermeneutic Medium as a Communication-Based Perspective on the Cartesian Problem in Epistemic Rhetoric." *DAI* 47 (March 1987): 3237A.

Uses Gadamer's notion of a hermeneutic medium as a "communication-based alternative" to a Cartesian dualist paradigm.

54. Bishop, Wendy. "Writing Teachers and Writing Process: Combining Theory and Practice." *ArEB* 29 (Spring 1987): 34–41.

Reviews the historical development of writing process theory, discusses differences in current theories, and suggests five goals for process-oriented workshops.

55. Blankenship, Jane, and Janet Kenner Muir. "On Imaging the Future: The Secular Search for 'Piety.' " *ComQ* 35 (Winter 1987): 1–12.

Discusses the role of rhetoric in imaging the future.

56. Bokeno, R. Michael. "The Rhetorical Understanding of Science: An Explication and Critical Commentary." *SSCJ* 52 (Spring 1987): 285–311.

Examines and challenges the view that science is fundamentally a rhetorical process.

57. Bontekoe, Ron. "The Function of Metaphor." *P&R* 20 (1987): 209–226.

Metaphor provokes suspension of judgment. The critics treated argue that metaphor communicates meaning, but that exegesis disables the work of metaphor.

58. Braet, Antoine. "The Classical Doctrine of *Status* and the Rhetorical Theory of Argumentation." *P&R* 20 (1987): 79–93.

By rereading *status*, Braet argues that classical rhetoric is not monological and not exclusive of the dialogism of dialectic.

59. Brenders, David A. "Fallacies in the Coordinated Management of Meaning: A Philosophy of Language Critique of Hierarchical Organization of Coherent Conversation and Related Theory." *QJS* 73 (August 1987): 329–348.

A critique of W. Barnett Pearce's coordinated management of meaning, treating it as a representative example of social action theories of meaning.

60. Britton, James. "Call It an Experiment: What Can We Expect Our Reading to Do for Our Writing?" *EEd* 19 (May 1987): 83–92.

Argues that we internalize our reading and thus the general schemata for constructing texts.

61. Brodkey, Linda. "Modernism and the Scene(s) of Writing." *CE* 49 (April 1987): 396–418.

   Argues that our image of the act of writing has been influenced by literary studies. A revision should be based on research into cognitive processes.

62. Brodkey, Linda. "Writing Critical Ethnographic Narratives." *A&E* 18 (June 1987): 67–76.

   Argues that the goal of critical ethnography is to help transform institutions such as schools through negative critique.

63. Brodkey, Linda. "Writing Ethnographic Narratives." *WC* 4 (January 1987): 25–50.

   Examines narrative choices in experimental (interpretive) and traditional (analytical) ethnographies.

64. Bruton, Dawn L., and Dan R. Kirby. "Written Fluency: Didn't We Do That Last Year?" *EJ* 76 (November 1987): 89–92.

   Examines written fluency as a multi-dimensional concept, "a construct valuable to teaching and to research in composing."

65. Bugniazet, Judith. "The Relationship between Character, Writer, and Reader: An Interview with Madeline L'Engle." *ALAN* 14 (Winter 1987): 45–47.

   L'Engle responds to questions about characters, concepts borrowed from science, and her blending of fact and fiction.

66. Burke, Kenneth. "A Comment on 'It Takes Capital to Defeat Dracula' [*CE* 48 (March 1986)]." *CE* 49 (February 1987): 221–222.

   Expresses appreciation for Coe's article and elaborates further on issues of attitude, analogy, *Dracula*, and artificial intelligence.

67. Canary, Daniel J., Brent G. Brossman, and David R. Seibold. "Argument Structures in Decision-Making Groups." *SSCJ* 53 (Fall 1987): 18–37.

   Analyzes and identifies four structures, focusing on the applicability of the taxonomy derived.

68. Carter, Michael. "A Rhetorical (and Teachable) Approach to Style." *TETYC* 14 (October 1987): 187–189.

   Reviews Milic's theories of stylistic monism and dualism. Defines style as a response to the rhetorical situation.

69. Chafe, Wallace, and Jane Danielwicz. *Properties of Spoken and Written Language.* CSW Report, no. 5. Berkeley, Calif.: CSW, 1987. ERIC ED 282 230. 31 pages

   Analyzes the spoken and written discourse of 20 professors and graduate students, noting increasing detachment with level of formality.

70. Chaoui, Mohamed. "The Rhetoric of Composition in Julien Guadet's *Elements et Theories.*" *DAI* 48 (September 1987): 493A.

   Assesses Guadet's theory of composition, drawing upon classical rhetoric and Roland Barthes.

71. Chapman, David W. "Conflict and Consensus: How Composition Scholars View Their Discipline." *BADE* 87 (Fall 1987): 1–3.

   Surveys 18 active scholars and concludes that research and teaching are symbiotic, that goals vary, that empirical research is limiting, and that many problems in the field are political.

72. Chase, Dennis. "The Best and Worst of the 'Nouvelle Vague': An Annotated Dictionary for the Bewildered." *ExEx* 32 (Spring 1987): 11–14.

   A compilation of jargon drawn from publications in the field of composition and rhetoric.

73. Chatelain, Daniele. "Frontiers of the Iterative." *Style* 21 (Spring 1987): 125–142.

   Argues that discourse should be extended beyond the realm of action in order to explore new frontiers between narrative and descriptive discourse.

74. Chen, Kuan-Hsing. "Beyond Truth and Method: On Misreading Gadamer's Practical Hermeneutics." *QJS* 73 (May 1987): 183–199.

Argues that Gadamer's hermeneutics has so far been applied to communications studies in excessively abstract and apolitical ways. Calls for concrete and political applications.

75. Cherwitz, Richard A., and James W. Hikins. *Communication and Knowledge: An Investigation in Rhetorical Epistemology*. Studies in Rhetoric/Communication. Edited by Carroll A. Arnold. Columbia, S.C.: University of South Carolina Press, 1986. 192 pages

Explores the connection between human claims to know and efforts to communicate what is known. Develops a theory of rhetorical knowledge, establishing the central role of communication in efforts to obtain knowledge.

76. Clark, Beth Hendry. "The Reliability of T-Unit Length in Two Modes of Written Discourse at Third-Grade Level." *DAI* 48 (October 1987): 855A.

Examines t-units as a measure of syntactic complexity over time, within discourse modes, and across modes such as narrative and argument.

77. Clifford, John, and John Schilb. "A Perspective on Eagleton's Revival of Rhetoric." *RR* 6 (Fall 1987): 22–31.

Explores the political benefits for composition studies in the "socialist inflection" of Eagleton's call in *Literary Theory* to critique a wide range of texts.

78. Coe, Richard M. "An Apology for Form; or, Who Took the Form Out of Process?" *CE* 49 (January 1987): 13–28.

Argues that a new rhetorical conception of form is needed within a process approach to composition.

79. Coe, Richard M. "Richard M. Coe Responds [to Burke, *CE* 49 (February 1987)]." *CE* 49 (February 1987): 222–223.

Expresses his agreement with Burke on the role of attitude in the pentad and discusses further the analog/digital distinction in communication.

80. Coe, Richard M. *Toward a Grammar of Passages*. Studies in Writing and Rhetoric. Carbondale, Ill.: Southern Illinois University Press, 1988. 128 pages

Extends Christensen's generative rhetoric. A two-dimensional graphic matrix analyzes the logical relations between statements by mapping coordinate, subordinate, and superordinate relationships. Concerned with questions about relations of form and function, thought and culture, cognitive and social processses.

81. Colley, Ann C. "A Defense of the I." *CEAF* 17 (1987): 10–13.

The use of "I" in writing does not confine the student writer.

82. Collier, James Lincoln. "Doing the Literary Tempo." *ALAN* 14 (Winter 1987): 1–2.

Collier details the procedure he and his brother follow in collaborating on their historical fictions, a procedure that requires a strict division of labor.

83. Comas, James N. "Toward a Rhetorical Historiography of the Discipline." *DAI* 48 (October 1987): 923A.

Since theoretical works shape the discipline's self-perception, an adequate understanding of the discipline is based on rhetorical readings of these works.

84. Cooper, Marilyn M. "Marilyn M. Cooper Responds [to Lyall, *CE* 49 (March 1987)]." *CE* 49 (March 1987): 359–360.

Supports the function of new models. Defends her use of ecology as a model for the study of the social context of writing.

85. Corder, Jim W. "Rhetoric and the Structure of the Field of English." *ET* 18 (Winter 1987): 4–7.

Argues that, by fragmenting the discipline of English, teachers have isolated themselves from their colleagues and from the community.

86. Cowen, Emory L., Arline Spinell, A. Dirk Hightower, and Bohdan S. Lotyczewski. "Author Reactions to the Manuscript Revision Process." *AmP* 42 (April 1987): 402–405.

   Revision is required in over 90 percent of published articles. Most authors approve, but they worry about the biases of editors and referees.

87. Crusius, Timothy W. "A Comment on 'that we have divided/In three our Kingdom': The Communication Triangle and *A Theory of Discourse* [*CE* 48 (March 1986)]." *CE* 49 (February 1987): 214–219.

   Criticizes Hunter's contention that the communication triangle cannot function adequately as a paradigm for written composition.

88. Cypert, Rick. "Memory: A Step toward Invention." Paper presented at the CCCC Convention, Atlanta, March 1987. ERIC ED 280 036. 14 pages

   Studies six assignments by freshman composition students to determine the "natural" and "artificial" memories on which their writing draws.

89. D'Angelo, Frank. "Prolegomena to a Rhetoric of Tropes." *RR* 6 (Fall 1987): 32–40.

   An interdisciplinary exploration of the ways metaphor, metonymy, synecdoche, and irony may be used in composing and critical reading.

90. Davis, Gayle B. "Women's Frontier Diaries: Writing for Good Reason." *WS* 14 (July 1987): 5–14.

   Discusses five functions of writing in diaries for white women settlers.

91. De La Perriere, Earleen. "Afro-American Indirections: Issues in the Signifyin Monkey and the Art of Coping." *DAI* 48 (August 1987): 421A.

Discusses the dominance of indirection patterns in Afro-American verbal arts, particularly in versions of the Signifyin Monkey.

92. Dieli, Mary. "Designing Successful Documents: An Investigation of Document Evaluation Methods." *DAI* 47 (April 1987): 3608A.

   Studies four current document evaluation methods and tests a new document evaluation method.

93. Donahue, Patricia. "Misreading Students' Texts." *Reader* 17 (Spring 1987): 1–12.

   Argues that students can be taught to revise the content of their essays by reading their drafts against cultural norms.

94. Donahue, Patricia, and Ellen Quandahl. "Freud and the Teaching of Interpretation." *CE* 49 (October 1987): 641–649.

   Argues that interpretation is integral to both reading and composition. Describes a sequence of assignments for a basic writing course based on reading Freud.

95. Dowdey, Diane. "Rhetorical Techniques of Audience Adaptation in Popular Science Writing." *JTWC* 17 (1987): 275–285.

   Writers of popular science essays use such techniques as focusing on real audiences, addressing an audience's misconceptions, and employing pronouns, literary allusions, comparisons, analogies, and examples.

96. Duffy, Thomas M., Theodore Post, and Gregory Smith. "Technical Manual Production: An Examination of Five Systems." *WC* 4 (October 1987): 370–393.

   Analyzes the production of technical manuals to identify the technical, rhetorical, and design factors contributing to the difficulty of producing usable manuals.

97. Dyson, Anne Haas. "Individual Differences in Beginning Composing: An Orchestral Vision of Learning to Compose." *WC* 4 (October 1987): 411–442.

Studies writers in primary grades to show that researchers should not evaluate growth linearly but from a holistic perspective.

98. Earls, Terrence D. "Something There Is That Doesn't Love a Dissertation, That Wants It Filed Away...." *EJ* 76 (February 1987): 49–52.

    Discusses the limitations of a dissertation that examines "whether peer evaluation of [student] writing could be as effective as teacher evaluation."

99. Elbow, Peter. "Closing My Eyes As I Speak: An Argument for Ignoring Audience." *CE* 49 (January 1987): 50–69.

    Argues that writer-based prose can be better than reader-based prose. Writers also need the contrary abilities to consider and to ignore audience.

100. Endres, Thomas Gerard. "A Dramatistic Analysis of Unmarried Mothers: Toward a Typology of Rhetorical Visions." *DAI* 47 (April 1987): 3608A.

    Uses Bormann's fantasy theme analysis to examine three rhetorical visions of unmarried mothers.

101. Fagan, William T. "Adult Illiterates Processing Narrative and Expository Text." *EQ* 20 (Summer 1987): 95–105.

    A study finding that adult illiterates processed narrative text more successfully than expository texts.

102. Farris, Christine R. "Current Composition: Beyond Process Versus Product." *EJ* 76 (October 1987): 28–34.

    Discusses recent composition theory and the emerging socio-contextual process approach.

103. Fisher, Walter R. *Human Communication as Narration: Toward a Philosophy of Reason, Value, and Action.* Studies in Rhetoric/Communication. Edited by Carroll A. Arnold. Columbia, S.C.: University of South Carolina Press, 1987. 210 pages

    Develops the theory that all human communication may be seen as narrative and that all human beings have the capacity to employ a sort of narrative logic. Argues that this logic ought to be the criterion by which communication is assessed.

104. Foss, Sonja, and Ann Gill. "Michel Foucault's Theory of Rhetoric as Epistemic." *WJSC* 51 (Fall 1987): 483–501.

    Discusses and applies five theoretical units derived from discursive formation, explaining the relationships among them, and the process by which rhetoric is epistemic.

105. Frederiksen, Carl H. "Knowledge Representation and Discourse: Producing and Communicating Meaning." Paper presented at the CCCC Convention, Atlanta, March 1987. ERIC ED 281 154. 34 pages

    Discusses how our analysis of discourse production and comprehension has shifted from text-centered analysis to the cognitive processes at work in knowledge production.

106. Freed, Richard, and Glenn J. Broadhead. "Discourse Communities and Instructional Norms." *CCC* 38 (May 1987): 154–165.

    Surveys rhetoric's interest in discourse communities. Illustrates two similar discourse communities and urges ethnographic perspectives toward student "cultures."

107. Fulk, Janet, Charles W. Steinfield, Joseph Schmitz, and J. Gerard Power. "A Social Information Processing Model of Media Use in Organizations." *ComR* 14 (October 1987): 529–552.

    Presents a model of how processes of social influence affect individuals' attitudes toward communication media within organizations. Suggests directions for future research.

108. Gabin, Rosalind J. "Aristotle and the New Rhetoric: Grimaldi and Valesio." *P&R* 20 (1987): 171–181.

Two readers of Aristotle differ on ontological, not logical grounds, which itself exemplifies the new rhetoric of dialectical opposition and linkage.

109. Gabin, Rosalind J. "Entitling Kenneth Burke." *RR* 5 (Spring 1987): 196–210.

Sees Burke's "language as a tool for action" as anticipating many of today's important literary movements. Maintains that Burke is far too complex for a simple label.

110. Gallow, DeDe. "Fiction as a Transition between Personal Narration and Exposition: Implications from Interviews with Professional Writers and College Student Writers." *DAI* 48 (August 1987): 323A.

Professional writers, unlike students, base both narration and exposition on personal experience and write to resolve personal conflicts.

111. Gaskill, William Hobart. "Revising in Spanish and English as a Second Language: A Process-Oriented Study of Composition." *DAI* 47 (April 1987): 3747A.

Studies L2 speakers' revising processes using video-recorded sessions. Analyzes the students' writing following Faigley and Witte's revision taxonomy.

112. Geisler, Cheryl. "Factors Affecting Precision: Discourse Constraints on Linguistic Choice in Narratives." *DAI* 47 (April 1987): 3748A.

Notes the effects of task and instruction on precision in writing and sees relationships between sentence-level phenomena and the structures of extended discourse.

113. Gibbs, Raymond, and Suzanne Delaney. "Pragmatic Factors in Making and Understanding Promises." *DPr* 10 (January–March 1987): 107–126.

Subjects' judgments of whether statements in texts were promises support Searle's analysis of promises. Contrary to Searle's analysis, however, promises may involve routine actions.

114. Giulani, Victoria, Elizabeth Bates, Barbara O'Connell, and Mario Pelliccia. "Recognition Memory for Forms of Reference: The Effects of Language and Text Type." *DPr* 10 (January–March 1987): 43–61.

In comparison with English speakers in earlier investigations, Italian-speaking subjects showed somewhat different patterns of recall of anaphoric devices such as nouns and pronouns.

115. Gonzalez, Alberto. "The Rhetoric of Apocalypse: An Inquiry into the Ascriptive Values in Chicano Self-Presentation." *DAI* 47 (April 1987): 3609A.

An image of "otherness" is descriptive of cultural alienation and reveals "new opportunity and potential."

116. Grassi, Ernesto. "Why Rhetoric Is Philosophy." *P&R* 20 (1987): 68–78.

Addresses the relationship between philosophy and rhetoric via Heidegger's critique of metaphysics. Language is rhetorical word play necessarily linked to the here and now.

117. Haas, Christina. "What Research with Computers Can Tell Us about the Uses of Reading in Writing." Paper presented at the CCCC Convention, Atlanta, March 1987. ERIC ED 284 252. 28 pages

Studies the revisions made by six freshmen and five skilled writers, noting the value of revising from hard copy.

118. Hagge, John. "The Process Religion and Business Communication." *JBC* 24 (Winter 1987): 89–120.

Argues that the process approach to writing suffers from methodological defects and from mistakes about the nature of language and mind, which may lead to contentless solipsistic courses.

119. Hall, William S., and William Nagy. "The Semantic-Pragmatic Distinction in the Investigation of Mental State Words: The Role of the Situation." *DPr* 10 (April–June 1987): 169–180.

Black children and white children showed equal familiarity with mental state words. However, there were differences in using such words to describe particular situations.

120. Hamilton-Wieler, Sharon. "Writing as a Thought Process: Site of a Struggle." Paper presented at the NCTE Convention, San Antonio, November 1987. ERIC ED 277 045. 13 pages

Examines the tensions between convention and choice in the language of disciplines. Viewed dialectically, these tensions are a struggle for linguistic growth.

121. Hample, Dale, and Judith Dallinger. "Cognitive Editing Standards." *HCR* 14 (Winter 1987): 123–144.

People's aggressiveness, interpersonal orientation, and gender can predict whether they will use the rationales of message effectiveness, principled objection, harm to the other, or argument avoidance.

122. Harker, W. John. "Literary Theory and the Reading Process: A Meeting of Perspectives." *WC* 4 (July 1987): 235–252.

Argues that literary theorists should pay greater attention to the implications of leading research, especially the interactive model of reader and text.

123. Harris, Joseph. "Egocentrism and Difference." Paper presented at the CCCC Convention, Atlanta, March 1987. ERIC ED 280 078. 12 pages

Opposes the cognitivist view of composition with a social view based particularly on the work of Flower and Bartholomae.

124. Harris, Joseph. "The Plural Text/The Plural Self: Roland Barthes and William Coles." *CE* 49 (February 1987): 158–169.

Analyzes the writings of Barthes and Coles and sees many similarities which form a basis for a theory and pedagogy of writing.

125. Harris, Joseph. "A Silent Voice, an Absent Ear: The Role of the Reader in Theories of Composing." *DAI* 47 (February 1987): 2927A.

Defines the opposing metaphors of writing as a transmitter of data and as a partner in a dialogue with a reader. Discusses the influence of these metaphors on composition theories.

126. Harrison, Teresa M. "Frameworks for the Study of Writing in Organizational Contexts." *WC* 4 (January 1987): 3–23.

Presents a theoretical rationale that includes rhetorical and organizational theory.

127. Hashimoto, I. "Voice as Juice: Some Reservations about Evangelical Composition." *CCC* 38 (February 1987): 70–80.

Warns composition teachers against emphasizing the nonrational nature of voice or equating successful writing with an authentic personal voice.

128. Hays, Janice N., Kathleen M. Brandt, and Kathryn H. Chantry. *The Effects of Friendly and Adversarial Audiences upon the Argumentative Writing of a Group of High School Seniors and College Students: A Developmental Perspective*. Urbana, Ill.: ERIC/RCS, 1987. ERIC ED 280 040. 79 pages

Studies argumentative essays written to both friendly and hostile audiences by 12 high school seniors, 24 college freshmen, and 16 juniors and seniors.

129. Herrmann, Andrea W. "Researching Your Own Students: What Happens When the Teacher Turns Ethnographer." *WI* 6 (Spring–Summer 1987): 114–128.

Describes the advantages and disadvantages of the teacher's assuming an additional role as an ethnographic researcher in a high school writing course.

130. Hesse, Douglas Dean. "The Story in the Essay." *DAI* 47 (February 1987): 3024A.

Argues that narrative not only illustrates points but also serves four other functions: to "present information, occasion the essay, and *be* the essay."

131. Hewitt, Leah. "Getting with the (Speech) Act: Autobiography as Theory and Performance." *SubStance* 16 (1987): 32–44.

   Posits a resemblance between Michel Leiris's autobiography, considered as a speech act, and J. L. Austin's theory, considered as a self-referential language act.

132. Horowitz, Rosalind, and S. Jay Samuels, eds. *Comprehending Oral and Written Language.* San Diego: Academic Press, 1987. 430 pages

   A collection of 13 essays that discuss the skills necessary for processing and comprehending language. Treats language and text analysis, the development of literacy, literacy and schooling, and factors influencing listening and reading.

133. House, Elizabeth B., and William J. House. "Problem Solving: The Debates in Composition and Psychology." *JAC* 7 (1987): 62–75.

   Compares two views of problem solving in composition (inventional versus cognitive process) to a parallel dispute in psychology.

134. Hua, Li Min. "Can Anyone Thunder? Writing within the Bounds of One's Authority." *EngR* 38 (1987): 6–9.

   Examines how writers use personal experience when composing and discusses similarities among American and Chinese students.

135. Hull, Glynda. "The Editing Process in Writing: A Performance Study of More Skilled and Less Skilled College Writers." *RTE* 21 (February 1987): 8–29.

   Compares writers' corrections of "consulting," "intuiting," and "comprehending" errors in self-written and standard essays under two conditions with or without receiving feedback on error location.

136. Hunter, Paul. "Paul Hunter Responds [to Crusius, *CE* 49 (February 1987)]." *CE* 49 (February 1987): 219–221.

   Defends his criticism of *A Theory of Discourse* because of its moralistic and positivistic language.

137. Jakobson, Roman. *Language in Literature.* Edited by Krystyna Pomorska and Stephen Rudy. Cambridge, Mass: Belknap Press, 1987. 592 pages

   The first comprehensive presentation in English of Jakobson's essays on language and literature.

138. Jensen, Marcia D. *Helical Thought Development and Chronology Revision: Intrapersonal Communication Processes Reflected in Memoirs.* Urbana, Ill.: ERIC/RCS, 1985. ERIC ED 281 258. 14 pages

   Argues that journals can be studied for the ways they illustrate theoretical descriptions of internal communication.

139. Johannesen, Richard L. "Richard M. Weaver's Uses of Kenneth Burke." *SSCJ* 52 (Spring 1987): 312–330.

   Explores some acknowledged and unacknowledged influences of two major theorists on each other.

140. Johnstone, Henry W., Jr. "Response [to Yoos and Arnold, *P&R* 20 (1987)]." *P&R* 20 (1987): 129–134.

   Responds to Yoos's and Arnold's definition of Johnstone's rhetoric as a "wedge" or an appeal that compels attention.

141. Karolides, Nicholas J., ed. "Composition: State of the Art." *WiEJ* 24 (October 1981): 1–36.

   Five articles survey the present status of writing instruction and scholarship. Also available as ERIC ED 278 989.

142. Keith, William Merrick. "Belief, Communication, and Logic: Toward a Theory of Rational Persuasion." *DAI* 47 (June 1987): 4232A.

   Posits a theory of persuasion that resolves present disagreements over the nature of rationality and that involves cognitive decision making.

143. Kellogg, Ronald T. "Writing Performance: Effects of Cognitive Strategies." *WC* 4 (July 1987): 269–298.

Using laboratory and field research, the study concludes that outlines improve writing quality, but drafts had no influence on quality or efficiency.

144. Keough, Colleen M. "The Nature and Function of Argument in Organizational Bargaining Research." *SSCJ* 53 (Fall 1987): 1–17.

Uses four current perspectives to analyze argumentation and human rationality in negotiations.

145. Killingsworth, M. Jimmie. "Thingishness and Objectivity in Technical Style." *JTWC* 17 (1987): 105–113.

Argues that a technical style comprised of nominalizations, strings of noun modifiers, passivity, indirectness, impersonality, and abstractions poorly represents the real world of technical communication.

146. Kinneavy, James L. "The Process of Writing: A Philosophical Base in Hermeneutics." *JAC* 7 (1987): 1–9.

Summarizes Heidegger's concept of forestructure as a basis for a broadened hermeneutical view of writing as process.

147. Kinneavy, James L. "William Grimaldi—Reinterpreting Aristotle." *P&R* 20 (1987): 183–200.

Argues that Grimaldi's "too expansive" reading of Aristotle's *Rhetoric* as a study of communication and discourse is not "historically valid."

148. Kleine, Michael. "What is it we do when we write articles like this one—and how can we get students to join us?" *WI* 6 (Spring–Summer 1987): 151–161.

Describes an in-depth study of the writing processes of eight college professors. Urges that findings be used in teaching research writing to students.

149. Kochan, Mary. "Revising Revisited." *EngR* 38 (1987): 2–5.

Discusses students' perceptions of revision.

150. Kong, Stephen King [pseud.]. "TIPS for Academic Publishing from the National Carnival of Theoreticians of English." *TETYC* 14 (May 1987): 152–154.

A satiric essay on contemporary jargon in composition theory.

151. LaCapra, Dominick. "History and Psychoanalysis." *CritI* 13 (Winter 1987): 222–251.

Examines both the history of psychoanalysis and the effect of psychoanalysis on history and criticism with some discussion of Lacan and the development of a new rhetoric.

152. Lalicker, William Benedict. "The Interdisciplinary Imagination in the Teaching of Writing." *DAI* 48 (September 1987): 639A.

Traces historical notions of imagination and demonstrates a new heuristic, based on themata theory of scientific creativity and using interdisciplinary imagination principles.

153. Langer, Judith A., and Arthur N. Applebee. *How Writing Shapes Thinking.* NCTE Research Report, no. 22. Urbana, Ill.: NCTE, 1987. 154 pages

A study of how seven teachers used writing in science, social studies, English, and home economics classes. Activities that involved writing led to better learning than activities involving only reading and studying.

154. Lawrence, Barbara. "Variations in Coherence and Overall Quality of a Written Composition as Influenced by the State of the Writer's Knowledge Structures." *DAI* 47 (March 1987): 3371A.

Findings correlate poor coherence and writing performance with the writer's commitment, study habits, and attitude toward the course.

155. Le Compte, Margaret D. "Bias in the Biography: Bias and Subjectivity in Ethnographic Research." *A&E* 18 (March 1987): 43–52.

Addresses the issue of credibility in ethnography, where the researcher is the main research instrument. Suggests ways to protect against bias.

156. Levin, Samuel R. "Catachresis: Vico and Joyce." *P&R* 20 (1987): 94–105.

As makers of catachresis, Vico and Joyce call into question classical definitions of catachresis. Catachresis becomes a nontrivial response to lexical gaps in language.

157. Levine, George. "Literary Science—Scientific Literature." *Raritan* 6 (Winter 1987): 24–41.

Explores arguments against scientific realism in light of problems in anti foundationalism. Literary criticism is an instrument of knowing "science," which is actually cultural production.

158. Levy, Fran Newmark. "Source of Initiation: An Influence on the Writing of Two Adolescents." *DAI* 47 (January 1987): 2438A.

A study comparing other-initiated writing and self-initiated writing. Measures the impact of the source on writing products, processes, and learning.

159. Limaye, Mohan R., and Roger D. Cherry. "Pragmatics, 'Situated' Language, and Business Communication." *JBTC* 1 (January 1987): 68–88.

Identifies politeness and other situational variables from speech act theory, with an eye toward business communication. Examines five and revises three business letters in light of principles derived from pragmatics.

160. Lung, Ching-Tung. "The Influence of Beliefs on Syllogistic Reasoning." *DAI* 47 (February 1987): 3531B.

Finds that, in solving syllogistic problems, students most often draw indeterminate conclusions when belief interferes.

161. Lyall, Laurence Hayden. "A Comment on 'The Ecology of Writing' [*CE* 48 (April 1986)]." *CE* 49 (March 1987): 357–359.

Resists Cooper's use of the term *ecology* as unnecessary in light of Burke's more encompassing model.

162. Lynn, Steven. "Reading the Writing Process: Toward a Theory of Current Pedagogies." *CE* 49 (December 1987): 902–910.

Applies a close reading to three representative theoretical statements from current writing pedagogy. Argues that examining conflicts and connections will reveal valuable insights.

163. Mack, Nancy Geisler. "False Consciousness and the Composing Process." *DAI* 47 (January 1987): 2490A.

Analyzes the social, economic, and political factors that alienate teachers and students from authentic composing.

164. Mandelbaum, Jennifer. "Couples Sharing Stories." *ComQ* 35 (Spring 1987): 144–170.

An analysis of a narration shared by two storytellers. Shows how the co-participants encounter and resolve the problem of having two tellers and a "knowing" participant present.

165. Mandler, Jean. "On the Psychological Reality of Story Structure." *DPr* 10 (January–March 1987): 1–29.

Despite variations in story structure, experimental subjects were able to identify invariant hierarchies in the schemata of traditional stories.

166. Marshall, James D. "The Effects of Writing on Students' Understanding of Literary Texts." *RTE* 21 (February 1987): 30–63.

Examines the effects of writing conditions (restricted, personal analytic, and formal analytic) on students' written products, writing processes, and later understanding of short stories.

167. Marston, Peter J. "Rhetorical Forms and Functions of Cosmological Argument." *DAI* 48 (August 1987): 249A.

This study produced three conclusions— one historical and two discourse-related— concerning motive and its close relationship to poetics.

168. Martin, Myra Jordan. "The Effects of Instruction in Metacognitive Strategies for Composing on Reading Achievement and Writing Achievement." *DAI* 48 (October 1987): 888A.

Suggests a method whereby students think about what is occurring during the writing process.

169. Mazzie, Claudia. "An Experimental Investigation of the Determinants of Implicitness in Spoken and Written Discourse." *DPr* 10 (January–March 1987): 31–42.

In a controlled communication task, discourse content had major effects on how explicit textual information was. Modality (spoken versus written language) had little effect.

170. McCarthy, Lucille Parkinson. "A Stranger in Strange Lands: A College Student Writing across the Curriculum." *RTE* 21 (October 1987): 233–265.

Examines the varied writing situations one student confronts during his freshman and sophomore years.

171. McCutchen, Deborah, Glynda A. Hull, and William L. Smith. "Editing Strategies and Error Correction in Basic Writing." *WC* 4 (April 1987): 139–154.

In two studies, basic writers showed two different editing strategies: a consulting strategy and an intuiting strategy.

172. McDaniel, Mark, and Mary L. Kerwin. "Long-Term Prose Retention: Is an Organiza-

tional Schema Sufficient?" *DPr* 10 (July–September 1987): 237–252.

Both proposition-specific and schema-related processing seem to be needed for successful long-term retention in tasks involving letter deletion and perspective changes.

173. McGuire, Michael, and Edith Slembek. "An Emerging Critical Rhetoric: Helmut Geissner's *Sprechwissenschaft*." *QJS* 73 (August 1987): 349–358.

An introduction to the work of the German communications theorist Helmut Geissner. A review essay treating five of his books.

174. Merrill, Stephen M. "Audience Adaptiveness in Job Application Letters Written by College Students: An Exploratory Study." *DAI* 48 (July 1987): 121A.

Studies how text elements influenced personnel officers' selecting job applicants from letters.

175. Miles, Curtis. "The Fourth 'R': The Final Four Determinants of Thinking." *JDEd* 10 (January 1987): 28.

Discusses the key role of communications competence in determining the nature and clarity of thinking.

176. Miller, Percy Wilson. "The Paragraph: Its Structure and Characteristic Features As Relates to Discourse Aim." *DAI* 48 (September 1987): 586A.

Analyzes the structure of randomly selected paragraphs as it relates to discourse aim. Makes recommendations for teaching paragraph structure.

177. Morley, Donald Dean. "Subjective Message Constructs: A Theory of Persuasion." *ComM* 54 (June 1987): 183–203.

Three studies indicate that the theory explains variance in belief. Valid operational measures can be constructed using subjective probabilities.

178. Morreale, Joanne. "*A New Beginning:* A Rhetorical Analysis of Televisual Political

Communications." *DAI* 48 (August 1987): 250A.

Examines President Reagan's videotaped 1984 campaign film. Finds a potential danger in political films' altering reality rhetorically.

179. Morse, Philip S. "Reminiscences of Writers—Pain and Poignancy." *EngR* 38 (1987): 12–14.

Explores the writing histories of 100 college students.

180. Murdock, Mary Cecelia. "Using Sociodrama to Examine the Creative Thinking Process and the Writing Process." *DAI* 48 (September 1987): 608A.

Examines what happens in the creative process and in the writing process, describing the relationship between them.

181. Naipaul, V. S. "On Being a Writer." *NYRB* 34 (23 April 1987): 7.

A personal statement. In defining himself as a writer, Naipaul recognizes the necessity of artificial literary forms and a separate writing self.

182. Nay-Brock, Paul. "Beyond Development Modelling Theory in Writing: Some Environmental or Sociological Forces." *EQ* 20 (Fall 1987): 194–204.

Advocates that schools go beyond the traditional parameters of a developmental modelling of writing and recognize the wide range of environmental factors at work across developmental grids.

183. Newell, George E., and Phyllis MacAdam. "Examining the Source of Writing Problems: An Instrument for Measuring Writer's Topic-Specific Knowledge." *WC* 4 (April 1987): 156–174.

Develops a theory-based rationale for measuring a writer's topic specific knowledge, formalizes a method for analyzing this knowledge, and provides a guide for using the method.

184. North, Stephen M. *The Making of Knowledge in Composition: Portrait of* Emerging Field. Upper Montclair, N.J.: Boynton/Cook, 1987. 352 pages

Examines the growth of the study of writing in the last two decades by focusing on eight major groups of knowledge makers: practitioners, historians, philosophers, critics, experimentalists, clinicians, formalists, and ethnographers.

185. North, Stephen M. "Research in Writing, Departments of English, and the Problem of Method." *BADE* 88 (Winter 1987): 13.

Analyzes writing research, finding eight major modes of inquiry clustered in three groups: practitioners, scholars, researchers.

186. O'Donnell, Angela M., Donald F. Dansereau, Thomas R. Rocklin, Celia O. Larson, Velma I. Hythecker, Michael D. Young, and Judith G. Lambiotte. "Effects of Cooperative and Individual Rewriting on an Instruction Writing Task." *WC* 4 (January 1987): 90–99.

In rewriting instructions on starting a car, the dyadic group and the individuals who had access to experimenter-provided instructions outperformed the individual writers who had no sample instructions to revise.

187. O'Keefe, Barbara, and Steven McCornack. "Message Design Logic and Message Goal Structure." *HCR* 14 (Fall 1987): 68–92.

An empirical study supports the hypothesis that message design logic correlates significantly with raters' predictions about the success or failure of the message.

188. Oring, Elliot. "Generating Lives: The Construction of an Autobiography." *JFR* 24 (September–December 1987): 241–262.

Examines some theoretical and practical problems of transforming interview transcriptions into a coherent text of a life history. Draws implications for the symbolic construction of voice in narrative.

189. Ortony, Andrew. "Cognitive Development and the Language of Mental States." *DPr* 10 (April–June 1987): 193–199.

Responds to the papers of Wellman and Estes, Olson and Torrance, and Hall and Nagy in *Discourse Processes* 10 (April–June 1987) and suggests areas for future research.

190. Osborn, Susan. "Revisioning the Argument: An Exploratory Study of Some Rhetorical Strategies of Women Student Writers." *Praxis* 1 (Spring/Summer 1987): 113–133.

Uses interviews and samples of women students' writing to discuss how women's styles work "in defiance of the code that defeats them."

191. Palmeri, Anthony. "Walter J. Ong's Perspectives on Rhetoric." Paper presented at the Eastern Communication Association, Syracuse, May 1987. ERIC ED 283 225. 52 pages

Reviews Ong's work, dividing it into three periods.

192. Park, Young Mok. "The Influence of the Task upon Writing Performance." *DAI* 48 (August 1987): 324A.

Finds mixed results for general and specific tasks.

193. Parker, Robert, and Vera Goodkin. *The Consequences of Writing: Enhancing Learning in the Disciplines.* Upper Montclair, N.J.: Boynton/Cook, 1987. 192 pages

Presents historical and philosophical background on the writing across the curriculum movement and case studies of writing in both academic and vocational classes. Includes samples of student writing.

194. Perdue, Virginia. "Confidence Versus Authority: Visions of the Writer in Rhetorical Theory." Paper presented at the CCCC Convention, Atlanta, March 1987. ERIC ED 280 058. 15 pages

Suggests that process-writing pedagogies attempt to reduce anxiety in students by building confidence, but they do not account for the social realities of discourse.

195. Peterson, Karen Eileen. "Relationships among Measures of Writer's Block, Writing Anxiety, and Procrastination." *DAI* 48 (November 1987): 1505B.

Concludes that writer's block, writing anxiety, and procrastination are positively related constructs. Better measures for these constructs need devising.

196. Piazza, Carolyn L. "Identifying Context Variables in Research on Writing: A Review and Suggested Directions." *WC* 4 (April 1987): 107–137.

Identifies context variables in written composition by using the theoretical perspectives of cognitive psychology, sociology, and anthropology.

197. Popken, Randell L. "A Study of Topic Sentence Use in Academic Writing." *WC* 4 (April 1987): 209–228.

Special content and coherence demands make topic sentences a standard in academic articles although not all writers in all fields use topic sentences.

198. Porush, David. "What Homer Can Teach Technical Writers: The Mnemonic Value of Poetic Devices." *JTWC* 17 (1987): 129–143.

Argues that technical writers should incorporate into their work devices of epic poetry because some contemporary research in cognition has confirmed their mnemonic value.

199. Pounds, Wayne. "Agents and Actions: An Excursion in Plain Style." *RR* 6 (Fall 1987): 94–106.

Affirms a revised plain style, concluding from an analytical study that it is teachable, "lucid, and capable of sustaining complexity of thought."

200. Prasse, Michael John. "The Model of Anaphoric Reference." *DAI* 48 (July 1987): 291B.

Experiments with a new model of anaphoric reference and concludes that previously read material relates to present material. Suggests three implications.

201. Puma, Vincent D. "The Effects of Degree of Audience Intimacy on Linguistic Features and Writing Quality in the Audience-Specified Essays of First-Year College Students." *DAI* 47 (March 1987): 3343A.

Results indicate an inverse relationship between quality and intimacy, suggesting differences in how writers adopt speaking and writing stances.

202. Puma, Vincent D. *Relationships between Writer-Audience Proximity, Register, and Quality in the Essays of First-Year College Students*. St. Augustine, Fla.: Flagler College Department of English, 1986. ERIC ED 282 217. 49 pages

Examines relationships among writer and audience proximity, register, and writing quality using 100 freshmen.

203. Qudah, Mahmoud A. "Cohesion and Interactivity in Scientific and Nonscientific Discourse." *DAI* 48 (September 1987): 643A.

Suggests that nonscientific texts are more cohesive, interactive, and readable than scientific texts.

204. Radner, Joan A., and Susan S. Lanser. "The Feminist Voice: Strategies of Coding in Folklore and Literature." *JAF* 100 (October–December 1987): 412–425.

Presents a theory and typology of women's strategies for coding ideas and feelings proscribed by the dominant culture. Draws implications for the analysis of narratives in different modes.

205. Rathjens, Dietrich. "The Problem of Synonymy: Bacon's Third Idol Expanded." *JTWC* 17 (1987): 373–384.

Argues that we should abolish the notion that words are synonymous and learn to make finer discriminations in meaning among words.

206. Raven, Mary Elizabeth. "A Situational Approach: Making Software More Functional." *JTWC* 17 (1987): 287–301.

Keeping readers and their needs in mind improve both computer software documentation and the design of word-processing software.

207. Redeker, Gisela. "Language Use in Informal Narratives: Effects of Social Distance and Listener Involvement." *DAI* 48 (November 1987): 1505B.

After examining 32 informal narratives, concludes that a friend's narrative style is more "mimetic" as contrasted with a stranger's more "diegetic" style.

208. Reid, Geneva Bryant. "The Use of the Perry Scheme in the Teaching of Freshman English." *DAI* 47 (June 1987): 4302A.

This study tests students' cognitive and writing apprehension levels. Results show that an appropriate curriculum could be designed to complement and challenge cognitive levels.

209. Roen, Duane, and Marvin Diogenes. "A Profound Proposal for Reform in Composition Instruction: The C-Team." *TETYC* 14 (May 1987): 137–141.

A satiric essay on the "New Paradigm" in composition instruction, which offers punishments for teachers and departments failing to conform.

210. Rosenfield, Irma Barbara. "Pauses in Oral and Written Narrative." *DAI* 48 (October 1987): 916A.

Confirms that pauses reflect narrative organization.

211. Rosenwald, Lawrence. "Common Myths about Diaries." *Raritan* 6 (Winter 1987): 97–112.

Discusses several myths about diaries: that they are "private," "artless," "subjective," "truthful," and have no audience but the writer.

212. Roth, Robert G. "The Evolving Audience: Alternatives to Audience Accommodations." *CCC* 38 (February 1987): 47–55.

Refers to three student writers' experiences, noting how audience may be created or invoked, defined or undefined, uniform or multiple, and external or imagined self projection.

213. Rowland, Robert C. "Narrative: Mode of Discourse or Paradigm?" *ComM* 54 (September 1987): 264–275.

Proposes three limitations on the narrative paradigm.

214. Rowland, Robert C. "On Defining Argument." *P&R* 20 (1987): 140–157.

Surveys the literature on argument as an epistemic method and a social process. Explores disagreements about definitions, theories, and methodologies for evaluating argument.

215. Rubens, Philip. "The Impact of Innovative Communication Technologies: On-Line Documentation, the Reader, and the Writer." *JBTC* 1 (September 1987): 5–20.

Argues that electronic information technologies ask us to question all text-preparation conventions and methods. Offers a set of conceptual problems.

216. Samuels, Marilyn Schauer. "Is Technical Communication 'Literature'? Current Writing Scholarship and Vico's Cycles of Knowledge." *JBTC* 1 (January 1987): 48–67.

Relates three premises of humanities and writing scholarship to Vico's theory and sees technical writing as both art and science, cognitive and interpretive.

217. Scholnick, Ellin K. "The Language of the Mind: Statements about Mental States." *DPr* 10 (April–June 1987): 181–192.

Responds to the papers of Wellman and Estes, Olson and Torrance, and Hall and Nagy in *Discourse Processes* 10 (April–June 1987) and suggests areas for future research.

218. Schroeder, Michael L. "Rhetoric in New Fiction." *DAI* 47 (March 1987): 3430A.

Uses Booth's rhetorical analysis to show that literary innovation gives writers a diversity of methods to effectively communicate ideas and values.

219. Sheehan, Anne Marie Harper. "Structure and Cohesion in Informative Writing by College Freshmen." *DAI* 48 (October 1987): 913A.

Finds structuring to be dynamic, changing over time during composition.

220. Sills, Caryl K. "The Writing Process of Experienced Writers in the Poetic and Transactional Modes: Similarities and Differences." *DAI* 48 (July 1987): 117A.

The six writers investigated used expressive writing in both modes, with purpose determining the roles adopted and the choices of genre.

221. Smith, Hugh T. "Composition via Strangulation." *TETYC* 14 (May 1987): 142–145.

A satiric essay on contemporary theories of composition.

222. Soter, Anna O. "New Perspectives in Composition Research and Instruction." *JCS* 19 (May–June 1987): 277–281.

A review of Miles Myers's *The Teacher-Researcher* and Anne Ruggles Gere's *Roots in the Sawdust*.

223. Soter, Anna O. "Recent Research on Writing: Implications for Writing across the Curriculum." *JCS* 19 (September–October 1987): 425–438.

Surveys "the major themes in research on writing" to define problems that remain in applying theory to practice, particularly in writing across the curriculum.

224. Spitzack, Carole, and Kathryn Carter. "Women in Communication Studies: A Typology for Revision." *QJS* 73 (November 1987): 401–423.

Reviews five research paradigms for women's communications, all of which are said to exclude women's communication from holding an appropriate place in the discipline.

225. Steinberg, Erwin R. "Erwin R. Steinberg Responds [to Vitanza, *CE* 49 (December 1987)]." *CE* 49 (December 1987): 928–930.

Clarifies his use of protocols.

226. Stephens, John, and Ruth Waterhouse. "Authorial Revision and Constraints on the Role of the Reader: Some Examples from Wilfred Owen." *PT* 8 (1987): 65–83.

Examines the temporal and spatial adjustments and concrete language that enhance readers' participation in meaning construction.

227. Sternglass, Marilyn S. "The Dual Role of Student/Research Subject: Effect of Context on a Study of Reading and Writing." Paper presented at the NCTE Convention, San Antonio, November 1986. ERIC ED 277 991. 9 pages

Examines changes in the behavior and attitudes of graduate students who became subjects in a study of reading and writing processes.

228. Sternglass, Marilyn S. "Instructional Implications of Three Conceptual Models of Reading/Writing Relationships." *EQ* 20 (Fall 1987): 184–193.

Claims that meaning is composed by both readers and writers resulting in a "new event, larger than the sum of its parts." This view is called the "transactional perspective."

229. Stotsky, Sandra. "Writing in a Political Context: The Value of Letters to Legislators." *WC* 4 (October 1987): 394–410.

Shows why letters are of great value to both writers and readers and why "civic writing" should be studied in more depth.

230. Straub, Richard E. "Writing as Authoring: A New Perspective for Evaluating Student Discourse." *DAI* 47 (May 1987): 4008A.

Proposes a theory of authoring that asks teachers to evaluate student discourse in terms of the writer's involvement, originality, belief, and dialogic thinking.

231. Strickland, James. "Computers, Invention, and the Power to Change Student Writing." *CC* 4 (April 1987): 7–26.

Compares the results of three heuristic studies. Finds no real differences between using pen, paper, or CAI for prewriting.

232. Swales, John, and Hazem Najjar. "The Writing of Research Article Introductions." *WC* 4 (April 1987): 175–191.

Although manual and style guides stress that introductions to research articles include statements of principal findings, actual practice in two fields does not support this advice.

233. Tanita Ratledge, Nancy Ellen. "Theoretical and Methodological Integrity of a Structurational Scheme for Coding Argument in Decision-Making Groups." *DAI* 47 (January 1987): 2373A.

Studies a scheme for coding argument in decision-making groups. The relationships among valence, argument, and strategy merit further study.

234. Tappmeyer, Mark Edward. "The Influence of Field Dependence/Independence in Writers' Goal Setting Strategies." *DAI* 48 (September 1987): 642A.

Finds that field-independent subjects tend to construct more composing-process goals and goals for elements of the rhetorical problem than field-dependent subjects.

235. Teich, Nathaniel. "Transfer of Writing Skills: Implications of the Theory of Lateral and Vertical Transfer." *WC* 4 (April 1987): 193–208.

Argues that the theory of lateral and vertical transfer as applied to writing is compatible with current conceptions of cognitive processes and with student-centered and direct, content-oriented instruction.

236. Tindale, Christopher W., and James Gough. "The Use of Irony in Argumentation." *P&R* 20 (1987): 1–17.

Investigates whether or not rhetorical strategy is different from irony as a literary trope.

237. Trapp, Robert, and Pamela J. Benoit. "An Interpretive Perspective on Argumentation: A Research Editorial." *WJSC* 51 (Fall 1987): 417–430.

Examines philosophical assumptions supportive of and contrary to an interpretive view of communication.

238. Trimbur, John. "Beyond Cognition: The Voices in Inner Speech." *RR* 5 (Spring 1987): 211–221.

Offers a "post-cognitivist" view of Vygotsky and Piaget. Proposes instead Bakhtin's idea that a "polyphony of [social] voices resonate in the writer's mind."

239. Udwin, Victor. "Reading and Writing: The Rhetoric of Reversal." *Reader* 18 (Fall 1987): 5–15.

Asserts that reading and writing are bound by the process of induction and deduction in the reader's response to a text.

240. Vacc, Nancy N. "Word Processor Versus Handwriting: A Comparative Study of Writing Samples Produced by Mildly Mentally Handicapped Students." *ExC* 54 (October 1987): 156–165.

Mildly mentally handicapped students spent more time on task using word processors instead of handwriting, but without any significant change in holistic scores.

241. van Dijk, Teun A. *Communicating Racism: Ethnic Prejudice in Thought and Talk.* Newbury Park, Calif.: Sage, 1987. 376 pages

Examines ethnic stereotypes and the ways in which they are diffused through interpersonal communication and intergroup interactions.

242. Vangelisti, Anita L. "Problem Solving: Issues for the Classroom." *ComEd* 36 (July 1987): 296–304.

Surveys recent research on problem solving in speech communication courses: conceptual developments, social and affective correlates, and potential teaching methods.

243. Vipond, Douglas, and Russell Hunt. "Shunting Information or Making Contact? Assumptions for Research on Aesthetic Reading." *EQ* 20 (Summer 1987): 131–136.

Argues that writing is a social process in which writers and readers try to make contact rather than being a process of passing information.

244. Vitanza, Victor J. "A Comment on 'Protocols, Retrospective Reports, and the Stream of Consciousness' [*CE* 48 (November 1986)]." *CE* 49 (December 1987): 926–928.

Questions Steinberg's use of protocols as reflections of cognitive processes in order to construct problem-solving models.

245. Voiku, Daniel J. "The One-Sided-Tripod and the New Pedagogy of Writing." *BADE* 86 (Spring 1987): 24–28.

Argues that emphasizing process and the student-centered teacher leads to a reification of the self and a new solipsism.

246. Von Der Osten, H. Robert. "Reading to Revise: Toward a Model of How and Why Freshman Read to Revise Their Own Drafts." *DAI* 47 (February 1987): 2931A.

Using case studies, discusses constructive revisers (revision driven by meaning) and reactive revisers (revision driven by the draft).

247. Waldrep, Tom, ed. *Writers on Writing, Volume 2.* New York: Random House, 1987. 352 pages

Essays by 24 rhetoricians on their practices as writers and teachers of writing.

248. Walker, Helen Louise. "Decentering: Its Place in the Writing Process." *DAI* 48 (September 1987): 643A.

Results indicate a significant correlation between audience awareness and overall writing effectiveness across writing tasks.

249. Wall, Susan V. "The Languages of the Text: What Even Good Students Need to

Know about Rewriting." *JAC* 7 (1987): 31–40.

A case analysis of work by a student in an epistemically oriented course stressing genuine re-seeing of a text.

250. Walzer, Arthur E. "Lloyd Bitzer's 'Rhetorical Situation': The 'Exigencies' of Academic Discourse." Paper presented at the CCCC Convention, Atlanta, March 1987. ERIC ED 280 059. 9 pages

Claims that Bitzer's concept, "rhetorical exigency," does not account for the nature of academic discourse.

251. White, Lauren L. "Modern Traditions of the Essay." *DAI* 48 (November 1987): 1195A.

Argues that the essay is a form of rhetoric, a view that accounts for it sermonic aim and protean nature.

252. Wilkes-Gibbs, Deanna. "Collaborative Processes of Language Use in Conversation." *DAI* 47 (March 1987): 3993B.

Concludes that speakers and listeners engaged in a conversation take the least resistive path, collaborating on meaning.

253. Williams, James D. "Covert Linguistic Behavior during Writing Tasks: Psychological Differences between Above-Average and Below-Average Writers." *WC* 4 (July 1987): 310–328.

Covert linguistic behavior (subvocal motor activity) functions as a memory aid, helping above average writers to focus on their topic, aim, and audience.

254. Williams, Patrick Swinny. "Quality in Linguistic Metaphors." *DAI* 48 (September 1987): 903B.

Argues that metaphor quality partly depends on comprehensibility, aptness, and novelty.

255. Winterowd, W. Ross. "'Chicken' and Poetry: The Unspeakable and the Unsayable." *JAC* 7 (1987): 76–80.

Meditations on the power and limits of language. Discusses rhetoric as the study of the unspeakable and unsayable.

256. Witte, Stephen P. "Pre-Text and Composing." *CCC* 38 (December 1987): 397–425.

Uses 50 protocols to make four tentative claims about the "nature and function of prewriting during composition."

257. Yarbrough, Donald B., and Ellen D. Gagne. "Metaphor and the Free Recall of Technical Text." *DPr* 10 (January–March 1987): 81–91.

Metaphoric language interfered with recall, especially with recall of information located close to the metaphors. Results support a two-stage model of metaphoric comprehension.

258. Yoos, George E. "Rhetoric of Appeal and Rhetoric of Response." *P&R* 20 (1987): 107–117.

The two rhetorics of appeal and of response imply different audiences. One-sided accounts of rhetoric usually favor the former, which is Aristotelian.

259. Zappen, James P. "Rhetoric and Technical Communication: An Argument for Historical and Political Pluralism." *JBTC* 1 (September 1987): 29–44.

Traces the changing associations of rhetoric, politics, ethics, and science since Plato. Proposes a pluralistic notion of technical communications that will accomodate both organizational and public interests.

260. Zumwalt, Glenda Ann. "An Empirical Application and Test of James L. Kinneavy's Theory of Discourse." *DAI* 47 (April 1987): 3689A.

Tests Kinneavy's assertion that aim determines the nature, structure, style, and logic of discourse by examining examples of discourse from 10 freshman composition anthologies.

See also 532, 635, 834, 837, 859, 883, 885,

897, 934, 966, 1078, 1192, 1430, 1446, 1656

2.2   RHETORICAL HISTORY

261. Abbott, Don P. "The Ancient Word: Rhetoric in Aztec Culture." *Rhetorica* 5 (Summer 1987): 251–264.

Analyzes the *huehuetlahtolli*, the Aztec speeches of the ancients, showing resemblances to European rhetoric and reflections of pre-literate Aztec culture.

262. Admodt, Terrie Dopp. "Righteous Armies, Holy Cause Apocalyptic Imagery, and the Civil War." *DAI* 47 (January 1987): 2627A.

A study of apocalyptic imagery in popular literature and art in northern and southern states during the Civil War.

263. Agamben, Giorgio. "The Thing Itself." *SubStance* 16 (1987): 18–28.

An article translated by Juliana Schiesari. Interprets the expression appearing in Plato's seventh letter as the "thing of thinking." Sees Plato's theory of linguistic significance as the subjects' first organic exposition.

264. Allen, Bobbie Jo. "Agricola's *De Re Metallia:* A Sixteenth-Century Link in the Evolution of Technical Writing." *DAI* 47 (February 1987): 2797A.

Uses Aristotle's *Rhetoric* and technical writing precepts of purpose, subject, and audience to show the evolution and applications of technical writing theories.

265. Autrey, Ken. "The Personal Journal in Composition Instruction: A History." Paper presented at the CCCC Convention, Atlanta, March 1987. ERIC ED 282 250. 12 pages

Notes the historical use of personal journals and their entry into writing textbooks in the late nineteenth and early twentieth centuries.

266. Benoit, William. "On Aristotle's Example." *P&R* 20 (1987): 261–267.

Argues that generalization mediates Aristotle's argument-by-example. Claims that Hauser would say it does not.

267. Berlin, James A. *Rhetoric and Reality: Writing Instruction in American Colleges 1900–1985.* Studies in Writing and Rhetoric. Carbondale, Ill.: Southern Illinois University Press, 1987. 236 pages

Continues the history begun in Berlin's *Writing Instruction in Nineteenth-Century American Colleges* (1986). Classifies movements and traditions under the headings of objective, subjective, and transactional rhetorics.

268. Blair, Carole. "The Statement: Foundation of Foucault's Historical Criticism." *WJSC* 51 (Fall 1987): 364–383.

Suggests the archeological approach as a useful critical perspective and applicable to rhetorical theory in general.

269. Carrington, Jane Laurel. "Erasmus and the Problem of Language." *DAI* 47 (February 1987): 3161A.

Examines Erasmus's ambivalent ideas about the polysemy of language.

270. Clifford, John. "Ideology into Discourse: A Historical Perspective." *JAC* 7 (1987): 121–130.

Both literature and composition formerly accepted positivist, formalist values. Now progressives in each area reject such assumptions and share a new epistemology.

271. Connors, Robert J. "Personal Writing Assignments." *CCC* 38 (May 1987): 166–183.

Traces the shift from impersonal to personal writing assignments from Aristotle to the present with emphasis on the nineteenth century.

272. Corbett, Edward P. J. "Teaching Composition: Where We've Been and Where We're Going." *CCC* 38 (December 1987): 444–452.

Surveys composition instruction since the 1940s, noting increased professionalism and changes in instructional emphases. Muses about improvements in the quality of instruction.

273. Cronkhite, Gary. "Aristotle's *Rhetoric* as an Historical Artifact, Being a Response to the Suggestion It Be Used as a Textbook." *ComEd* 36 (July 1987): 286–289.

Argues that the *Rhetoric* is only of historical interest, having little to offer to those needing practical, sound advice and theory.

274. Crowley, Sharon. "The Teaching of Writing: What Good Is Theory?" *ArEB* 29 (Spring 1987): 29–33.

Reviews the historical development of writing pedagogy's theoretical basis and argues for rethinking our goals.

275. Donelson, Ken. "English Becomes a Subject: 1894." *ET* 18 (Winter 1987): 24–26.

Discusses American education before and after the 1894 report of the Committee of Ten, which advocated a new direction in curriculum.

276. Douglas, George H., and Herbert W. Hildebrandt, eds. *Studies in the History of Business Writing*. Urbana, Ill.: Association for Business Communication, 1985.

A collection of 14 essays that develop a central theme: written communication was the medium for transmitting information in the business world. Traces the historical roots of business communication and analyzes specific applications from the sixteenth to the twentieth century.

277. Eden, Kathy. "Hermeneutics and the Ancient Rhetorical Tradition." *Rhetorica* 5 (Winter 1987): 59–86.

Examines the development of hermeneutics within the rhetorical tradition between the fourth century B.C. and the first century A.D. Treats Plato, Aristotle, Cicero, Quintilian, and Demetrius.

278. Enos, Richard Leo. "The Classical Tradition(s) of Rhetoric: A Demur to the Country Club Set." *CCC* 38 (October 1987): 283–291.

Argues for the acceptance in classical rhetoric of second-order instrumental scholarship.

279. Enos, Richard Leo. *The Literate Mode of Cicero's Legal Rhetoric*. Carbondale, Ill.: Southern Illinois University Press, 1987. 144 pages

Examines the relationship between Cicero's oral and written skills and his legal argumentation. Argues that Cicero developed a "literate mind," enabling him to construct arguments both compelling and appealing. Examines Cicero's use of writing as an aid to composing and editing speeches.

280. Grego, Rhonda Carnell. "Science, Late Nineteenth-Century Rhetoric, and the Beginnings of Technical Writing Instruction in America." *JTWC* 17 (1987): 63–78.

Argues that engineering departments were dissatisfied with early twentieth-century technical writing courses because they stressed methods of scientific exposition rather than practical methods of technical argumentation.

281. Grierson, Don. "Battling Censors, Chiding Home Office: Harrison Salisbury's Russian Assignment." *JQ* 64 (Summer–Autumn 1987): 313–316.

Salisbury was severely censored while in Moscow, but was able to vindicate himself upon returning to the U.S. after Stalin's death. He won a Pulitzer Prize with his articles about Russia.

282. Hagaman, John. "Rhetorical Invention and Advanced Literacy: An Historical Perspective." Paper presented at the CCCC Convention, Atlanta, March 1987. ERIC ED 280 082. 14 pages

Argues that students should be taught both cognitive and social approaches to invention.

283. Hancock, Donald H. "Ideas about Adult Learning in Fifth- and Fourth-Century B.C. Athens." *DAI* 47 (May 1987): 3943A.

Concludes that modern adult education lacks the concern for "communal and transcendental human interests" important to many ancient Greeks.

284. Hanks, William F. "Discourse Genres in a Theory of Practice." *AmE* 14 (November 1987): 668–692.

Describes the rise of new discourse genres in documents of eighteenth-century colonial Yucatan. Shows them to reflect new, hybrid forms of action.

285. Harmon, Joseph E. "The Literature of Enlightenment: Technical Periodicals and Procedures in the Seventeenth and Eighteenth Centuries." *JTWC* 17 (1987): 397–405.

Traces the origin of technical periodicals and describes their early characteristics. They were aimed at a general readership, were multi-disciplinary in subject matter, and were written in a plain style.

286. Haun-Montiel, Margaret E. "Twentieth-Century Neo-Aristotelian Criticism: Five Theorists." *DAI* 48 (October 1987): 924A.

Provides an account of the views of Lane Cooper, R. S. Crane, Elder Olson, Wayne C. Booth, and Ralph W. Rader on Aristotle's *Poetics*.

287. Hauser, Gerard A. "Reply to Benoit [*P&R* 20 (1987)]." *P&R* 20 (1987): 268–272.

Defends his reading of Aristotle's argument-by-example by making a distinction between "epistemological requirements" and "formal reasoning."

288. Heckel, David. "Francis Bacon's New Science: Rhetoric and the Transformative Power of Print." Paper presented at the CCCC Convention, Atlanta, March 1987. ERIC ED 283 194. 12 pages

Suggests that typographic literacy allowed Bacon to see nature as "text to be read."

289. Henry, Susan. "'Dear Companion, Ever-Ready Co-Worker': A Woman's Role in a Media Dynasty." *JQ* 64 (Summer-Autumn 1987): 301–312.

Eliza Otis, wife of a *Los Angeles Times* publisher, was active in newspaper work as revealed in the letters, journals, and autobiographies of family members since 1882.

290. Jarratt, Susan C. "The First Sophists and the Uses of History." *RR* 6 (Fall 1987): 67–78.

Argues that sophists suffer from "two millenia of neglect." Examines contemporary versions of sophists to make their useful contributions more relevant to composition studies.

291. Jensen, J. Vernon. "Rhetorical Emphases in Taoism." *Rhetorica* 5 (Summer 1987): 219–229.

Explains the rhetorical emphasis in six principles of Taoism.

292. Johnson, Nan. "English Composition, Rhetoric, and English Studies at Nineteenth-Century Canadian Colleges and Universities." *EQ* 20 (Winter 1987): 296–304.

Reviews the study of rhetoric and English composition.

293. Johnson, Nan. "Origin and Artifact: Classical Rhetoric in Modern Composition Texts." *EQ* 19 (Fall 1986): 207–215.

Reviews canons of classical and modern rhetoric. Concludes that instruction in rhetoric has changed little.

294. Kantor, Ken. "Teaching Writing since Dartmouth: Broadening the Context." *EEd* 19 (October 1987): 171–180.

Argues that the personal growth model developed at Dartmouth has proven difficult to implement.

295. Le Tourneau, Mark. "General and Special Topics in the *De Baptismo* of Tertullian." *Rhetorica* 5 (Winter 1987): 87–105.

Analyzes the topics in Tertullian's *De Baptismo*, classifying them according to taxonomies in Cicero's *De Inventione* and *Topica*. Reveals frequent use of antithesis and dense clusters of topics.

296. Locker, Kitty O. " 'As Per Your Request': A History of Business Jargon." *JBTC* 1 (January 1987): 27–47.

Offers preliminary explanations for the sources and persistence of American and British business jargon, noting variation over time and stressing the inexperience, misguided assumptions, and habits of writers.

297. McClish, Glen A. "Rhetoric and the Rise of the English Novel." *DAI* 48 (November 1987): 1211A.

Demonstrates the pervasive nature of the eighteenth-century's ambivalent attitude toward rhetoric.

298. McKerrow, Raymie E. "Richard Whately and the Revival of Logic in Nineteenth-Century England." *Rhetorica* 5 (Spring 1987): 163–185.

Analyzes Whately's *Elements of Logic*, explaining its historical context and its defense of syllogistic logic.

299. Myers, Greg. "Greg Myers Responds [to Ramage and Bean, *CE* 49 (February 1987)]." *CE* 49 (February 1987): 211–214.

Clarifies his argument that collaborative learning is not necessarily liberating, as proponents claim.

300. O'Banion, John. "Narration and Argumentation: Quintilian on *Narratio* as the Heart of Rhetorical Thinking." *Rhetorica* 5 (Autumn 1987): 325–351.

Argues that Quintilian considered narration as the basic rhetorical process, explaining its dialectical relationship with argument and its role in arrangement.

301. Plochmann, George Kimball, and Franklin E. Robinson. *A Friendly Companion to Plato's Gorgias*. Carbondale, Ill.: Southern Illinois University Press, 1987. 640 pages

A detailed analysis of the *Gorgias*. Reflects on the book's unity, sweep, and philosophic implications.

302. Poulakos, Takis. "Isocrates's Use of Narrative in the *Evagoras*: Epideictic Rhetoric and Moral Action." *QJS* 73 (August 1987): 317–328.

Isocrates's oration on the life of the Cyprian king Evagoras demonstrates his attempts to expand the epideictic form to give it political purpose.

303. Prill, Paul. "Rhetoric and Poetics in the Early Middle Ages." *Rhetorica* 5 (Spring 1987): 129–147.

Discusses how Carolingian authors adapted rhetorical principles and the *progymnasmata* to the analysis and writing of poetry.

304. Purcell, William M. "Transsumptio: A Rhetorical Doctrine of the Thirteenth Century—Explication and Application." *DAI* 47 (May 1987): 4082A.

Establishes *transsumptio* as a concept with which to organize the study of tropes and to restore metaphor to the status of a trope.

305. Quintilian. *Quintilian on the Teaching of Speaking and Writing*. Edited by James J. Murphy. Landmarks in Rhetoric and Public Address. Carbondale, Ill.: Southern Illinois University Press, 1987. 200 pages

Translations from books 1, 2, and 10 of the *Institutio Oratoria* with an introductory essay by James Murphy.

306. Ramage, John D., and John C. Bean. "A Comment on 'Reality, Consensus, and Reform in the Rhetoric of Composition Teaching' [*CE* 48 (February 1986)]." *CE* 49 (February 1987): 209–211.

Argues that Myers is uncritically reductive in assuming that collaborative learning leads to monolithic groupthinking.

307. Ried, Paul E. "The Boylston Professor in the Twentieth Century." *QJS* 73 (November 1987): 474–481.

Examines the evolution of the Boylston Professorship from being a chair of rhetoric to one of poetry. Covers the period from the retirement of Adams Sherman Hill to the present.

308. Riegelman, Milton. "Today's Scholar: 'A Good Finger, a Good Neck, an Elbow, but Never a Man.' " *CHE* 34 (2 September 1987): A128.

Argues that educators should heed Ralph Waldo Emerson's 150-year-old argument against overspecialization and for scholarly "thoroughness."

309. Roochnik, David L. "Plato's Critique of Postmodernism." *P&L* 11 (October 1987): 282–289.

Analyzes Plato's attack on postmodernism, acknowledging the historical absurdity implicit in the analysis. Indicates that one aspect of Plato's genius was his "prescience" of later genres.

310. Scott, Patrick, ed. "Victorians on Rhetoric and Prose Style." *Dictionary of Literary Biography 57: Victorian Prose Writers after 1867* (Detroit: Gale Research, 1987): 377–509.

Reprints excerpts and essays on rhetoric and style written by Whately, de Quincey, Spencer, Lewes, Bain, Saintsbury, Symonds, Pater, Harrison, and others.

311. Sharratt, Peter. "Recent Work on Peter Ramus (1970–1986)." *Rhetorica* 5 (Winter 1987): 7–58.

A critical account of books and articles on Ramus since 1970, including new books that alter views of Ramus. Uses a computerized catalog of Ramus's works.

312. Thompson, Kenneth W., ed. *The History and Philosophy of Rhetoric and Political Discourse, Volume I*. Exxon Educational Foundation Series on Rhetoric and Political Discourse. Lanham, Md.: University Press of America, 1987. 130 pages

Three essays explore the meaning and purpose of rhetoric in the seventeeth, eighteenth, and nineteenth centuries. One essay examines rhetoric in light of the changing boundaries involved in liability and torts in American political life.

313. Thompson, Kenneth W., ed. *The History and Philosophy of Rhetoric and Political Discourse, Volume II*. Exxon Educational Foundation Series on Rhetoric and Political Discourse. Lanham, Md.: University Press of America, 1987. 118 pages

Five essays treat the rhetoric of the Greeks, Romans, and medieval writers.

314. Thompson, Kenneth W., ed. *Rhetoric and the Founders, Volume III*. Exxon Educational Foundation Series on Rhetoric and Political Discourse. Lanham, Md.: University Press of America, 1987. 102 pages

A *festschrift* for Dumas Malone, the eight essays in this collection discuss two papers written by Malone.

315. Thoreau, Henry D. *Thoreau's Comments on the Art of Writing*. Edited by Richard Dillman. Lanham, Md.: University Press of America, 1987. 66 pages

A collection of Thoreau's comments on the art and process of writing.

316. Toohey, Margaret L. "English Studies in the U.S.: Origin and Evolution." *DAI* 48 (December 1987): 1452A.

Examines the rapid, nonparallel evolution of English studies, including the decline of rhetoric, oratory, and philology.

317. Vitanza, Victor J. "Critical Sub/Versions of the History of Philosophical Rhetoric." *RR* 6 (Fall 1987): 41–66.

Argues through a "methodology of provocation" that we need to reclaim nontraditional, antagonistic, suspicious, sophistic rhetorics to debunk conventional ideas of knowledge, truth, and power.

318. Wallace, Trudy, and Herbert J. Walberg. "Personality Traits and Childhood Environ-

ments of Eminent Essayists." *GCQ* 31 (Spring 1987): 65–69.

Catalogues the cognitive, affective, physical, and environmental traits of famous essayists from the fourteenth to the twentieth centuries.

319. Walzer, Arthur E. "Logic and Rhetoric in Malthus's *Essay on the Principle of Population*, 1798." *QJS* 73 (February 1987): 1–17.

Claims that Malthus imitated the argumentative techniques of Newton's *Principia* to refute the optimism of Condorcet and Godwin.

320. Welch, Kathleen E. "A Critique of Classical Rhetoric: The Contemporary Appropriation of Ancient Discourse." *RR* 6 (Fall 1987): 79–86.

Maintains that classical rhetoric has been reductively misinterpreted lately, making Aristotle appear as a "logic-chopping automaton." Blames scholarly decontextualizing and proposes alternatives.

321. Winterowd, W. Ross. "The Purification of Literature and Rhetoric." *CE* 49 (March 1987): 257–273.

A historical description of how the division between rhetoric, literature, and composition has developed.

See also 54, 108, 147, 251, 259, 739, 1140

2.3 POLITICAL, RELIGIOUS, AND JUDICIAL RHETORIC

322. Appel, Edward C. "The Perfected Drama of Reverend Jerry Falwell." *ComQ* 35 (Winter 1987): 26–38.

Uses Burke's "principles of perfection" and nine "indexes of dramatic intensity" to study the tragic-symbol preaching of the Reverend Jerry Falwell.

323. Arneson, Patricia Ann. "Political Perspectives on Revolution: A Mythic Analysis of the Public Discourse of Presidents Ronald Reagan and Daniel Ortega." *DAI* 48 (December 1987): 1355A.

Uses Burke's dramatistic pentad to discuss agency in President Reagan's discourse, purpose in President Ortega's, and the importance of myth.

324. Asonevich, Walter J. "George Washington's Speeches and Addresses: Origins of an American Presidential Rhetoric." *DAI* 48 (December 1987): 1454A.

Provides a historical, literary, and oral analysis of Washington's rhetoric.

325. Bennett, Diane Tobin. "Public Communication in Crisis: A Case Study of the Rhetorical Dimensions of the Abdication of Edward VIII." *DAI* 48 (November 1987): 1054A.

A rhetorical analysis of crisis rhetoric suggests that it simplifies and structures reality for the public.

326. Berezov, Jack Lewis. "Single-Line Proverbs: A Study of the Sayings Collected in Proverbs 10–22:16 and 25–29." *DAI* 48 (November 1987): 1226A.

Examines the syntax and structure of sayings in Proverbs and classifies them into seven types.

327. Birdsell, David S. "A Coordinated Approach to the Master Tropes." *DAI* 48 (July 1987): 7A.

Uses a pluralistic approach to study four master tropes. Finds a relationship between "information and form" and "argument and poetic." Demonstrates the approach with an analysis of President Reagan's rhetoric on the Soviet Union.

328. Birdsell, David S. "Ronald Reagan on Lebanon and Grenada: Flexibility and Interpretation in the Application of Kenneth Burke's Pentad." *QJS* 73 (August 1987): 267–279.

Uses President Reagan's 27 October 1983 televised foreign policy address to show that Burke's pentad works best when applied flexibly, recognizing ambiguity of five terms.

329. Bostdorff, Denise M. "Making Light of James Watt: A Burkean Approach to the Form and Attitude of Political Cartoons." *QJS* 73 (February 1987): 43–59.

A Burkean study of 83 cartoons about the former Secretary of the Interior. Sees metaphor, irony, synecdoche, and metonymy as organizing principles.

330. Boswell, Parley Ann. "'Unspeakable rich mercy': Text and Audience in Three Puritan Sermons." *DAI* 48 (November 1987): 1241A.

Examines the rhetoric of three sermons by Cotton, Hooker, and Shepard, discovering compositional strategies that suggest roles for speakers and audience in the ongoing Christian drama.

331. Branham, Robert J., and W. Barnett Pearce. "A Contract for Civility: Edward Kennedy's Lynchburg Address." *QJS* 73 (November 1987): 424–443.

Argues that Kennedy's 1983 address at Liberty Baptist College successfully created a rhetorical situation in which he and Reverend Jerry Falwell could practice increased mutual civility.

332. Brown, Daniel Stewart, Jr. "A Radical Republican in the United States Senate: The Antislavery Speaking of Benjamin Franklin Wade (Ohio)." *DAI* 48 (December 1987): 1355A.

Analyzes Wade's rhetorical strategies in six speeches. His rhetorical proofs, affectives, quality, and ethics reveal both strengths and weaknesses.

333. Cardona, Ivan. "Aging in America: A Propositional Analysis of Selected Congressional Speeches of Representative Claude Pepper." *DAI* 47 (March 1987): 3238A.

Discusses pleas and recommendations in Pepper's program to improve quality of life for the elderly.

334. Casey, Michael John. "Ronald Reagan's Epideictic Rhetoric within the Context of the State of the Union Addresses during the Cold War, 1945–1985." *DAI* 47 (April 1987): 3791A.

Analyzes President Reagan's use of epideictic rhetoric in his inaugural addresses, his state of the Union addresses, and his speech about the downing of a Korean airliner.

335. Casey, Michael Wilson. "The Development of Necessary Inferences in the Hermeneutics of the Disciples of Christ/Churches of Christ." *DAI* 47 (April 1987): 3608A.

Examines the shift from George Campbell's inductive approach to Richard Whately's syllogistic approach in the rhetoric of Alexander Campbell, a leader of the Disciples of Christ.

336. Charland, Maurice. "Constitutive Rhetoric: The Case of the *Peuple Quebecois*." *QJS* 73 (May 1987): 133–150.

Studies how Burke's principle of "identification" functions in the rhetoric of the Quebec sovereignty movement.

337. Clark, E. Culpepper, and Raymie E. McKerrow. "The Historiographical Dilemma in Myrdal's American Creed: Rhetoric's Role in Rescuing a Historical Moment." *QJS* 73 (August 1987): 303–316.

Historians influenced by Myrdal's 1944 study, *An American Dilemma*, presented improved race relations as inevitable, thus overlooking the drama of the civil rights struggle.

338. Clark, Rebecca Leigh. "Changing Perceptions in Sex and Sexuality in Traditional Women's Magazines, 1900–1980." *DAI* 48 (September 1987): 749A.

Examines the depiction of sex and sexuality in the nonfiction of *Ladies' Home Journal* and *Good Housekeeping* from 1900 to 1980.

339. Coleman-Burns, Patricia Wendolyn. "A Rhetorical Analysis of the National Organization for an American Revolution (NOAR)." *DAI* 48 (October 1987): 778A.

32 THEORY AND RESEARCH

Uses the work of Cathcart, Burke, Brock, and McGee to analyze the rhetoric of NOAR in three periods.

340. Cornfield, Michael. "Book Review Essay: Presidential Rhetoric and the Credibility Gap." *ComR* 14 (August 1987): 462–469.

Reviews Ericksons's *Reagan Speaks* and Zarefsky's *President Johnson's War on Poverty*. Describes the "presidential communicative burden" of meeting both mass and elite audiences' expectations.

341. DeChamplain, Mitties McDonald. "Restoring the Myth of the Presidency: A Rhetorical Study of Televised Campaign Commercials in the 1976 Presidential Contest." *DAI* 48 (October 1987): 778A.

Uses constructs of myth and mythic adequacy to analyze television advertisements.

342. Enholm, Donald K., David Curtis Skaggs, and W. Jeffrey Welsh. "Origins of the Southern Mind: The Parochial Sermons of Thomas Craddock of Maryland, 1744–1770." *QJS* 73 (May 1987): 200–218.

Finds evidence of what Weaver considered the roots of Southern thinking in the sermons of an eighteenth-century Anglican clergyman.

343. Enrique, Sandoval. "The Metaphoric Style in the Politically Censored Theatre." *DAI* 47 (January 1987): 2376A.

Examines three instances of repression: France under Nazi rule, South Africa under apartheid, and Chile under a military dictatorship.

344. Fink, Evelyn Carol. "Political Rhetoric and Strategic Choice in the Ratification Conventions on the U.S. Constitution." *DAI* 48 (December 1987): 1531A.

Argues that traditional rhetoric as political argument is a necessary component of any model of political decision making that predicts change in democratic politics.

345. Fish, Stanley. "Critical Legal Studies: Unger and Milton." *Raritan* 7 (Fall 1987): 1–20.

Argues that Unger's construction of "community" does not resolve modern antinomies between public and private, individual and society, except by positing "God."

346. Floyd, Christina. "Where There's a Will There's a Way: Legal Minds Grapple with Plain Language." *ETC* 44 (Fall 1987): 280–287.

Describes how courts determine a testator's intent when the language of a will establishes provisions that are illegal or impossible to carry out.

347. Foley, Michael. "The Languages of Contention: Political Language, Moral Judgment, and Peasant Mobilization in Contemporary Mexico." *DAI* 47 (June 1987): 4500A.

Concludes that political discourse helps determine the parameters of choice in labor organizations.

348. Gaber, Julia Ellen. "Lamb of God or Demagogue? A Burkean Cluster Analysis of the Selected Speeches of Minister Louis Farrahkan." *DAI* 47 (May 1987): 3908A.

Analyses three speeches composed before, during, and after Farrahkan's alliance with Jesse Jackson. Traces the evolution of motivation, techniques, and labels.

349. Gerardi, Pamela Dettart. "Assurbanipal's Elamite Campaigns: A Literary and Political Study." *DAI* 48 (September 1987): 722A.

Traces changes in Assyrian historical writing, including the use of topical arrangement in the discussion of military campaigns.

350. Gill, Ann Marie. "The Epistemic Role of Rhetoric in *Pring v. Penthouse*." *DAI* 47 (April 1987): 3709A.

Categorizes rhetoric-as-epistemic claims in speech communities and develops an "epistemic rhetorical theory" of inducement able to be used for pedagogical purposes.

351. Goody, Jack. "Writing, Religion, and Revolt in Bahia." *VLang* 20 (Autumn 1986): 318–343.

Concludes that introducing writing into a culture opens the way for converts into its religion.

352. Green, Steven Joe. "Political Communications in the Soviet Media: An Analysis of Channels and Patterns of Political Communication in Soviet Journals." *DAI* 47 (June 1987): 4501A.

Focuses on journals that participate in political discussions, thus providing a list of political message sources.

353. Guempel, Stephen Robert. "Charlotte Perkins Stetson Gilman, a Voice for Progress and Reflection: A Rhetorical Analysis of Selected Addresses, 1883–1892." *DAI* 47 (March 1987): 3238A.

Analyzes six speeches that convey Gilman's vision of perfectability. Discusses her rhetorical strategies and the "historical underpinnings of contemporary feminism."

354. Hamilton, Barbara Bova. "The Rhetoric of a Judicial Document: The Presentence Investigation, Document Design, and Social Context." *DAI* 48 (October 1987): 856A.

Examines document design and its effect on probation officers and judges.

355. Hardesty, Martha Ellen. "Language, Culture, and Romaji Reform: A Communications Policy Failure of the Allied Occupation of Japan." *DAI* 47 (February 1987): 2799A.

Analysis suggests that the proposed American language reform of Japan failed because American ethnocentrism and propaganda prohibited a clear assessment of the target culture and language.

356. Harding, Susan. "Convicted by the Holy Spirit: The Rhetoric of Fundamental Baptist Conversion." *AmE* 14 (February 1987): 167–181.

Argues that rhetoric, not ritual, is the primary vehicle of conversion.

357. Hatfield, Stephen Gill. "The Rhetorical Function of Selected Vice/Virtue Lists in the Letters of Paul." *DAI* 48 (October 1987): 943A.

Analyzes the functions of vice and virtue lists, their scope, their origin, their relationship to the history of rhetoric, and their specific rhetorical features.

358. Hayden, Robert M. "Turn-Taking, Overlap, and the Task at Hand: Ordering Speaking Turns in Legal Settings." *AmE* 14 (May 1987): 251–270.

Contrasts the sequencing of speaking turns in courts in India with those in the West, illuminating the effects of rhetorical practice on legal processes.

359. Hendricks, Janet Wall. "Images of Tradition: Ideological Transformations among the Shuar." *DAI* 47 (March 1987): 3466A.

Considers the role of language in changing the system of government among the Shuars of Ecuador to a hierarchical, federal system.

360. Hennen, Cathy L. "Campaigning against Communism: The Rhetoric of Walter P. Reuther, 1946–1948." *DAI* 47 (April 1987): 3609A.

Uses Bitzer's theory to analyze Reuther's four arguments against Communism. Discusses four rhetorical strategies and four positions.

361. Hockenhull, Brenda Rae. "The Use of Series in the Book of Amos." *DAI* 48 (October 1987): 944A.

Concludes that the series arrangement of Amos is an effective rhetorical structure.

362. Houglum, Robert Michael. "A Rhetorical Perspective of the Survivalist Movement of the Pacific Northwest." *DAI* 47 (March 1987): 3239A.

Uses historical critical methods to examine survivalist rhetoric, describing its key features.

363. Jeffres, Leo W., Jean Dobos, and Mary Sweeney. "Communication and Commitment to Community." *ComR* 14 (December 1987): 619–643.

Examines decisions by residents that commit them to neighborhoods and communities. Studies the relationships among communication processes, beliefs and attitudes, and commitments to community.

364. Johnson, Charles LeRoy. "The Rhetoric of Retailing Religion: A Comparative Analysis of the Rhetoric of Electric and Non-Electric Church Ministers." *DAI* 48 (July 1987): 7A.

Using a "standard" for sermons, a Toulmin model, and comparative analysis, finds little difference among sermons in the two groups.

365. Johnson, Raymond Eugene, Jr. "The Rhetorical Question as a Literary Device in Ecclesiastes." *DAI* 47 (April 1987): 3787A.

Explores the impact of rhetorical questions in Ecclesiastes upon the structure, argument, and mood of the book.

366. Kaid, Linda Lee, and John Boydston. "An Experimental Study of the Effectiveness of Negative Political Advertising." *ComQ* 35 (Spring 1987): 193–201.

Negative newspaper and television advertising reduces the image of targeted politicians among members of the opposite political party and, to a lesser extent, of their own party.

367. Katriel, Tamar. "Rhetoric in Flames: Fire Inscriptions in Israeli Youth Movement Ceremonials." *QJS* 73 (November 1987): 444–459.

The use of fire inscriptions in Israeli ceremonies derives from, and mediates between, secular European custom and traditional Judaism.

368. Kelly, Claire Callaghan. "The Representation of the Trinity according to the Filioque Doctrine." *DAI* 47 (June 1987): 4215A.

Surveys the development of the filioque doctrine through the seventeenth century, focusing on "medieval iconographic origins and imagery."

369. Kirk Whillock, Rita Gayle. "An Abductive View of American Civil Religion through the Use of Q-Methodology." *DAI* 47 (April 1987): 3610A.

Finds five emergent typologies of distinct patterns of belief, two of which have direct links to religious typologies.

370. Koser, Ruth Elaine. "Hermeneutics of the Book of Revelation for Preaching." *DAI* 48 (October 1987): 957A.

Explores the metaphoric, apocalyptic, linguistic, and historical possibilities within Revelation, suggesting strategies for preaching.

371. Krug, Linda Teresa. "Stylizing, Culturizing, and Image-Action: The Dialectic Forces of the Metaphoric Experience." *DAI* 48 (December 1987): 1356A.

Uses symbolic action and language action perspectives to analyze the "multidimensionality of metaphoric experience." President Reagan's image serves as an example.

372. Lewandowski, Monica Ann. "A Credible Candidate: The Campaign Oratory of Geraldine A. Ferraro." *DAI* 48 (November 1987): 1055A.

Analyzes Ferraro's public presentations of self and the press's responses to them.

373. Lewis, William F. "Telling America's Story: Narrative Form and the Reagan Presidency." *QJS* 73 (August 1987): 280–302.

Argues that narrative dominates President Reagan's rhetoric, which exhibits story-based truth, an emphasis on morality, and a grounding in common sense.

374. Lindsey, Suzanne E. "The Land for the People! The Rhetoric of the Irish National Land League as Response to a Rhetorical Situation." *DAI* 47 (June 1987): 4233A.

The complexity of the rhetorical situation necessitated both coercive and discursive measures.

375. Lloyd, Douglas Emory. "Patterns of Interrogative Rhetoric in the Speeches of the Book of Job." *DAI* 47 (January 1987): 2616A.

Examines the assumption that attention to linguistic details such as interrogative rhetoric can reveal thought as expressed in texts.

376. Lutz, Nancy Melissa. "Authoritative Discourse: Language and Ideology in Adonara, Eastern Indonesia." *DAI* 47 (January 1987): 2636A.

Argues that the discourses of Indonesian authority are tied to military and bureaucratic penetration into Indonesia's interior, making Indonesian a language of authority backed by force.

377. Maley, Yon. "The Language of Legislation." *LSoc* 16 (March 1987): 25–48.

Argues that decisions about language in legislative discourse are essentially decisions about the roles of law and legislation.

378. McFadden-Preston, Claudette. "The Rhetoric of Minister Louis Farrakhan: A Pluralistic Approach." *DAI* 47 (June 1987): 4233A.

Finds a pluralistic approach useful in examining the public discourse of Farrakhan, which in turn reveals the Nation of Islam's theological ideology.

379. McKiernan, John Edward. "Rhetorical Strategies of Charles Colson: Apologia as Apologetics." *DAI* 47 (February 1987): 2799A.

Uses Burke to describe Colson's purposes for apologia and apologetics: transcendence, differentiation and bolstering, and attacking and replacing secular values.

380. Michel, Thomas Arthur. "The Guardian Angel Movement: 1979–1984." *DAI* 47 (January 1987): 2371A.

An analysis of the Guardian Angel movement's public, its organization, and its opposition reflects its rhetorical skill.

381. Morris, Richard Joseph. "Memorializing among Americans: The Case of Lincoln's Assassination." *DAI* 47 (June 1987): 4233A.

Examines the rhetorical responses to Lincoln's assassination as well as cemetarial and iconographic forms produced between 1620 and 1986.

382. Muir, Janet Kenner. "Political Cartoons and Synecdoche: A Rhetorical Analysis of the 1984 Presidential Campaign." *DAI* 47 (June 1987): 4234A.

Explores theoretical, pragmatic, and artistic dimensions of political cartoons.

383. Murphy, John Michael. "Renewing the National Covenant: The Presidential Campaign Rhetoric of Robert F. Kennedy." *DAI* 48 (August 1987): 250A.

An analysis of Kennedy's rhetoric indicates that its form is the jeremiad, uniting "diverse moral concerns" and supporting the social structure.

384. Neelley, Edwin Edward, Jr. "Alben W. Barkley: The Image of the Southern Political Orator." *DAI* 48 (August 1987): 251A.

Focuses on the political and cultural climate of the South and Barkley's creation of an *ethos* as a regional speaker.

385. Nicholson, Barbara L. "The Pentagon Papers Case: Perelman's Practical Reasoning Redefined." *DAI* 48 (December 1987): 1356A.

Tests Perelman's idea of a universal audience and concludes that the concept needs refining.

386. Olson, Kathryn Marie. "Toward Uniting a Fellowship Divided: A Dramatistic Analysis of the Constitution-Writing Process of the Evangelical Catholic Church in America." *DAI* 48 (July 1987): 7A.

Identifies three key terms—newness, unity, and inclusiveness—and discusses their use in the rhetoric of the Commission for a New Lutheran Church.

387. Olson, Lester C. "Benjamin Franklin's Pictorial Representations of the British Colonies in America: A Study in Rhetorical Ideology." *QJS* 73 (February 1987): 18–42.

Franklin's 1765 engraving "Magna Britannia" was an attempt to persuade Parliament to abolish the Stamp Act, while also appealing to American conservatives.

388. Pearce, W. Barnett, Stephen W. Littlejohn, and Alison Alexander. "The New Christian Right and the Humanist Response: Reciprocated Diatribe." *ComQ* 35 (Spring 1987): 171–193.

Studies the interaction of the ideological conflict between the Christian Right and its opponents.

389. Penman, Robyn. "Discourse in Courts: Cooperation, Coercion, and Coherence." *DPr* 10 (July–September 1987): 201–218.

Contrary to Gricean assumptions, individuals in court may not always try to adhere to the cooperative principle. Courtroom maneuvers frequently coerce individuals to be cooperative.

390. Petchesky, Rosalind Pollack. "Fetal Images: The Power of Visual Culture in the Politics of Reproduction." *FS* 13 (Summer 1987): 263–292.

Argues that *The Silent Scream* presents a "cultural representation" as medical evidence by using an aural "moral text" to distort the visual "medical text."

391. Peterson, Tarla Rai. "Conceptual Metaphor in Soil Conservation Service Rhetoric and Farmers' Responses." *DAI* 47 (April 1987): 3611A.

An analysis of metaphorical concepts surrounding the frontier myth shows that farmers and the Soil Conservation Service interpret the myth differently.

392. Phillips, William Sherman. "The Christian Preacher as Poet: A Method for Exposi-

tion of Narrative Portions of Scripture Based on Aristotle's *Poetics.*" *DAI* 47 (March 1987): 3241A.

Demonstrates how Aristotelian poetics meets expository or interpretive needs and exhortatory or applicative needs for narrative exposition of Scripture.

393. Piipo, John Paul. "Metaphor and Theology: A Multidisciplinary Approach." *DAI* 47 (January 1987): 2623A.

Argues that a metaphorical use of language often best expresses religious knowledge and experience.

394. Preston, Charles Thomas. "A Rhetorical Analysis of Ronald Reagan's November 19, 1981, Address on Strategic Arms Reduction." *DAI* 47 (January 1987): 2372A.

Using Burke's dramatistic method, suggests that President Reagan's success in transformation, entitlement, and identification helped listeners deal with the arms race better than the discourse of nuclear freeze advocates did.

395. Reed, Thomas Vernon. "Reading the Left, Writing Politics: Literature, History, and the Rhetoric of American Political Culture." *DAI* 48 (July 1987): 162A.

Describes a problem faced by the American Left in finding rhetorical forms to engage and displace the dominant political culture.

396. Reid, Gwendoline Lilian. "Winston S. Churchill's Theory of Public Speaking as Compared to His Practice." *DAI* 48 (November 1987): 1056A.

Discerns seven principles of Churchill's theory that also informed his public oratory.

397. Riches, Suzanne Volmar. "Threads through a Patchwork Quilt: The Wedding Shower as a Communication Ritual and Rite of Passage for Mormon Women." *DAI* 48 (August 1987): 251A.

Wedding showers serve as a communication ritual that initiates young women into the world of Mormon womanhood by creating and maintaining group life.

398. Rosteck, Henry Thomas, Jr. "Rhetorical Analysis and Television Documentary: The Case of 'See It Now' and McCarthyism." *DAI* 48 (November 1987): 1057A.

Analyzes four "See It Now" documentaries as responses to McCarthyism. Suggests that tropes, rhetorical depiction, and intertextuality can be useful *topoi* for analyzing television discourse.

399. Rutledge, Kay Ellen. "Prophesying after the Event: Analyzing Persuasion by Combining Kenneth Burke's Pentad and Hugh Rank's Intensify/Downplay Schema." *DAI* 47 (February 1987): 2801A.

Devises an instrument for analyzing public addresses to determine a speaker's perception of events.

400. Shipley, David Stiles. "The Rhetorical Drama of Lyndon B. Johnson: A Burkean Analysis." *DAI* 48 (August 1987): 251A.

Analyzes President Johnson's Vietnam rhetoric during the period 1964 and 1965.

401. Simons, Herbert W., and Aram A. Aghazarian, eds. *Form, Genre, and the Study of Political Discourse*. Studies in Rhetoric/Communication. Edited by Carroll A. Arnold. Columbia, S.C.: University of South Carolina Press, 1986. 385 pages

Eleven essays explore the problems and possibilities of a generic approach to the study of rhetoric with special focus on political rhetoric. Some essays explore form or genre theory in various fields. Several essays concern a particular political discourse genre, the presidential inaugural.

402. Smith, Carolyn. "Toward a Rhetoric of Presidential Press Conferences." *DAI* 48 (December 1987): 1356A.

Develops methods for analyzing evaluations of presidential press conferences.

403. Smith, Christine Marie. "Weaving: A Metaphor and Method for Women's Preaching." *DAI* 48 (November 1987): 1238A.

Finds that the metaphor of "weaving" suits the particular qualities and demands of preaching from a feminist perspective.

404. Snowball, William David. "Change and Continuity in the Rhetoric of the Moral Majority." *DAI* 48 (August 1987): 252A.

Finds that, although the organization addressed the same agenda over time, its rhetoric became less confrontational and more secular to reach a broader audience.

405. Snyder, Lewis Leroy. "Alexander Campbell as a Change Agent within the Stone-Campbell Movement from 1830–1840." *DAI* 48 (November 1987): 1057A.

Uses Brown's model of social intervention to analyze Campbell's rhetoric and to discuss his intentional shaping of the movement.

406. Sproule, J. Michael. "Propaganda Studies in American Social Science: The Rise and Fall of the Critical Paradigm." *QJS* 73 (February 1987): 60–78.

Studies the rise of "propaganda analysis" in America after World War I and its replacement by the "communication research" paradigm during World War II.

407. Stevens, Leland Robert. "The Americanization of the Missouri Synod as Reflected within the *Lutheran Witness*." *DAI* 48 (October 1987): 965A.

Examines how editorial choice and management contributed to the Americanization of the Missouri Synod.

408. Tetley, Ann. "Social Movements as Worldmaking: A Theoretical and Practical Analysis of the Rhetoric of the British Women's Suffrage Movement through the Perspectives of Charles Stewart and Nelson Goodman." *DAI* 48 (December 1987): 1357A.

Constructs and tests a method for analyzing, comparing, and contrasting rhetorics of social movements.

409. Tulis, Jeffrey K. *The Rhetorical Presidency*. Princeton, N.J.: Princeton University Press, 1987. 208 pages

Argues that modern presidents' opportunities for direct rhetorical appeal to the public has created a "fundamental change" in the national political system.

410. Underwood, Charles Fred. "The Indian Witness: Narrative Style in Courtroom Testimony." *DAI* 47 (January 1987): 2640A.

Discusses how Lakota oral narrative style creates problems both in courtrooms and in the development of federal Indian policy.

411. Watson, Duane Fredrick. "Rhetorical Criticism of Jude and 2 Peter." *DAI* 47 (March 1987): 3454A.

Concludes that both Jude and 2 Peter admirably conform to the conventions of Greco-Roman rhetoric for invention, arrangement, and style.

412. Wells, Robert V. "A Structure for Successful Trial Technique: The Plaintiff's Case." *DAI* 48 (August 1987): 252A.

An analysis of successful lawyers' rhetoric reveals similar perceptions and ways of resolving rhetorical problems.

413. Williamson, Loretta Louise. "Art and Propaganda during the French Wars of Religion." *DAI* 47 (April 1987): 3597A.

Examines "the role of the image in propaganda" and the "relationship of image to text" in sixteenth-century French woodcuts and engravings.

414. Zagacki, Kenneth Stephen. "Rhetoric, Redemption, and Reconciliation: A Study of Twentieth-Century Postwar Rhetoric." *DAI* 47 (March 1987): 3242A.

Examines postwar presidential speeches to identify common purposes and uses for postwar rhetoric.

415. Zalampas, Mehale Athanasi. "Adolf Hitler and the Third Reich in Selected American Magazines, 1923–1939." *DAI* 48 (September 1987): 733A.

Reconstructs the images of Hitler and the Third Reich presented to readers of American general magazines until Germany's attack on Poland.

See also 313, 314, 319, 488, 682, 909

2.4   COMPUTER AND LITERACY STUDIES

416. Allen, Thomas J., and Oscar Hauptman. "The Influence of Communication Technologies on Organizational Structure." *ComR* 14 (October 1987): 575–587.

Choosing one new information technology over another has an impact on research and development project teams within organizations. Gives implications for technical communication research.

417. Aman, James R., and Lee Mountain. "In Word Processing and Programming, Does Sex Rear Its Head?" *Leaflet* 86 (Fall 1987): 28–31.

Concludes that there are no significant statistical differences between the sexes in attitudes toward word processing or programming.

418. *Annual Report on LSCA Special Activities, FY 1985*. Washington, D.C.: Office of Educational Research and Improvement, 1985. ERIC ED 284 549. 299 pages

A collection of seven reports providing information about the Library Services and Construction Act. Includes a report by Adrienne Chute, "Meeting the Literacy Challenge," abstracted as ERIC ED 284 549, that focuses on federal efforts to fight illiteracy.

419. Bloom, Allan. *Closing of the American Mind*. New York: Simon & Schuster, 1987. 392 pages

Argues that widespread relativism is the central problem in today's higher education. Intellectual standards have been corrupted by democratic demands for equality. Universities should restore a core curriculum based on the great books of the Western tradition, in particular ancient philosophy.

420. Bloom, Allan. "Thoughts on Reading: Ayn Rand, Pop Psychology, and a New Enemy of the Classics." *CHE* 33 (6 May 1987): 96.

Regrets that most college students select "pop" films and books over classical literature. Argues that this problem stems from such causes as feminism and teachers who were educated in the 1960s.

421. Brookfield, Stephen D. "E. D. Hirsch's *Cultural Literacy*: A Cocktail-Party View of Higher Education." *CHE* 34 (16 September 1987): B2.

Argues that memorizing book titles may produce short-term social success, but reality requires other, more complex skills.

422. Broyles, Shelia Leigh. "The Efficacy of Word-Processing Systems as an Aid to Disabled Writers." *DAI* 47 (February 1987): 3559B.

Finds that both attitude and formal writing ability improved when students with writing difficulties used word processors.

423. Buchanan, James P. "Allan Bloom and *The Closing of the American Mind:* Conclusions Too Neat, Too Clean, and Too Elite." *CHE* 34 (16 September 1987): B2.

Finds that Bloom's book has "wit and stylistic elegance," but humanists must also admit that we live in a technological world.

424. Catlin, Janet Green. "Their Solitary Way: Student Perception and Performance." *JT* 22 (Spring 1987): 25–29.

Argues that the speed and isolated nature of students' perceptions allow their reading and writing to remain opinionated, "illogical," and "weakly substantiated."

425. Coles, Nicholas, and Susan V. Wall. "Conflict and Power in the Reader Responses of Adult Basic Writers." *CE* 49 (March 1987): 298–314.

Discusses the unique features of the writing of adult basic writers as they are introduced to the academic discourse community.

426. Collins, Allan, and John Seely Brown. *The Computer as a Tool for Learning through Reflection.* Center for the Study of Reading Technical Report, no. 376. Urbana, Ill.: University of Illinois, 1986. ERIC ED 281 503. 32 pages

Describes how the computer focuses students' attention on their own thought processes and learning.

427. Crew, Louie. "Abusing Literacy to Colonize Minds: Eight Scenes from a Travesty." Paper presented at the CCCC Convention, Atlanta, March 1987. ERIC ED 280 062. 13 pages

Suggests that literacy may be equated, not with a set of skills, but with a certain behavior to be achieved, namely passive obedience to authority.

428. Crismore, Avon, and Larry Mikulecky. "Investigating a Process Model of Literacy in the Workplace." Paper presented at the IRA, Anaheim, May 1987. ERIC ED 282 189. 39 pages

Studies the literacy activities of exemplary nurses and electronics technicians. Findings support the process model of Flower and Hays.

429. Dalton, David W., and Michael J. Hannafin. "The Effects of Word Processing on Written Composition." *JEdR* 80 (July–August 1987): 338–342.

Word processing had little effect on able learners compared to pen-and-paper techniques. It was most effective for low-achieving students.

430. Daniell, Beth. "Ong's Great Leap: The Politics of Literacy and Orality." *DAI* 47 (March 1987): 3417A.

Concludes that Ong's literacy theory is ethnocentric. Proposes an alternative literacy model based on discourse communities.

431. Daniell, Beth. "The Uses of Literacy Theory: The Great Leap and the Rhetoric of Retreat." Paper presented at the CCCC Convention, Atlanta, March 1987. ERIC ED 281 197. 16 pages

    The "Great Leap" theory of literacy may have been a contributing factor in the academy's retreat from social issues.

432. Denham, Robert H. "From the Editor: Notes on Cultural Literacy." *BADE* 1988 (Winter 1987): 1–8.

    Argues that Hirsch's *Cultural Literacy* raises crucial questions about curriculum, ideologies, the ends of education, and motives for learning but does not answer them adequately.

433. Dever, Susan Young. "Contributions of Linguistic, Cognitive Processing, and Instructional Research to Computer-Assisted Spelling Instruction." *DAI* 48 (October 1987): 855A.

    Details research from three fields and examines how computer programs incorporate them into their design and content.

434. Edwards, Bruce L., Jr. "Process and the Digitized Word: Toward an Epistemology of Computerized Literacy." Paper presented at the CCCC Convention, Atlanta, March 1987. ERIC ED 280 035. 14 pages

    Discusses ways in which computerized writing may affect the utility and meaning of reading and writing in future generations.

435. Fagan, Edward, and Patrick Detterbeck. "Status Report: Micros for Word Processing." *EngR* 38 (1987): 10–13.

    Reviews the status of word processing in college writing instruction.

436. Feldman, Paula, and Buford Norman. *Wordworthy Computer*. New York: Random House, 1987. 192 pages

    Designed for teachers of literature and language, this guide outlines, explains, and illustrates the uses of microcomputers in teaching and research. Includes a bibliography.

437. Finn, Chester E., Jr., and Diane Ravitch. "Survey Results: U.S. 17-Year-Olds Know Shockingly Little about History and Literature." *ASBJ* 174 (October 1987): 31–33.

    Reviews the findings of their book *What Do Our 17-Year-Olds Know?* (1987) and suggests new reading and writing strategies for improving literacy.

438. Fleigel, Richard. "The Codes of Literacy." *DAI* 47 (March 1987): 3411A.

    Distinguishes between "local" and "collegiate" literacy, examining the influence of environment and sociolinguistic codes on each type of literacy.

439. Forman, Sid. "Why Buy a Computer?" *CalE* 23 (September–October 1987): 22, 29.

    Computers are useful for writers and teachers, and they are fun.

440. Frederking, Robert Eric. "Natural Language Dialogue in an Integrated Computational Model." *DAI* 48 (July 1987): 186B.

    Proposes a computational system, Psli3, which resolves complex elliptical natural language problems.

441. Froese, Victor. "Illiteracy: What Is It?" *EQ* 20 (Fall 1987): 175–177.

    Presents statistics from the *Southam News* survey revealing that five million Canadians are functionally illiterate. This group is divided according to educational background, interest in seeking assistance, and degree of illiteracy.

442. Gadomski, Kenneth E. "Culture Shock: Men's and Women's Myths of Literacy in Academe." Paper presented at the NCTE Convention, San Antonio, November 1986. ERIC ED 277 043. 21 pages

    Examines 200 personal narratives of college freshmen writers, finding that males understand literacy through an autonomy myth, females through a participation myth.

443. Geiger, Aryeh Joseph. "Motivating Individuals and Community toward Utilizing Literacy Services: An Action Research Study." *DAI* 48 (October 1987): 893A.

Explores methods by which people are encouraged to use community resources. Focuses on the role of an "external catalyst," someone from outside the community.

444. Graff, Harvey J. *The Legacies of Literacy: Continuities and Contradictions in Western Culture.* Bloomington, Ind.: Indiana University Press, 1987. 512 pages

A history of the dimensions and meanings of literacy in the Western world.

445. Haas, Christina. "Computers and the Writing Process: A Comparative Protocol Study." Paper presented at the Conference on Computers and Research, Pittsburgh, May 1986. ERIC ED 281 219. 24 pages

Reports on a study of 15 experienced writers accustomed to composing on a computer. Examines how computer composing differed from pen and paper composing.

446. Hargrave, Susanne, ed. *Literacy in an Aboriginal Context.* Working Papers of the Summer Institute of Linguistics, vol. 6. Darwin, Australia: Summer Institute of Linguistics, 1981. ERIC ED 282 425. 153 pages

Prints five papers on literacy in an Australian aboriginal context.

447. Hartwell, Patrick. "Creating a Literate Environment in Freshman English: Why and How." *RR* 6 (Fall 1987): 4–20.

Argues against a skills-oriented view of literacy in favor of one "embedded in social relationships, a matter of metacognition, metalinguistic awareness, and deep experiential learning."

448. Hayakawa, S. I. "Why the English Language Amendment." *EJ* 76 (November 1987): 14–16.

Hayakawa's personal history helps explain his position on designating English as the official U.S. language.

449. Haynes, Kathleen J. M. "A Study of the Ecological Validity of Procedures in Staging, T-Unit Roles, and Discourse Matrix Diagramming and an Examination of the Criteria for Usability for User Documentation for Microcomputers." *DAI* 47 (February 1987): 2780A.

Uses discourse analysis procedures to predict difficulties with the writing in computer manuals.

450. Hays, Richard R. "Relationships between Literacy Level and Job-Related Reading Self-Concept." *DAI* 47 (May 1987): 4038A.

Investigates relationships between literacy level and global self-concept, employment, income, age, and gender among 100 students enrolled at a vocational technical college.

451. Hirsch, E. D., Jr. *Cultural Literacy: What Every American Needs to Know.* Boston: Houghton Mifflin, 1987. 251 pages

Argues that Americans must change the educational system if we are to attain a high level of cultural literacy, "the network of information that all competent readers possess."

452. Hirschorn, Michael. "Best-Selling Book Makes the Collegiate Curriculum a Burning Public Issue." *CHE* 34 (16 September 1987): A1, A22.

Allan Bloom's *The Closing of the American Mind* has stirred interest in the "great books" approach to education, but critics charge that the approach is naive.

453. Holdstein, Deborah H. *On Composition and Computers.* Technology and the Humanities. New York: MLA, 1987. 104 pages

Provides information on how to use computers in writing courses and what kinds of considerations teachers should take into account before adopting computer-aided instructional software. Discusses some political and practical issues associated with teachers' developing their own software.

454. Holtzberg, Margaret. "'It Was a World': The Rhetoric of Tradition in the Occupational

Nostalgia of Hot Metal Printers." *DAI* 48 (September 1987): 719A.

Studies the rhetoric of tradition brought about by technological change and what it can tell us about nostalgia.

455. Hudson, Joyce, and Noreen Pym, eds. *Language Survey*. Working Papers of the Summer Institute of Linguistics, vol. 11. Darwin, Australia: Summer Institute of Linguistics, 1984. ERIC ED 282 436. 183 pages

Prints three surveys of the literacy needs of Australian Aborigines.

456. Jacobson, Robert L. "Against Towering Odds, Latin American Countries Combat Problems of Illiteracy." *CHE* 33 (29 July 1987): 1, 24.

Many Latin American countries are losing their struggle against illiteracy, but others such as Argentina and Mexico are succeeding.

457. Jacoby, Larry L., and C. A. G. Hayman. "Specific Visual Transfer in Word Identification." *JEPL* 13 (July 1987): 456–463.

Visual details such as typeface affect word identification.

458. Jeremiah, Milford A. "An Analysis of Students' Writing." Paper presented at the NCTE Convention, San Antonio, November 1986. ERIC ED 280 065. 14 pages

Explains why the study of sociological factors is germane to evaluations of students' writing ability.

459. Johnson, Jean Flanigan. "A New Ethnography in Literacy Studies: A Reconsideration." *WI* 6 (Spring-Summer 1987): 102–113.

Analyzes major differences between traditional ethnography and the new ethnography in literacy studies. Examines questions of objectivity and validity stemming from these differences.

460. Kerr, Stephen T. "Instructional Text: The Transition from Page to Screen." *VLang* 20 (Autumn 1986): 369–392.

Points out problems in surface design and interface design when text is converted from printed to electronic forms.

461. "Kids Ain't Writin' Right." *ASBJ* 174 (April 1987): 16, 20, 22.

Reviews the findings of the NAEP's *Writing Report Card* and summarizes its recommendations.

462. Kirsch, Irwin S., and Ann Jungeblut. *Literacy: Profiles of America's Young Adults*. Princeton, N.J.: NAEP, ETS, 1986. ERIC ED 275 692. 79 pages

A large survey in 1985 found that 21- to 25-year-olds were unable to perform well on tasks of moderate complexity.

463. Kirsch, Irwin S., and Ann Jungeblut. *Literacy: Profiles of America's Young Adults*. Princeton, N.J.: NAEP, ETS, 1986. ERIC ED 275 701. 436 pages

Presents the research methodology and findings of a large survey of the literacy skills of young adults aged 21 to 25.

464. Kriegel, Leonard. "Writers and Ethnicity." *PR* 54 (Winter 1987): 115–120.

Argues that no writer can be understoood solely by ethnic groupings because writers belong simultaneously to many groups.

465. Langer, Judith A. *Literate Communication and Literacy Instruction*. Urbana, Ill.: ERIC/RCS, 1986. ERIC ED 276 020. 24 pages

Takes a sociological approach to literacy instruction and gives examples of how to apply this perspective.

466. Langer, Judith A. *A Sociocognitive Perspective on Literacy*. Urbana, Ill.: ERIC/RCS, 1986. ERIC ED 274 988. 39 pages

Advocates incorporating social practices and literacy as a way of thinking into our perspective on literacy.

467. Larrimore, B., ed. *Papers in Literacy*. Working Papers of the Summer Institute of Linguistics, vol. 12. Darwin, Australia: Sum-

mer Institute of Lingusitics, 1984. ERIC ED 282 427. 185 pages

Prints four papers discussing literacy education for Australian aborigines.

468. Leeson, Lee Ann. "Literacy Education as Social Practice: Functional and Cultural Literacy in the Workplace and Classroom." *DAI* 48 (August 1987): 324A.

Analyzes the conflicting claims of programs and discusses several features of social structures.

469. Lofty, John Sylvester. "Time to Write: The Influence of Temporality on Learning to Write in a Maine Fishing Community." *DAI* 47 (April 1987): 3688A.

An ethnographic study of patterns of alienation between home and school. Concludes that students' resistance to learning how to write was related to cultural experiences of time.

470. Lu, Minzhan. "Silence to Words: Writing as Struggle." *CE* 49 (April 1987): 437–448.

Reflects on the effects a childhood in China and a career as a composition teacher in the U.S. had on the author's development as a writer.

471. Lutz, Jean A. "A Study of Professional and Experienced Writers Revising and Editing at the Computer and with Pen and Paper." *RTE* 21 (December 1987): 398–421.

Finds significant differences between experienced writers who revise using a computer and those who use pen and paper.

472. Maik, Linda L., and Thomas A. Maik. "Perceptions of Word Processing in Composition Classes: First-Year and Upper-Level Students Compared." *CC* 4 (August 1987): 7–16.

A comparison of student responses to word processing showed increased confidence and a better attitude toward writing after the experience.

473. Maloney, Ann Carroll. "The Identification of the Components of a Curriculum Planning Schema for Microcomputer-Assisted Writing Instruction." *DAI* 47 (April 1987): 3650A.

A descriptive survey of the literature of curriculum planning for writing. No schema for integrating the microcomputer into the writing curriculum was found.

474. McPhail, Irvine P. "Literacy as a Liberating Experience." *EQ* 20 (Spring 1987): 9–15.

Traces the origins of the literacy tools used by W. E. B. Dubois and Malcolm X to indigenous African cultures. Relates literacy to social action, self-education, and liberation.

475. Mellix, Barbara. "From Outside, In." *GR* 41 (Summer 1987): 258–267.

An autobiographical reflection on Black English and university education.

476. "NAEP: Students Aren't Literate Enough." *ASBJ* 174 (June 1987): 14.

Reviews the findings of *Learning to Be Literate in America* and summarizes its recommendations.

477. Norvig, Peter. "A Unified Theory of Influence for Text Understanding." *DAI* 48 (November 1987): 1418B.

Combines an inference program, Faustus, with a powerful computer language, Kodiak, to properly draw inferences from a variety of texts.

478. Nystrom, Christine. "Literacy as Deviance." *ETC* 44 (Summer 1987): 111–115.

Argues that we watch television rather than read or write because writing contradicts the "logic of the senses," while television restores sensory logic and experience.

479. Pappas, Christine C., and Elga Brown. "Learning to Read by Reading: Learning How to Extend the Functional Potential of Language." *RTE* 21 (May 1987): 160–184.

Argues that "an essential factor" in acquiring literacy is an early understanding of the registers of written language.

480. Rachal, John R. "Freedom's Crucible: William T. Richardson and the Schooling of the Freedmen." *AdEd* 37 (Fall 1986): 14–22.

Describes the Port Royal Experiment, a federal effort in basic adult education, begun early in the Civil War for some 10,000 freed slaves on South Carolina's Sea Islands.

481. Ravitch, Diane, and Chester E. Finn, Jr. *What Do Our Seventeen-Year-Olds Know? The First National Assessment of What American Students Know about History and Literature.* New York: Harper & Row, 1987. 224 pages

Reports on the 1986 NAEP, asserting that students know best literary and historical information translated by popular culture. They know least about the cultural figures, events, and themes emphasized in schools.

482. Rice, Ronald E., and Gail Love. "Electronic Emotion: Socioemotional Content in a Computer-Mediated Communication Network." *ComR* 14 (February 1987): 85–108.

Using a computer-mediated network affects both the content and structure of written communication.

483. Ross, Sandra, and Mark Wiley. "The Politics of Literacy." *WI* 7 (Fall 1987): 3–6.

Defines "the politics of literacy," citing Allan Bloom and E. D. Hirsch, Jr., and describes some of its controversial facets.

484. Roy, Alice. "The English Only Movement." *WI* 7 (Fall 1987): 40–47.

Reports on the status of the English Only and Official English movements in the U.S. Discusses the "melting pot" and related myths and urges respect for "linguistic diversity."

485. Sadler, Lynn Veach. "The Computers-and-Effective Writing Movement: Computer-Assisted Composition." *BADE* 87 (Fall 1987): 28–33.

Presents a history of computers in the classroom, distinguishing between computer-assisted instruction and computer-assisted composition. Calls for more research and heuristic packages.

486. Selfe, Cynthia L. "Redefining Literacy: The Multi-Layered Grammars of Computers." Paper presented at the CCCC Convention, Atlanta, March 1987. ERIC ED 280 034. 32 pages

Argues that teachers must realize how the multi-layered grammars of computers affect definitions of literacy.

487. Shetty, Yolan L. "Writing-as-Process and Problem Solving." Paper presented at the CCCC Convention, Atlanta, March 1987. ERIC ED 284 289. 15 pages

Focuses on CAI, arguing that writing-as-process is distinct from problem solving and that keyboarding is not composing.

488. Smitherman-Donaldson, Geneva. "Toward a National Public Policy on Language." *CE* 49 (January 1987): 29–36.

Proposes that language professionals develop a national public policy on language to promote wider communication and counteract reactionary sociolinguistic forces.

489. Staton, Jana, Roger Shuy, Joy Kreeft Peyton, and Leslee Reed. *Dialogue Journal Communication: Classroom, Linguistic, Social, and Cognitive Views.* Perspectives in Writing Research. Norwood, N.J.: Ablex, 1987. 388 pages

Illustrates from four perspectives how dialogue journals represent a "personal literacy" prior to and more comprehensive than the literacies emphasized and assessed in schools. Student motivated and controlled writing provides information about how students think, manage social interactions, and use language to get things done.

490. Straw, Stanley B. "Questions of Literacy." *EQ* 20 (Winter 1987): 271–272.

Distinguishes between literate activities and the nuts and bolts of reading.

491. Stuckey, J. Elspeth. "Literacy and Class Structure in America." *DAI* 47 (January 1987): 2581A.

Uses sociolinguistic theory to offer a literacy program that rejects "traditional literary pedagogy."

492. Suhor, Charles. "ERIC/RCS Report: Understanding Literacy—An Overview." *LArts* 64 (October 1987): 659–663.

Charts characteristics of preliterate, literate, and multiliterate cultures according to their world views, arts, language, education, social memory, social attitudes, and work.

493. Trimbur, John. "Cultural Literacy and Cultural Anxiety: E. D. Hirsch's Discourse of Crisis." *JTW* 6 (Fall-Winter 1987): 343–355.

Defines cultural literacy as "a strategic move to contain the flow of power by concentrating it in traditional forms of knowledge." Sees crisis discourse as a "holding action" against change.

494. Tuman, Myron. *A Preface to Literacy: An Inquiry into Pedagogy, Practice, Progress.* Tuscaloosa, Ala.: University of Alabama Press, 1987. 288 pages

Addresses within a broad cultural context two basic questions: what is literacy and why is it valuable? Chapters on the nature of literacy, modern literacy education, the role of praxis, the ontogeny of literacy, the revisionist critique of literacy, literacy and social reproduction, and the future of literacy.

495. Vik, Gretchen N. "Computer Screen Design Strategies." *JBTC* 1 (September 1987): 21–28.

Discusses research-based strategies for screen formatting, screen readability, and the use of graphics and color.

496. Walker, Roland W. "Towards a Model for Predicting the Acceptance of Vernacular Literacy by Minority-Language Groups." *DAI* 48 (December 1987): 1445A.

Discusses which sociolinguistic variables best predict the acceptance of vernacular literacy among minority-language groups.

497. Walters, Keith, Beth Daniell, and Mary Trachsel. "Formal and Functional Approaches to Literacy." *LArts* 64 (December 1987): 885–868.

Examines two major trends in literacy research to define a context that enables students from a variety of backgrounds to become literate.

498. Weinstein-Shr, Gail. "From Mountaintops to City Streets: An Ethnographic Investigation of Literacy and Social Progress among the Hmong of Philadelphia." *DAI* 47 (May 1987): 4004A.

Explores the relationship between literacy and social progress using a community profile and portraits of three individuals.

499. Winterowd, W. Ross. "Literacy: 'Kultur' and Culture." Paper presented at the CCCC Convention, Atlanta, March 1987. ERIC ED 281 233. 11 pages

Advocates Paulo Freire's conception of culture for educators. Cultural literacy can only be achieved through "problem-posing education."

500. Winterowd, W. Ross. "Literacy: 'Kultur' and Culture." *LArts* 64 (December 1987): 869–874.

Examines the seeming paradox between Hirsch's "kultur. . . a given" and Freire's "culture… [that is] always becoming, being made."

501. Woodring, Paul. "Let's Go Back to the Dictionary Definition: Illiteracy Is the Inability to Read and Write." *CHE* 33 (6 May 1987): 48.

Argues that "illiteracy," a word often misused, has become a problem because of changing educational methods and the increasing demands of modern society.

502. Zeidel, Robert Frederic. "The Literacy Test for Immigrants: A Question of Progress." *DAI* 47 (June 1987): 4498A.

Traces the development of literacy testing for immigrants between 1890 and 1917.

503. Zernik, Uri. "Strategies in Language Acquisition: Learning Phrases in Context." *DAI* 48 (September 1987): 815B.

Examines how computers might acquire language as human beings do. Models, in a program, how second language speakers acquire language through lexical content.

504. Zorn, Jeff. "The 1985 NAEP *Reading Report Card.*" *CalE* 23 (January–February 1987): 10–11.

Reports on the NAEP study. Questions the study's classification of students and their skills.

See also 32, 215, 288, 712, 847, 1143, 1144, 1617, 1625, 1630, 1727, 1746, 1797, 1798

2.5 ADVERTISING, PUBLIC RELATIONS, AND BUSINESS

505. Aalberts, Robert J., and Lorraine J. Krajewski. "Claim and Adjustment Letters: Theory Versus Practice and Legal Implications." *ABCAB* 50 (September 1987): 1–5.

Describes a study comparing what business communication textbooks say about claim and adjustment letters with actual sample letters. The study also explores applicable legal theories.

506. Axley, Stephen R. "Communication Consultants and Consulting: A Survey of ABC Members." *ABCAB* 50 (June 1987): 8–15.

Reports the results of a survey describing consultants' backgrounds, client organizations, educational needs, resources, and fees.

507. Bostian, Lloyd R., and Ann C. Thering. "Scientists: Can They Read What They Write?" *JTWC* 17 (1987): 417–427.

Twenty-nine international scientists processed the nominal style more slowly than

the active one and preferred the active style over the nominal.

508. Cassidy, John C. "The Role of the Corporate Speechwriter in Public Policy Spokemanship." *ABCAB* 50 (June 1987): 24–28.

Describes the methodology and results of a survey of corporate speechwriters about their role in communicating public issues.

509. Darsey, Nancy, and Jean Dorrell. "The Demography and Professional Status of the ABC Member, 1985 Compared with 1968." *ABCAB* 50 (March 1987): 3–7.

Reports the results of a questionnaire assessing the status of both academic and business members of the ABC.

510. Darsey, Nancy, and Jean Dorrell. "The Demography and Professional Status of the ABC Member, 1985 Compared with 1968." *ABCAB* 50 (June 1987): 2–7.

Reports the results of a questionnaire assessing the status of members of the ABC. Includes charts omitted from the March 1987 issue of *ABCAB*.

511. David, Fred R., and Daniel S. Cochran. "Characteristics of Boundary-Spanning Communicators." *JTWC* 17 (1987): 165–177.

Based on a study of managerial personnel at four large banks. Attempts to describe the characteristics of individuals who facilitate and filter the flow of information within an organization.

512. DeConinck, James, and Dale Level. "An Analysis of Current Perspectives of the Influence of Communication in Successful Organizations." *ABCAB* 50 (March 1987): 7–11.

Applies the contingency perspective of communication to an analysis of corporate communication as discussed in *Megatrends, In Search of Excellence*, and *Theory Z*.

513. Forman, Janis. "Computer-Mediated Group Writing in the Workplace." *CC* 5 (November 1987): 19–30.

Describes research on group writing practices of managers who use electronic messages within the company. Gives conclusions and directions for future research.

514. Freed, Richard C. "A Meditation on Proposals and Their Backgrounds." *JTWC* 17 (1987): 157–163.

Based on research in large management consultant firms. Defines the proposal-as-genre and argues the importance of the background section for demonstrating the writer's qualifications.

515. Frohlich, David M. "On the Organisation of Form-Filling Behaviour." *IDJ* 5 (1986): 43–59.

Analyzes the processes by which eight people filled out a government form.

516. German, Carol J., and William R. Rath. "Making Technical Communication a Real-World Exercise: A Report of Classroom and Industry-Based Research." *JTWC* 17 (1987): 335–346.

Student research into on-the-job communication tasks suggests "that practicing professionals need individual, group, oral, and written communication skills in somewhat equal measure."

517. Golen, Steven P., John L. Waltman, and Shirley A. White. "Processors or Producers? Secretaries as Communicators." *ABCAB* 50 (June 1987): 32–34.

Describes a study of secretaries' communication roles in organizations.

518. Goodin, Edward H., and Skip Swerdlow. "The Current Quality of Written Correspondence: A Statistical Analysis of the Performance of Thirteen Industry and Organizational Categories." *ABCAB* 50 (March 1987): 12–16.

Analyzes 800 business letters and memos from 13 industries and organizations. Summarizes communications and writing deficiencies and draws conclusions.

519. Hayes, Laurie Schultz. "Measuring the Rhetorical Sensitivity of Technical Communicators." *TWT* 14 (Spring 1987): 192–207.

Discusses a survey measuring attitudes toward communication among members of the Society for Technical Communication.

520. Heckler, Susan Elizabeth. "Processing of Advertisements: The Role of Thematic Relationships in the Comprehension and Memory of Verbal and Visual Information." *DAI* 48 (July 1987): 175A.

Integrates the perspectives of academics and practitioners regarding the memory and comprehension of marketing communications.

521. Holdstein, Deborah H., and Tim Redman. "Writing Research in the Technical Writing Classroom: The Blind Leading the Double-Blind." *JTWC* 17 (1987): 355–365.

A double-blind research design in the writing classroom divides students into competing peer review teams and provides teachers with a method for pursuing their own research.

522. Horne, Mike, Jonathan Roberts, and Douglas Rose. "Getting There: An Assessment of London Transport's Endeavour to Improve Bus Passenger Information Literature for Central London, 1979–1985." *IDJ* 5 (1986): 3–27.

Traces the development of a new London bus map that led to "a radical rethink of the whole concept of bus route cartography." Includes diagrams.

523. Jenkins, Susan, and John Hinds. "Business Letter Writing: English, French, and Japanese." *TESOLQ* 21 (June 1987): 327–349.

Compares and contrasts the form and content of English, French, and Japanese business request letters. Uses textbooks to gather data and places letters in a linguistic and social context.

524. Jones, David Blodgett. "Directiveness in Promotional Communications." *DAI* 48 (November 1987): 1263A.

Finds that the wording or "directiveness" of a persuasive communication may influence a receiver's responses to content.

525. Kallendorf, Craig, and Carol Kallendorf. "Careful Negligence: Cicero's Low Style and Business Writing." *BRMMLA* 41 (1987): 33–49.

Presents Cicero's low style as a prescriptive mode for business writing that emphasizes thought and substance over language.

526. Keller-Cohen, Deborah. "Literate Practices in a Modern Credit Union." *LSoc* 16 (March 1987): 7–24.

Observes that clients have limited access to documents that guide transactions. Argues that better access during transactions enables better understanding by clients.

527. Keller-Cohen, Deborah. "Organizational Contexts and Texts: The Redesign of the Midwest Bell Telephone Bill." *DPr* 10 (October–December 1987): 417–428.

In the process of redesigning bills, corporate practice played a greater part than did customers' experiences with phone bills.

528. Knouse, Stephen B. "Confidentiality and the Letter of Recommendation: A New Approach." *ABCAB* 50 (September 1987): 6–8.

Examines research on confidentiality of letters of recommendation, describes current solutions to the problem, and recommends employing a situational framework.

529. Krohn, Franklin B. "Military Metaphors: Semantic Pollution of the Market Place." *ETC* 44 (Summer 1987): 141–145.

Shows how the use of military metaphors in marketing education creates an unethical and adversarial relationship between business and the consumer. Promotes alternative diction.

530. Lieberman, Jay. "Implications of Adult Learning Characteristics and Learning Styles for the Design of Software Documentation." *TWT* 14 (Spring 1987): 219–231.

A review of the literature suggests that software documentation should be organized flexibly, should focus on possible problems users will encounter, and should relate to the user's experience.

531. Little, Sherry Burgus, and Margaret C. McLaren. "Profile of Technical Writers in San Diego County: Results of a Pilot Study." *JTWC* 17 (1987): 9–23.

Discusses the responses of 122 writers in the San Diego area to a questionnaire asking them about tasks performed, documents produced, skills possessed, and working conditions.

532. Mattina, Anne F. "Shattered Silence: The Rhetoric of an American Female Labor Reform Association." *DAI* 47 (January 1987): 2371A.

Tests Karlyn Kohrs Campbell's argument that neo-Aristotelian rhetorical criticism is not valid in analyzing women's discourse. Concludes that traditional methods are not useful.

533. McDowell, Earl E. "Perceptions of the Ideal Cover Letter and Ideal Resume." *JTWC* 17 (1987): 179–191.

Surveys attitudes held by recruiters, teachers, and students about cover letters and resumes, including how much time they take to process, how long they should be, and how important mechanics are.

534. Megginson, Jayne Margaret. "The Rhetoric of Lee Iacocca: The Man, the Myth, the Message." *DAI* 48 (August 1987): 250A.

Uses the theoretical principles of Bormann, Bitzer, Burke, Aristotle, and Campbell to examine Iacocca's rhetoric.

535. Miller, Allie F. "An Empirical Study of the Effects of Information Formats on the Prediction of Financial Distress." *DAI* 47 (April 1987): 3803A.

Investigates the use of graphic versus tabular displays in decision making.

536. Mirel, Barbara. "Designing Field Research in Technical Communication: Usability Testing for In-house User Documentation." *JTWC* 17 (1987): 347–354.

Describes a three-pronged design for testing in-house user manuals: user logs, observations, and surveys.

537. Moorhead, Alice E. "Designing Ethnographic Research in Technical Communication: Case Study Theory into Application." *JTWC* 17 (1987): 325–333.

Describes the value of ethnographic methods and discusses the constraints on this kind of research, especially as they affect the ethnographic study of technical communication.

538. Murray, Denise F. "Requests at Work: Negotiating the Conditions for Conversation." *MCQ* 1 (August 1987): 58–83.

Draws on speech-act theory and conversation analysis to account for how requests by one party may be negotiated by the requestee.

539. Office of Consumer Affairs. *How Plain English Works for Business: Twelve Case Studies.* Washington, D.C.: U.S. Government Printing Office, March 1984. ERIC ED 277 033. 108 pages

Describes language simplification projects initiated by insurance and other companies. Gives information on payoffs of the projects.

540. Ralphs, Lenny T. "A Field Study of the Relationship of Management Communication Style to Organizational Commitment and Employee Satisfaction." *DAI* 47 (June 1987): 4444A.

Finds that value and stay commitment, supervisor satisfaction, work, pay, coworkers, and promotion are positively related to an employee-centered management communication style. Contrasts this style with boss-centered styles.

541. Rosen, Jay. "The Presence of the Word in TV Advertising." *ETC* 44 (Summer 1987): 152–154.

Advertisers use visual images to "create the presence of a word." Overt visualization of connotations increases a viewer's awareness of deeper meanings because the surface level disappears.

542. Senf, Carol A. "Technical Writing as a Career." *TWT* 14 (Winter 1987): 68–76.

Provides information about careers in technical writing, job opportunities, salaries, necessary training and experience, and types of work available.

543. Shear, Marie. "Little Cat Feet: Subtle Sexism and the Writer's Craft." *ABCAB* 50 (March 1987): 17–18.

The author describes her own unconscious use of sexism in her writing of annual report copy for a nonprofit agency.

544. Sides, Charles H. "Commentary: Land of Milk and Honey: Technical Writing in Israel." *JTWC* 17 (1987): 367–372.

This writing consultant to an Israeli computer company feels that technical writers hold second-place positions in Israel, but there are many opportunities to upgrade their status.

545. Simmons, Carolyn Jean. "Effects of Missing Information on Product Evaluations." *DAI* 47 (May 1987): 4139A.

Examines how product evaluations are formed when some attribute information is not available.

546. Spinks, Nelda, and Barron Wells. "Letters of Application and Resumes: A Comparison of Corporate Views." *ABCAB* 50 (September 1987): 9–16.

Describes results of a survey of corporate personnel officers about their preferences in letters of applications and resumes. Compares results with those of a 1978 survey.

547. Stegman, John Davis. "A Rhetorical Investigation of Selected 1982 Corporate Annual Reports." *DAI* 48 (July 1987): 8A.

Examines the rhetoric in 50 corporate annual reports.

548. Thorpe, Judith Mosier. "The Role of Persuasion for a Corporate Spokesman: An Analysis of the Arguments Lee Iacocca Presented on Behalf of Chrysler Corporation to the American Consumer and to the Congress from 1979 to 1982." *DAI* 47 (January 1987): 2374A.

Suggests that Iacocca tended to rely on statistical arguments.

549. Torobin, Jack. "Media Style: A New Perspective on the Use and Implementation of Media for Interpersonal Communication in Organizations." *DAI* 48 (October 1987): 973A.

Examines the influence of communicator traits, task characteristics, organizational status, and channel predispositions on media styles.

550. Walker, Peter, Sylvia Smith, and Alan Livingston. "Predicting the Appropriateness of a Typeface on the Basis of Its Multi-Modal Features." *IDJ* 5 (1986): 29–42.

Studies relationships between characteristics of various typefaces and various professions.

551. Young, John Howard. "Planning and Action: Practices and Discourses of Managing Change." *DAI* 48 (November 1987): 1261A.

Scrutinizes the planning documents of a Brazilian subsidiary to discover the ways in which plans for change had been articulated over a 20-year period.

See also 159, 206, 276, 296, 366, 682, 727, 947, 1436, 1440

2.6   LITERATURE, FILM

552. Achebe, Chinua. "Achebe on Editing." *WLWE* 27 (Spring 1987): 1–4.

Discusses collecting and using oral tradition field material.

553. Anderson, Chris. *Style as Argument: Contemporary American Nonfiction.* Carbondale, Ill.: Southern Illinois University Press, 1987. 224 pages

A rhetorical approach to the literary nonfiction of Wolfe, Capote, Mailer, and Didion. The technique of these writers is a response to the problem of conveying experiences that conventional rhetoric cannot evoke.

554. Atherton, John. "The Confessions of a Poetry Eater." *CHE* 33 (25 February 1987): 96.

A narrative spoof set in a science-dominated world. Describes the decline and fall of a promising young scientist who becomes addicted to literature.

555. Backscheider, Paula R. "Women Writers and the Chains of Identification." *SNNTS* 19 (Fall 1987): 245–262.

Argues that society increasingly circumscribed the writing range of eighteenth- and nineteenth-century women novelists by identifying the writers with their material.

556. Barley, James. "An Exploration in Comparative Metrics." *Style* 21 (Fall 1987): 359–376.

A study of comparative metrics can give a broader perspective on the rhythmical structure of an individual language.

557. Becker, John E. "Science and the Sacred: From Walden to Tinker Creek." *Thought* 62 (December 1987): 400–413.

Compares Thoreau's use of sacred language with Dillard's use of scientific language.

558. Bishop, Edward L. "Metaphors and the Subversive Process of Virginia Woolf's Essays." *Style* 21 (Winter 1987): 573–588.

Discusses Woolf's use of verb metaphors and their effects on the reader.

559. Blackall, Jean Frantz. "Edith Wharton's Art of Ellipsis." *JNT* 17 (Spring 1987): 145–159.

Argues that the novelist seeks to cultivate a special relationship between herself and the reader through the use of ellipsis.

560.   Blain, Derrel R. "A Mathematical Model for Alliteration." *Style* 21 (Winter 1987): 607–625.

Discusses how mathematical description can be used to measure alliteration and assonance by a computer.

561.   Blair, Carole, and Martha Cooper. "The Humanist Turn in Foucault's Rhetoric of Inquiry." *QJS* 73 (May 1987): 151–171.

Defends Foucault against Walter Fisher's charge that he is "anti-humanist." Argues that Foucault's "humanist" method permits people to assert freedom from the prevailing social order.

562.   Boone, Joseph A. "How Feminist Criticism Changes the Study of Literature." *CHE* 33 (8 July 1987): 76.

"Rereading through sex-conscious eyes has. . . initiated a wholesale reinterpretation of all literature" and allows students to realize the "multiplicity of. . . contexts in their own lives."

563.   Brooks, Peter. "The Idea of a Psychoanalytic Literary Criticism." *CritI* 13 (Winter 1987): 334–348.

Argues that "psychoanalytic criticism can and should be textual and rhetorical."

564.   Burgoyne, Robert James. "History and Narrative in the Film-Text: A Study of Bertolucci's *1900*." *DAI* 47 (February 1987): 2771A.

Analyzes fictional film techniques that model the historical process.

565.   Cather, Willa. *Willa Cather on Writing*. 2d ed. Critical Studies on Writing as an Art. Lincoln, Neb.: University of Nebraska Press, 1987. 126 pages

Cather critiques her own fiction and that of Sarah Orne Jewett, Stephen Crane, Katherine Mansfield, among others.

566.   Chase, Kathleen. "Legend and Legacy: Some Bloomsbury Diaries." *WLT* 61 (Spring 1987): 230–233.

Woolf refers to the diary as a letter to oneself. It is a first cousin to letter writing, biography, autobiography, history, and even the novel and the play.

567.   Clippinger, Anne Elizabeth. "Ironic Functions of Interior Monologue in the Stream-of-Consciousness Novel." *DAI* 48 (October 1987): 918A.

Beginning with speech-act theory, stylistics, and reader-response criticism, this study treats text as a complex form of speech resulting from a discourse situation.

568.   Copjec, Joan Karen. "Apparatus and Umbra: A Feminist Critique of Film Theory." *DAI* 47 (June 1987): 4212A.

Examines the relationships among "spectator, film-text, technological, economic, and other intersecting discourses."

569.   Coplan, David B. "Eloquent Knowledge: Lesotho Migrants' Songs and the Anthropology of Experience." *AmE* 14 (August 1987): 413–433.

Oral literary forms such as the *sefela*, sung poetry of Basotho migrant workers, provide opportunities for self-conscious, reflexive accounts of social experience.

570.   Crawford, David Wright. "The Development of a Playwriting Philosophy as Demonstrated in the Writing of a Full Length Script." *DAI* 48 (September 1987): 515A.

Examines the act of creation, both "sequentially and in chronological order," and develops a nonprescriptive, methodological approach to this art.

571.   Culler, Jonathan. "Poststructuralist Criticism." *Style* 21 (Summer 1987): 167–180.

Contextualizes poststructuralist criticism. Applies deconstruction and psychoanalytic criticism. Considers implications on the "New Pragmatics" critique of theory.

572. De Lancey, Mark. "Interpreting Deconstruction: The Cause of Clarity." *Style* 21
(Summer 1987): 192–207.

   "Deconstruction confirms the interpreter's
   central premise—that the text says one
   thing but means something else—and thus
   justifies the enterprise founded on it."

573. Delany, Samuel. "The Semiology of Silence." *SFS* 14 (July 1987): 134–163.

   An interview with Delany on his writing
   and the relationships between science fiction and other types of texts.

574. DelGaudio, Sybil. "Clothing Signification
in the Films of Josef Von Sternberg." *DAI* 47
(April 1987): 3592A.

   Examines the use of clothing as a narrative
   technique that stresses concealment, sexual
   ambiguity, and ornamentation.

575. Donoghue, Francis J. "Author and Re-
viewer in the Later Eighteenth Century: The
Role of Popular Criticism in the Careers of
Sheridan, Sterne, Goldsmith and Smollett."
DAI 48 (August 1987): 397A.

   Analyzes the transition from a patronage
   system in the early 1700s to an open market
   at mid-century.

576. Eden, Rich. "Master Tropes in Satire."
Style 21 (Winter 1987): 589–606.

   Discusses the use of the four "master
   tropes" in satire and how they blur the reader's perspective.

577. Elgin, Suzette Haden. "Women's Language and Near Future Science Fiction: A
Reply." *WS* 14 (December 1987): 175–181.

   Describes the process of constructing the
   women's language for Elgin's "near future" novel, *Native Tongue*.

578. Elimimian, I. I. "The Rhetoric of J. P.
Clark's *Ivbie*." *WLWE* 27 (Autumn 1987):
161–173.

   Examines ceremonial, forensic, and political discourse as they develop themes in the
   work.

579. Everson, Philip Andrew. "Proof Revisions
in Three Novels by Charles Dickens: *Dombey
and Sons, David Copperfield*, and *Bleak
House*." *DAI* 48 (December 1987): 1459A.

   Discusses how last minute revisions, resulting from printing requirements, affected the meanings of Dickens's serial
   novels. Also discusses his usual habits of
   composition.

580. Falk, Thomas. "The Diary: A First Reality
in the Creative Process." *WLT* 61 (Spring
1987): 183–185.

   Examines the diaries of five major Austrian
   writers. Correspondence is a diarylike
   work.

581. Fenno, Shelley. "Unity and the Three
Principles of Composition in a No Play." *DAI*
47 (February 1987): 2804A.

   Identifies structural categories, narrative,
   and musical effects. Analyzes the play, *Ta-
   kasago*.

582. Feyerabend, Paul. "Creativity: A Dangerous Myth." *CritI* 13 (Summer 1987): 700–
711.

   Argues that "the view that culture needs
   individual creativity is not only absurd but
   also dangerous."

583. Flannery, Kathryn T. "What Makes This
Text Literature? The Meaning of Style in Productions of Richard Hooker's and Francis
Bacon's Work." *DAI* 48 (December 1987):
1459A.

   Analyzes the works of Hooker and Bacon
   to understand the relationships between literary productions and conceptions of literacy in terms of political and social affilia-
   tions.

584. Fore, Steven James. "The Perils of Patrio-
tism: The Hollywood War Film as Generic and
Cultural Discourse." *DAI* 47 (March 1987):
3215A.

   A close analysis of nine exemplary texts.

585. Franke, Thomas L. "The Art of Verbal
Performance: A Stylistic Analysis of Langston

Hughes's 'Feet Live Their Own Life.' " *Lang&S* 19 (Fall 1986): 377–406.

Analyzes Hughes's literary style and concludes that it belongs to a well defined system of language use that, whether African or American in origin, is characteristic of Black English speakers.

586. Freedman, Carl. "Marxist Theory, Radical Pedagogy, and the Reification of Thought." *CE* 49 (January 1987): 70–82.

Discusses the implications for English teachers of the split between the theorists and the pedagogues of the academic literary left.

587. Freedman, Carl. "Science Fiction and Critical Theory." *SFS* 14 (July 1987): 180–200.

Argues that science fiction, by insisting on "the primacy of historical specificity," ought to be the genre most privileged by "genuinely critical" or dialectical theory.

588. Gallop, Jane. "Reading the Mother Tongue: Psychoanalytic Feminist Criticism." *CritI* 13 (Winter 1987): 314–329.

Asserts that psychoanalytic feminist criticism joins feminism with psychoanalysis as well as poststructuralism and American feminist social science.

589. Gaonkar, Dilip Parameshwar. "Deconstruction and Rhetorical Analysis: The Case of Paul de Man." *QJS* 73 (November 1987): 482–498.

Surveys the function of rhetoric in the theories of Paul de Man. A review essay treating five of his books.

590. Gaughan, Richard T. "Mr. Hyde and Mr. Seek: The Utterson Antidote." *JNT* 17 (Spring 1987): 184–197.

Discusses the way Hyde's and Utterson's use of various levels of discourse define and constitute social order.

591. Goatly, Andrew. "Interrelations of Metaphor in Golding's Novels: A Framework for the Study of Metaphoric Interplay." *Lang&S* 20 (Spring 1987): 125–144.

Proposes a framework and terminology for studying how two or more metaphors affect each other's interpretations and how these interpretations may be related. Illustrates with Golding's novels.

592. Graff, Gerald. *Professing Literature: An Institutional History*. Chicago: Chicago University Press, 1987. 315 pages

A history of educational theories and practices in the field of literary studies. Recounts the arguments supporting different literary theories and argues for "a more explicitly historicized and cultural kind of literary study that would make [critical] disagreements part of what is studied."

593. Grubb, Shirley Carr. "Women, Rhetoric, and Power: The Women of Shakespeare's *Richard III* as Collective Antagonist." *DAI* 48 (November 1987): 1058A.

Applies classical rhetorical terminology to the language women use with Richard.

594. Gunning, Thomas Robert. "D. W. Griffith and the Narrator-System: Narrative Structure and Industry Organization in Biograph Films, 1908–1909." *DAI* 47 (February 1987): 2772A.

Explains Griffith's ground-breaking combination of cinematic elements to create a new "filmic discourse."

595. Hall, Peter C., and Richard D. Erlich. "Beyond Topeka and Thunderdome: Variations on the Comic-Romance Pattern in Recent Science Fiction Film." *SFS* 14 (November 1987): 316–325.

Explores tendencies away from comic romance and toward both irony and myth in recent, post-apocalyptic science fiction films.

596. Harris, Wendell V. "Critical Discussions." *P&L* 11 (October 1987): 300–314.

A review of Felperin's *Beyond Deconstruction*, Mailloux's *Interpretive Conventions*, and Scholes's *Textual Power: Liter-*

ary Theory and the Teaching of English. Finds that these books reflect and participate in de-emphasizing deconstruction and "allied poststructuralist endeavors."

597. Hawkinson, Kenneth Steven. "Three Novels by W. Somerset Maugham: An Analysis Based on the Rhetoric of Wayne C. Booth." *DAI* 47 (January 1987): 2370A.

Applies Booth's rhetorical approach in *The Rhetoric of Fiction* to provide an extended example of his theory and to explain Maugham's popularity despite his rejection by critics.

598. Heisserer, Gary Lawrence. "The Historical Drama of the Holocaust: Assessing the Transformation from Reality to Record." *DAI* 48 (November 1987): 1058A.

Applies a theoretical discussion of historiography, drama criticism, and Holocaust studies to five plays.

599. Herman, Vimala. "How to See Things with Words: Language Use and Descriptive Art in John Clare's 'Signs of Winter.' " *Lang&S* 20 (Spring 1987): 91–109.

Studies the linguistic and rhetorical choices that create Clare's descriptive art. Argues that Clare was a deliberate craftsman.

600. Hiles, Jane. "A Margin for Error: Rhetorical Context in *Titus Andronicus*." *Style* 21 (Spring 1987): 62–75.

Uses Aristotle's and Cicero's discussions of rhetorical occasion to show how various characters fail to use the appropriate mode of discourse in specific situations.

601. Hollinger, Veronica. "Deconstructing the Time Machine." *SFS* 14 (July 1987): 201–221.

Argues that time travel deconstructs classical notions about the nature of time. Examines how Wells deconstructs "the metaphysics of presence" in *The Time Machine*.

602. Hungerford, Lynda. "Dialect Representation in *Native Son*." *Lang&S* 20 (Winter 1987): 3–15.

Argues that, by using different literary techniques to represent the Black English Vernacular spoken by two groups of black characters, Wright demonstrated his sympathy for communist literature.

603. Hurst, Mary Jane. "Characterization and Language: A Case Study of *As I Lay Dying*." *Lang&S* 20 (Winter 1987): 71–88.

Argues that case grammar is a legitimate tool for literary analysis. Concludes that, for *As I Lay Dying*, such analysis reveals consistency of voice and character.

604. Jackson, Selwyn. "Distance and the Communication Model." *JNT* 17 (Spring 1987): 225–233.

Creates a communication model to discuss levels of distance in *Moll Flanders*.

605. Jacobs, Naomi. "Person and Persona: Historical Figures in 'Recombinant' Science Fiction." *SFS* 14 (July 1987): 230–240.

Evaluates the contemporary trend of combining ready-made "figures from all time periods and levels of reality [pop culture, history, archetype, myth] within new fictional contexts."

606. Jameson, Fredric. "Shifting Contexts of Science Fiction Theory." *SFS* 14 (July 1987): 241–247.

Explores issues and trends in current European and American science fiction criticism.

607. Katz, David Robert. "The Search for Cinema: A History of Ontological Cinema Theory from 1900–1960." *DAI* 47 (March 1987): 3216A.

Divides early ontologies into three categories: a Western approach (cinema as "high art"), a Soviet approach (serve practical needs), and Bela Balazs's combination of the two.

608. Kinney, Clare R. "Fragmentary Excess, Copious Death: *The Waste Land* as Anti-Narrative." *JNT* 17 (Fall 1987): 273–285.

Argues that the notes of the poem are fictional fragments that the reader must resolve into a linear narrative to discover the narrative "ends."

609. Kitch, Sally L. "Gender and Language: Dialect, Silence, and the Disruption of Discourse." *WS* 14 (July 1987): 65–78.

Challenges Derrida's idea that language is phallogocentric by examining the relationships between silence and expressive speech in texts by Hurston and Arnow.

610. Klinger, Barbara Gail. "Cinema and Social Process: A Contextual Theory of the Cinema and Its Spectators." *DAI* 47 (February 1987): 2772A.

Drawing upon the work of Bakhtin, Eco, and Foucault, this study posits a contextual theory for text-spectator relationships.

611. Knapp, Steven, and Walter Benn Michaels. "Against Theory 2: Hermeneutics and Deconstruction." *CritI* 14 (Autumn 1987): 49–68.

Argues that "conventions play no role in determining meaning"; furthermore, conventions do not "give an autonomous identity that will allow [the text] to mean more than its author intends."

612. Knepp, Bettina L. "The Diary as Art: Anais Nin, Thornton Wilder, Edmund Wilson." *WLT* 61 (Spring 1987): 223–230.

Nin and Wilder consider the diary therapeutic and recuperative. Wilson's tetralogy is autobiographical and narrative.

613. Kramarae, Cheris. "Present Problems with the Language of the Future." *WS* 14 (December 1987): 183–186.

Points to the importance of *la parole feministe* in science fiction.

614. Kucich, Greg. "The Poetry of Mind in Keat's Letters." *Style* 21 (Spring 1987): 76–94.

Discusses the poet's use of letter writing as a means of inventing patterns or rhetorical structures for future poems.

615. Langland, Elizabeth. "Patriarchal Ideology and Marginal Motherhood in Victorian Novels by Women." *SNNTS* 19 (Fall 1987): 381–394.

Applies Bakhtin's theories to Victorian novels written by women, revealing a dialogic between dutiful daughters and marginal mothers and exploring the narrative space opened by that dialogic.

616. Lehman, Patricia V. "Text Act and Tradition: Salutations and Status in the Paston Family, 1440–1495." *DAI* 47 (April 1987): 3749A.

Concludes that variations in the salutations of Paston family letters provide clues to fifteenth-century family relationships.

617. Lily, Ian K. "Some Structural Variants in the Russian and German Ottava Rima." *Style* 21 (Fall 1987): 377–386.

Proposes that comparative versification studies can be more productive than contrastive ones.

618. Limburg, Kay Bosgraaf. "Quantitative Analyses of the Style of Woolf's *Orlando*." *Lang&S* 19 (Summer 1986): 250–279.

Uses several quantitative techniques to analyze the style of *Orlando: A Biography* at the sentence-semantic, syntactic, and lexical levels. Finds significant differences between chapters and sections.

619. Lobb, Edward. "Imaginary History: The Romantic Background of George Bowering's *Burning Water*." *SCL* 12 (1987): 112–128.

Analyzes the author's perception and creation of history.

620. Lobo, Luiza. "Women Writers in Brazil Today." *WLT* 61 (Winter 1987): 49–54.

Most Brazilian women writers are from the upper and middle classes and break through a repressive ideology with humor and a counterideological perspective on society.

621. LoVerso, Marco P. "Dialectic, Morality, and the Deptford Trilogy." *SCL* 12 (1987): 69–89.

Explicates Robertson Davies's dialectical process between the self and the material world.

622. Lowenthal, Cynthia Jeanne. "Lady Mary Wortley Montagu and the Eighteenth-Century Familiar Letter." *DAI* 48 (October 1987): 928A.

Examines the nature of the familiar letter as exemplified by one of its "premier" practitioners.

623. Maduakor, Obi. "Rhetoric as Technique: Language in Soyinka's *The Road*." *WLWE* 27 (Spring 1987): 27–34.

Examines the word play and wit of the character Professor, a rhetorician and dialectician.

624. Malloy, Carolyn Frances. "Gustavo Sainz: The Writer and the Text." *DAI* 48 (December 1987): 1463A.

Evaluates Sainz's contribution to Mexican narrative. Examines his views on language and its function, the social purpose of literature, and the writing process.

625. Mannix, Patrick James. "Available Means: Manifestations of Aristotle's Three Modes of Rhetorical Appeal in Anti-Nuclear Fiction." *DAI* 47 (April 1987): 3751A.

By arousing emotions like pity, fear, and hope, anti-nuclear fiction mobilizes "its audience's active support for the ideas it presents."

626. McHale, Brian. "Postmodernist Lyric and the Ontology of Poetry." *PT* 8 (1987): 19–44.

Examines presented objects in projected textual worlds.

627. McPherson, Dolly Aimee. "Order out of Chaos: The Autobiographical Works of Maya Angelou." *DAI* 47 (January 1987): 2627A.

Identifies recurrent themes that connect Angelou with both Afro-American and American cultural traditions of autobiography.

628. Miall, David S. "Authorizing the Reader." *EQ* 19 (Fall 1986): 186–195.

Discusses confusion among the authority of the text, the authority of the reader, and a student's own reading. Suggests concentration on the student's reading for more effective learning.

629. Miller, J. Hillis. "The Ethics of Reading." *Style* 21 (Summer 1987): 181–191.

Questions whether there is an ethical obligation in reading and to whom the obligation is directed.

630. Miller, J. Hillis. "Presidential Address 1986: The Triumph of Theory, the Resistance to Reading, and the Question of the Material Base." *PMLA* 102 (May 1987): 281–291.

An explanatory defense of deconstruction that emphasizes the necessity of recognizing the "rhetorical or tropological dimension of language" in reading and writing.

631. Miller, Marilyn Jeanne. "Literary Diaries: Their Tradition and Their Influence on Modern Japanese Fiction." *WLT* 61 (Spring 1987): 207–210.

Diary writing in Japan dates back to the eighth century, with periods since then greatly influencing contemporary Japanese poetry and prose.

632. Miller, R. Baxter. "A Deeper Literacy: Teaching *Invisible Man* from Aboriginal Ground." Paper presented at the CCCC Convention, Atlanta, March 1987. ERIC ED 279 021. 15 pages

An analysis of Ellison's beliefs concerning texts and literacy as projected in *The Invisible Man*.

633. Monaghan, Peter. "Is That a Sonic Boom, or Spokane Going Up?" *CHE* 34 (11 November 1987): A3.

Paul Brians's study of 1000 war novels and stories reveals a dismaying "mythology" about nuclear holocaust. Most people evade the subject's horrors.

634. Moss, Leonard. "Rhetorical Addition in *King Lear* (Part One)." *Lang&S* 20 (Winter 1987): 16–29.

Posits the rhetorical technique of "addition" or "cumulation" as the device Shakespeare used to develop tension, fact, and idea in *King Lear*. See also *Lang&S* 20 (Spring 1987).

635. Moss, Leonard. "Rhetorical Addition in *King Lear* (Part Two)." *Lang&S* 20 (Spring 1987): 171–184.

Concludes research described in an earlier article, *Lang&S* 20 (Winter 1987).

636. Neupert, Richard John. "The End: Notions of Closure in the Cinema." *DAI* 47 (January 1987): 2347A.

Categorizes films as closed text, open story, and open discourse.

637. Pearson, Roberta E. "'The Modesty of Nature': Performance Style in the Griffith Biographs." *DAI* 48 (September 1987): 494A.

Using three paradigms, including a formalist textual approach, examines performance style in D. W. Griffith films from 1908 to 1913.

638. Pelias, Ronald J., and James VanOosting. "A Paradigm for Performance Studies." *QJS* 73 (May 1987): 219–231.

Surveys research on "performance studies" and compares them to the older concept of "oral interpretation." Discusses research in terms of text, event, performer, and audience.

639. Perrin, Patricia Elizabeth. "A Change of Vision: The Emergence of the Systems Paradigm in the Visual, Literary, and Dramatic Arts." *DAI* 47 (May 1987): 3897A.

Argues that early twentieth-century artists, writers, and filmmakers were just as involved with determining the nature of reality as scientists and philosophers were.

640. Peterson, James Donald. "In Warhol's Wake: Minimalism and Pop in the American Avant-Garde Film." *DAI* 47 (March 1987): 3216A.

These films "trigger perceptual and cognitive processes on the part of the viewer, and these processes should be the focus" of film analysis.

641. Piper, David. "The 'World' Metaphors of English Education." *EQ* 19 (Winter 1986): 282–290.

Discusses the value of "world" metaphors used to explore language processing: narrative worlds, possible worlds, text worlds, and so on.

642. Pollard-Gott, Lucy. "Fractal Repetition Structure in the Poetry of Wallace Stevens." *Lang&S* 19 (Summer 1986): 233–249.

Explains fractal mathematics in lay terms and shows that repetition in Stevens's poetry approximates this particular structure. Discusses the implications of this characteristic for the study of style.

643. Popovich, George Lee. "Structural Analyses of Selected Modern Science Fiction Films." *DAI* 48 (November 1987): 1060A.

Surveys science fiction films from 1960 to 1981 and posits 12 categories that differ from traditional literary comparisons.

644. Renan, Yael. "Figurative Language and the Establishment of Norms in Modern Fiction." *Lang&S* 20 (Winter 1987): 63–70.

Suggests that the opposing tensions found in the figurative language of modern novels support the reversal of conventional values.

645. Reuter, Kathleen Alice. "The Language of *Middlemarch*." *DAI* 48 (August 1987): 400A.

Examines the vocabulary, diction, and syntax that characterize the narrator and that create artistic effects.

646. Richetti, John J. "Voice and Gender in Eighteenth-Century Fiction: Haywood to Burney." *SNNTS* 19 (Fall 1987): 263–272.

Analyzes the constraints on the use of language by female characters and novelists.

Eliza Haywood, Fanny Burney, and others exploited those constraints.

647. Riffaterre, Michael. "The Intertextual Unconscious." *CritI* 13 (Winter 1987): 371–385.

Argues that, while "meaning is wholly present in the text, significance rests on the inseparability of a visible sign from its repressed intertextual homologue."

648. Roberts, Constance Janine. "An Application of Erving Goffmann's Frame Analysis to Literature and Performance: A Study of Vladimir Nabokov's *Pale Fire.*" *DAI* 47 (March 1987): 3241A.

Uses frame analysis to examine Nabokov's novel and Frank Galati's performance to explain it.

649. Roemer, Marjorie Godlin. "Which Reader's Response?" *CE* 49 (December 1987): 911–921.

Argues that English teachers using reader-response techniques must consciously support a plurality of readings in the classroom and avoid unconsciously purveying values.

650. Rosen, Charles. "Romantic Originals." *NYRB* 34 (17 December 1987): 22–31.

Reviews five collections of works by Balzac, Byron, and Wordsworth. Discusses the revelations afforded by studying revision in the multiple versions of texts provided by critical and variorum editions.

651. Sawicki, Joseph. "'The Mere Truth Won't Do': Esther as Narrator in *Bleak House.*" *JNT* 17 (Spring 1987): 209–224.

Argues that the character-narrator's rhetorical strategies "deconstruct" some of the thematic issues in the novel.

652. Schulz, H.-J. "Science Fiction and Ideology: Some Problems of Approach." *SFS* 14 (July 1987): 165–179.

Calls for a critical approach to paraliterary science fiction that is sensitive to its "peculiar socio-cultural milieu" and to its "formal and ideological complexity."

653. Shen, Yeshayahu. "On the Structure and Understanding of Poetic Oxymoron." *PT* 8 (1987): 105–122.

Examines the semantic features and cognitive processing complexity of oxymorons.

654. Shoos, Diane L. "Speaking the Subject: The Films of Marguerite Duras and Alain Resnais." *DAI* 47 (January 1987): 2347A.

Examines films using psychoanalytic theory. Concludes that they "refute the notion of the self" as an essence that controls discourse.

655. Simpson, Louis P. "Lionel Trilling and the Agency of Terror." *PR* 54 (Winter 1987): 18–35.

Considers Trilling's vacillation between his imaginative and critical writing. Views cultural studies as a function of poesis.

656. Skinner, John. "The Oral and the Written: Kurtz and Gatsby Revisited." *JNT* 17 (Winter 1987): 131–143.

Suggests that, while the similarities between *The Heart of Darkness* and *The Great Gatsby* have been noted, they differ in their written and oral modes.

657. Smith, Michael William. "Reading and Teaching Irony in Poetry: Giving Short People a Reason to Live." *DAI* 48 (July 1987): 40A.

Results indicate that understanding irony begins with recognizing what is not ironic.

658. Spacks, Patricia Meyer. "Female Changelessness; or, What do Women Want?" *SNNTS* 19 (Fall 1987): 273–283.

Argues that male novelists create changeless and compliant female characters, reducing their complexity to differentiate them from men and to make them comprehensible to men.

659. Stampfl, Barry. " 'As Ifs': Against Knowing in Conrad: Two Types of Anti-Conjectural Simile." *JNT* 17 (Winter 1987): 107–114.

Suggests that the simile can act as a form of coming closer to knowing or as a form of circling an unstable knowing.

660. Stark, Heather Alexandra. "Keeping Track of Characters in Narrative." *DAI* 47 (June 1987): 5080B.

Concludes that pronouns and scene cues such as *then* and *meanwhile* affect readers' attention to characters in narrative.

661. Staub, Michael Eric. "From Speech to Text: The 1930s Narratives of John Neihardt, Tillie Olsen, and James Agee." *DAI* 48 (October 1987): 965A.

Examines Neihardt, Olsen, and Agee's struggle to translate the speech and sounds of dispossessed people into print.

662. Stecker, Robert. "Apparent, Implied, and Postulated Writers." *P&L* 11 (October 1987): 258–271.

Discusses Wayne Booth's suggestion to distinguish between the writer of a work and its narrator and to distinguish both writer and narrator from the author.

663. Sterk, Helen Mae. "Functioning Fictions: The Adjustment Rhetoric of Silhouette Romance Works." *DAI* 47 (January 1987): 2373A.

Finds that the eight-step narrative schema of Silhouette romances constrain roles for women and men; an alternate series does not. The two series exemplify Plato's base and noble rhetorics.

664. Subramini. "Indo-Fijian Writing." *WLWE* 27 (Spring 1987): 143–151.

Examines oral traditions, image and self-image, and historical consciousness.

665. Sultana, Niloufar. "The Principle of Chapter- and Volume-Division in *Tristram Shandy*." *Lang&S* 20 (Spring 1987): 185–202.

Concludes that Sterne's playing with structural conventions highlights the problem of realism in fiction and its relationship to life.

666. Tarlinskaja, Marina. "Rhythm and Meaning: 'Rhythmical Figures' in English Iambic Pentameter, Their Grammar, and Their Links with Semantics." *Style* 21 (Spring 1987): 1–35.

Structurally classifies rhythmical figures in English verse and discusses the different ways poetic genres use them for semantic and stylistic purposes.

667. Thorpe, James. *The Sense of Style: Reading English Prose*. Hamden, Conn.: Shoe String Press, 1987. 185 pages

Analyzes exemplary selections of English prose from the Renaissance to Joyce. Shows how diction, mechanics, and syntax affect readers' interpretations. Depicts reading as the "performance" of a text and writing as the "signing" of a text.

668. Tinter, Adeline R. "The Narrative Structure of *Old New York:* Text and Pictures in Edith Wharton's Quartet of Linked Short Stories." *JNT* 17 (Winter 1987): 76–82.

Lists several devices of continuity and variation that achieve an overarching narrative structure for the four stories.

669. Tomasulo, Frank Peter. "The Rhetoric of Ambiguity: Michelangelo Antonioni and the Modernist Discourse." *DAI* 47 (April 1987): 3592A.

"Modernist paradigms of textual structuration are explored in interdisciplinary fashion to show Antonioni's relationship to realism and modernism."

670. Visser, Carla. "Historicity in Historical Fiction: *Burning Water* and *The Temptations of Big Bear*." *SCL* 12 (1987): 90–111.

Analyzes George Bowering's and Rudy Wiebe's narrativizations of history.

671. Warnick, Barbara. "The Narrative Paradigm: Another Story." *QJS* 73 (May 1987): 172–182.

Criticizes Walter Fisher's "narrative paradigm" as a model for rhetorical criticism. Fisher's model is said to be ambiguous on narrative rationality and sources of critical judgment.

672. Weis, Lyle P. "Bipolar Paths of Desire: D. C. Scott's Poetic and Narrative Structures." *SCL* 12 (1987): 35–52.

Analyzes cultural context as a force shaping narrative and rhetorical patterns.

673. Whiteside, Anna, and Michael Issacharoff, eds. *On Referring in Literature.* Bloomington, Ind.: Indiana University Press, 1987. 224 pages

Illustrates close links between reference and interpretation. Examines types of literary references, showing what it is and how it works.

674. Wiemer, Annegret. "Foreign L(Anguish), Mother Tongue: Concepts of Language in Contemporary Feminist Science Fiction." *WS* 14 (December 1987): 163–173.

Summarizes contemporary feminist theories of the differences in the social contract of power, language, and meaning, relating them to works of science fiction by women.

675. Wihl, Gary. "Why the Interpretive Community Has Banished Literary Theory." *P&L* 11 (October 1987): 272–281.

Attacks Stanley Fish's contention that "theory's day is dying." Demonstrates the limited validity of Fish's use of certain speech-act conventions.

676. Winkler, Karen J. "Evolution of Poststructuralism Owes Much to Derrida, Cixous, and Others." *CHE* 34 (25 November 1987): A6, A8.

Offers brief descriptions of the work of major French poststructuralists, including Lacan, Barthes, Kristeva, and Irigaray.

677. Winkler, Karen J. "Literary Critic's Early Writings for Pro-Nazi Newspaper Stir Controversy." *CHE* 34 (9 December 1987): A5–6.

Paul de Man, a deconstruction theorist, wrote literary articles in 1942 for a Nazi newspaper. Scholars debate what this means for the theory he helped popularize.

678. Winkler, Karen J. "Poststructuralism: An Often-Abstruse French Import Profoundly Affects Research in the United States." *CHE* 34 (25 November 1987): A6-A9.

Poststructuralism, introduced to U.S. scholars in 1968, now embraces scholars in diverse disciplines from anthropology to law and literature.

See also 73, 122, 151, 178, 188, 211, 297, 309, 390, 679, 712, 747, 777, 816

2.7 READING

679. Bartlett, Bertrice. "Negatives, Narrative, and the Reader." *Lang&S* 20 (Winter 1987): 41–62.

Analyzes the uses of negatives to structure readers' processes of understanding, and thus adding the drama of comprehension to the drama of the story proper.

680. Beach, Richard, and Linda Wendler. "Developmental Differences in Response to a Story." *RTE* 21 (October 1987): 286–297.

Compares the inferences high school and college writers make about a character's actions, perceptions, and goals.

681. Begg, Ian, and Andrea Snider. "The Generation Effect: Evidence for Generalized Inhibition." *JEPL* 13 (October 1987): 553–563.

Generated words are sometimes remembered better and sometimes not as well as read words. Suggests that the demand to generate hurts reading.

682. Belmore, Susan M. "Determinants of Attention during Impression Formation." *JEPL* 13 (July 1987): 480–489.

When reading, people pay more attention to early information and inconsistent information than to late or consistent information. Discusses the implications for advertising, jury selection, and voting.

683. Boyle, Owen Frank. "The Effect of Cognitive Mapping on Reading Comprehension and Written Expression." *DAI* 47 (January 1987): 2522A.

A study exploring the effects of cognitive mapping indicates that mapping groups made higher holistic gain scores for summarization and cohesion.

684. Britton, Bruce K., and Shawn M. Glynn. *Executive Control Processes in Reading.* Hillside, N.J.: Erlbaum, 1987. 328 pages

Eleven essays treat the subprocesses of reading that require executive control to function optimally. Includes a review of empirical research and an examination of executive control processes in studying, inferencing, schema use, and learning.

685. Brown, Tracy L., Thomas H. Carr, and Marc Chaderjian. "Orthography, Familiarity, and Meaningfulness Reconsidered: Attentional Strategies May Affect the Lexical Sensitivity of Visual Code Formation." *JEPH* 13 (February 1987): 127–139.

Considers the linguistic properties of printed words to which the visual system is sensitive during its encoding operations.

686. Carrell, Patricia L. "Content and Formal Schemata in ESL Reading." *TESOLQ* 21 (September 1987): 461–481.

Using high-intermediate ESL learners, this experiment examines the significance of content schemata versus formal schemata in reading comprehension. Indicates that content schemata affects reading more than formal schemata.

687. Cate, Laureen Connelly. "The Interrelationship of Reading and Writing: Consequential Effects Attributable to Integration of Directional Writing Components into a Selected Collegiate Reading Program." *DAI* 47 (March 1987): 3380A.

An infusion of writing favorably affected reading. Suggests modifications for the present curriculum.

688. Clark, James M. "Understanding Pictures and Words: Comment on Potter, Kroll, Yachzel, Carpenter, and Sherman [*JEPG* 115 (September 1986)]." *JEPG* 116 (September 1987): 307–309.

Suggests that meaning may be better explained by a dual coding model rather than by either a lexical or conceptual model.

689. Courtis, John K. "Fry, Smog, Lix and Rix: Insinuations about Corporate Business Communication." *JBC* 24 (Spring 1987): 19–27.

A readability study of 65 Canadian annual corporate reports. Finds them written beyond the fluent reading levels of 92% of adults and 56% of investors.

690. Cupples, Linda. "Individual Differences in Reading Ability." *DAI* 48 (September 1987): 901B.

Finds that skilled readers are more able to access syntactic knowledge than unskilled readers.

691. Davidson, A., and G. Green. *Linguistic Complexity and Text Comprehension: A Reexamination of Readability and Alternative Views.* Hillside, N.J.: Erlbaum, 1987. 296 pages

Eleven papers examine the relationship between the linguistic complexity of texts and their readability.

692. Dixon, Peter. "The Processing of Organizational and Component Step Information in Written Directions." *JML* 26 (February 1987): 24–35.

Suggests that when readers are given component steps first, they guess at possible outcomes. Organizational information early on reduces reading comprehension time.

693. Dixon, Peter. "The Structure of Mental Plans for Following Directions." *JEPL* 13 (January 1987): 18–26.

Describes a process of studying reading comprehension while it occurs. Demonstrates that prior knowledge has dramatic effects on comprehension.

694. Frost, Ram, Leonard Katz, and Shlomo Bentin. "Strategies for Visual Word Recognition and Orthographical Depth: A Multilin-

gual Comparison." *JEPH* 13 (February 1987): 104–115.

> The directness with which an orthography represents the phonology of its language determines the relative use of orthographic versus phonological codes in reading.

695. Glenberg, Arthur M., Marion Meyer, and Karen Lindem. "Mental Models Contribute to Foregrounding during Text Comprehension." *JML* 26 (February 1987): 69–83.

> Suggests that mental models and the spatial structure of events described in narrative texts influences comprehension.

696. Grant-Davie, Keith A. *Readers' Perceptions of Writers' Aims in Ironic Discourse*. Urbana, Ill.: ERIC/RCS, 1984. ERIC ED 283 154. 41 pages

> Compares the reading protocols of six graduate students and five freshmen reading ironic texts, finding in general that both groups used similar strategies.

697. Healy, Alice F., William L. Oliver, and Timothy P. McNamara. "Detecting Letters in Continuous Text: Effects of Display Size." *JEPH* 13 (May 1987): 279–290.

> Letter detection is more difficult in four-word displays than in one-word displays. Letter detection is also more difficult in correctly spelled, familiar words than in misspelled ones.

698. Horning, Alice S. "Readability: Reading/ Writing Tools for Measurement." *JAC* 7 (1987): 101–111.

> Compares the effects on readability of increasing syntactic and/or semantic redundancy in professional texts. Uses standard formulas, propositional analysis, and cloze tests.

699. Levy, Betty Ann, Susan Newell, Judy Snyder, and Kurt Timmins. "Correction to Levy *et al*. [*JEPL* 12 (October 1986)]." *JEPL* 13 (April 1987): 186.

> An editorial correction of an earlier article in which two reading graphs were transposed.

700. Lorch, Robert F., Elizabeth P. Lorch, and Ann M. Mogan. "Task Effects and Individual Differences in On-Line Processing of the Topic Structure of a Text." *DPr* 10 (January–March 1987): 63–80.

> Topic sentences occasioned slower reading more than nontopic sentences did. Patterns shown by good recallers in processing topic sentences differed from those of poor recallers.

701. Maclay, Connie M. "An Investigation of the Use of Computer-Assisted Instruction in Teaching Sight Word Recognition to Adult Beginning Readers in a Prison Setting." *DAI* 47 (May 1987): 3964A.

> Results indicate that, for 11 subjects, the number of correct responses on the word sets increased while the response time decreased.

702. Martin, Nadine. "Variables Influencing the Occurrence of Naming Errors: Implications for Models of Lexical Retrieval." *DAI* 48 (October 1987): 1175B.

> After testing models of lexical retrieval, concludes that the interactive activation model best explains how phonological and semantic variables influence error.

703. McCann, Robert S. "On the Locus of Word-Frequency Effects in Word Recognition: Evidence from the Processing of Novel Letter Strings." *DAI* 48 (November 1987): 1536B.

> Challenges existing theories of word recognition, which associate word-frequency effects with lexical memory differences. Suggests at least two loci for such effects.

704. McCann, Robert S., and Derek Besner. "Reading Pseudohomophones: Implications for Models of Pronunciation Assembly and the Locus of Word-Frequency Effects in Naming." *JEPH* 13 (February 1987): 14–24.

Nonwords with pronunciations identical to real words show that meaning resides between lexical representations, not in lexical representation.

705. McGrath, Mary Ann. "Reading and Writing: A Positive Link." *CET* (1987): 22–27.

Draws on current reading-writing research to suggest a procedure for observing, documenting, and sharing the interrelatedness of reading and writing.

706. Morris, Mary K. "Phonologic and Lexical Routes to Reading: A Comparison of Impaired, Normal, and Superior Readers." *DAI* 48 (October 1987): 1157B.

Finds that poor, as opposed to normal and superior, readers are hindered more by phonology than by lexis.

707. Nelson, Douglas L., Jose J. Canas, Maria Teresa Bajo, and Patricia D. Keelean. "Comparing Word Fragment Completion and Cued Recall with Letter Cues." *JEPL* 13 (October 1987): 542–552.

Both fragment completion and letter-cued recall depend on lexical search. Cued recall also involves semantic search.

708. O'Hear, Michael F., Richard N. Ramsey, and Valli E. Pherson. "Location of Main Ideas in English Composition Texts." *RTE* 21 (October 1987): 318–326.

Concludes that main idea statements and clues exist in English composition textbooks and are comparable to those found in sociology textbooks.

709. Ormrod, Jeanne Ellis. "Differences between Good and Poor Spellers in Reading Style and Short-Term Memory." *VLang* 20 (Autumn 1986): 437–447.

Finds that good spellers read faster and have better short-term memories than poor spellers.

710. Potter, Mary C., and Judith F. Kroll. "Conceptual Representation of Pictures and Words: Reply to Clark [*JEPG* 116 (September 1987)]." *JEPG* 116 (September 1987): 310–311.

Argues for the conceptual model rather than a dual coding model as most appropriate to describe language processing.

711. Ritchie, David, Vincent Price, and Donald F. Roberts. "Television, Reading, and Reading Achievement." *ComR* 14 (June 1987): 292–315.

Reappraises the relationship between television and reading achievement.

712. Sawyer, Wayne. "Literature and Literacy: A Review of Research." *LArts* 64 (January 1987): 33–39.

A review of recent major theoretical statements on the role of narrative in reading and on the connection between literature and literacy. Bibliography included.

713. Silkebakken, Gail Patricia. "The Effect of Student-Generated Analogies on Reading Comprehension." *DAI* 48 (September 1987): 619A.

Results of this study suggest that self-generated analogies can be an effective mechanism for transferring knowledge from a familiar to an unfamiliar domain.

714. Squire, James R., ed. *The Dynamics of Language Learning: Research in Reading and English*. Urbana, Ill.: NCTE, ERIC/RCS, 1987. 425 pages

Twenty-seven papers originally presented at the National Conference on Research in English Mid-Decade Seminar (1985). Focuses on the skills and processes that influence the development of children's competence in reading, writing, and the related language arts. Essays also treat the gap between research and classroom practice. Also available as ERIC ED 274 967.

715. Tierney, Robert J., Patricia L. Anders, and Judy Nicols Mitchell. *Understanding Readers' Understanding: Theory to Practice*. Hillside, N.J.: Erlbaum, 1987. 344 pages

Fifteen papers address current issues in reading comprehension from cognitive and linguistic perspectives. Three sections treat the text, knowledge of the world and inference, and instructional issues.

716. Tuman, Myron C. "Reflexive Cloze-Testing: A Look inside the Psycholinguistic Process." *Lang&S* 19 (Summer 1986): 280–292.

To determine the relationship between authorial intention (and understanding) and the public meaning of a text, the author used cloze tests to measure how well students could recall two assignments written for freshman composition class.

717. Vellutino, Frank R. "Dyslexia." *SAm* 256 (March 1987): 34–41.

Suggests that dyslexia is a linguistic rather than a perceptual deficiency, treatable through remedial reading instruction.

718. Vipond, Douglas, and Russell A. Hunt. "Aesthetic Reading: Some Strategies for Research." *EQ* 20 (Fall 1987): 178–183.

Points out the necessity of using a range of tasks and measures to study variations in readers, texts, and situations when conducting research in aesthetic reading.

719. Walker, Robert. "What Electronic Books Will Have to Be Better Than." *IDJ* 5 (1986): 72–74.

Increased accessibility of electronic texts may hinder their readability.

720. Whyte, Sarah S. *The Connection of Writing to Reading and Its Effect on Reading Comprehension*. Cambridge, Mass.: Lesley College Graduate School, 1985. ERIC ED 278 940. 28 pages

Argues that reading and writing reinforce each other. Dictation, paraphrasing, abstracting, and peer conferencing all contribute to reading comprehension and learning.

See also 15, 29, 166, 226, 239, 759, 852, 864, 873, 987

2.8 LINGUISTICS, GRAMMATICAL THEORY, AND SEMANTICS

721. Adams, John K. "Semantic Information in the Long-Term Memory Traces of Nouns." *DAI* 47 (June 1987): 5077B.

Examines in three experiments the concept of memory trace. Finds that only nouns crucial to understanding are encoded and accessed.

722. Allport, Alan, Donald G. MacKay, Wolfgang Prinz, and Eckart Scheerer, eds. *Language Perception and Production: Relationships between Listening, Speaking, Reading, and Writing*. Cognitive Science Series. San Diego: Academic Press, 1987. 512 pages

Studies the possible representations, timing mechanisms, sequencing mechanisms, and neural substrates for the perception and production of language in its written, lipread, and spoken forms.

723. Andersen, Peter A., Myron W. Lustig, and Janis F. Andersen. "Regional Patterns of Communication in the United States: A Theoretical Perspective." *ComM* 54 (June 1987): 128–144.

Provides a foundation for systematic study and outlines theoretical and methodological requirements for a program of research.

724. Anderson, John R., and Lynne M. Reder. "Effects of Number of Facts Studied on Recognition Versus Sensibility Judgments." *JEPL* 13 (July 1987): 355–367.

Questions the view that language processing is a faculty that occupies a place separate from memory.

725. Appel, Gabriela. "L1 and L2 Narrative and Expository Discourse Production: A Vygotskyan Analysis." *DAI* 47 (June 1987): 4373A.

Examines the nature of the text recall process and finds that differences between L1 and L2 speakers are not absolute.

726. Baily, Nathalie Hutchins. "The Importance of Meaning over Form in Second Language System Building: An Unresolved Issue." *DAI* 48 (September 1987): 639A.

Studies interlanguage development to infer language learning principles. Concludes that meaning constrains language learning more than form.

727. Barton, Ben F., and Marthalee S. Barton. "Simplicity in Visual Representation: A Semiotic Approach." *JBTC* 1 (January 1987): 9–26.

Reviews notions of visual simplicity within Charles Morris's semiotic framework of interacting syntactic, semantic, and pragmatic levels, levels whose incompatibilities can often be revealed.

728. Baugh, John. "Research Currents: The Situational Dimension of Linguistic Power in Social Context." *LArts* 64 (February 1987): 234–240.

Discusses the complexity of diverse linguistic power and the need for speakers of nonstandard English to have access to standard English.

729. Besner, Derek, and Nancy Hildebrandt. "Orthographic and Phonological Codes in the Oral Reading of Japanese Kana." *JEPL* 13 (April 1987): 335–343.

Suggests that lexical access based upon visual or orthographic information is a feature of word recognition in all orthographies.

730. Besnier, Nicholas Guy. "Spoken and Written Registers in a Restricted-Literacy Setting." *DAI* 47 (January 1987): 2737A.

Analyzes differences between speech and writing in Tuvaluan, a Polynesian language.

731. Bleasdale, Fraser A. "Concreteness-Dependent Associative Priming: Separate Lexical Organization for Concrete and Abstract Words." *JEPL* 13 (October 1987): 582–594.

Argues that lexical representations for concrete concepts and their labels are organized differently from abstract concepts and their labels.

732. Bonaventura, Anna Maria. "Effects of Cooperative Learning Methods on the Achievement of Limited-English Speaking Students in the English as a Second Language Classroom." *DAI* 48 (November 1987): 1100A.

Four instruments measured individual characteristics of second language learning variables. Although learning interest was a significant effect, the study found no significant interaction effect.

733. Bowie, David Greenfield. "Converting Thought to Oral Narrative Composition in a Second Language." *DAI* 48 (November 1987): 1135A.

Employs protocol analysis to explore the relationship between thought and language. Discusses applying the technique to instruction and testing.

734. Bruce, Harry. "Language of the U.S. Military." *ETC* 44 (Fall 1987): 295–296.

Presents current examples of doublespeak in the U.S. military. Argues that current practices are more dangerous than earlier doublespeak.

735. Chanawangsa, Wipah. "Cohesion in Thai." *DAI* 48 (December 1987): 1446A.

Describes how classes are connected, what devices are used for cohesion, and how these devices make different parts of a text hang together.

736. Chodchoey, Supa W. "Strategies in Thai Oral Discourse." *DAI* 47 (January 1987): 2369A.

Examines the organization of Thai oral discourse, a particle that functions as a highlight marker, and the use of referential devices.

737. Chomsky, Noam. *The Chomsky Reader.* Edited by James Peck. New York: Pantheon, 1987. 492 pages

Contains an interview with Noam Chomsky and a collection of his essays, three of which deal with language.

738. Clyne, Michael. "Constraints on Code Switching: How Universal Are They?" *Ling* 25 (1987): 739–764.

Presents data suggesting that bilinguals use nonlanguage-specific processing, in which case indexing and code switching and its constraints are surface-structure phenomena.

739. Cmiel, Kenneth J. "Democratic Eloquence: Language, Education, and Authority in Nineteenth-Century America." *DAI* 47 (May 1987): 4171A.

Addresses the question, how did Americans think about correct and incorrect English?

740. Coates, Jennifer. *Women, Men, and Language.* White Plains, N.Y.: Longman, 1986. 178 pages

An analysis and historical survey of sex-related linguistic behavior.

741. Connor, Ulla, and Robert B. Kaplan, eds. *Writing across Languages: Analysis of L2 Text.* Second Language Professional Library. Reading, Mass.: Addison-Wesley, 1987. 202 pages

A collection of 10 essays focusing on recent research in linguistics, psycholinguistics, and rhetoric. Urges an interdisciplinary approach in examining second language writing and the ways readers interact with it.

742. Corse, Sandra. "The Nonverbal Interplay in Written Texts." *TETYC* 14 (October 1987): 181–186.

Semiotic descriptions of sign, index, and icon offer helpful perceptions about student essays.

743. Coulmas, Florian. "Why Linguists Should Deal with 'Good Language' and 'Bad Language.' " Paper presented at the Conference on Vernacular Languages for Modern Societies, Bad Hamburg, West Germany, June 1985. ERIC ED 276 286. 32 pages

Contrary to disciplinary methodology, linguists should evaluate languages according to their suitability for different forms of communication in response to social need.

744. diVirgilio, P. S. "In Search of Deep Semiotic Structures: The Genesis of *Das Schloss.*" *Lang&S* 19 (Fall 1986): 315–324.

Describes and evaluates the relationship between surface and deep structures in *Das Schloss* as evidenced by the shift in the ontological roles of the subject and object in the deep structure.

745. Drummond, Samuel Joseph. "A Historical Critique of the Problem of Conditional Discourse in Hebrew." *DAI* 47 (April 1987): 3787A.

Describes, analyzes, and compares the classical Western tradition of Hebrew grammar since 1813.

746. Embler, Weller. "Notes Toward a Theory of Metaphor." *ETC* 44 (Summer 1987): 163–170.

Discusses the psychological uses and effects of metaphor, mixed metaphor, extended figures, epigrammatic metaphor, allegory and fable, personification, synesthesia, and analogy.

747. Fabb, Nigel, Derek Attridge, Alan Durant, and Colin MacCabe, eds. *The Linguistics of Writing: Arguments between Language and Literature.* New York: Methuen, 1987. 325 pages

A collection of 18 essays presented at The Linguistics of Writing conference held at Strathclyde University, July 1986. Discussions explore areas of agreement and dispute in modern theoretical linguistics and the study of texts, assessing the achievements of the interdisciplinary study of literary language since *Style in Language* (1960).

748. Fasold, Ralph W. "Are Black and White Vernaculars Diverging? Papers from the NWAVE XIV Panel Discussion." *AS* 62 (Spring 1987): 3–80.

Papers of the Fourteenth Annual Colloquium on New Ways of Analyzing Variations in English (1985) trace the differentiating processes of Black English and its continued linguistic divergence.

749. Freeman, Sue. "Verbal Response Data as Predictors of Social Structure." *DAI* 48 (December 1987): 1551A.

Studies whether long-term patterns of social structure can be reconstructed best from observations of interaction or from verbal reports by participants in the interaction.

750. Ginn, Doris O. "Who Needs Linguistics Anyway?" *SCETCJ* 20 (Spring 1987): 6–9.

Identifies subspecialties in the discipline of linguistics and advocates the value of language study.

751. Graesser, Arthur C., and Patricia L. Hopkinson. "Differences in Interconcept Organization between Nouns and Verbs." *JML* 26 (April 1987): 242–253.

Examines the semantic interrelatedness between simple nouns and verbs.

752. Hall, Christian. "Revision Strategies in L1 and L2 Writing Tasks: A Case Study." *DAI* 48 (November 1987): 1187A.

Data indicate that revising strategies are recursive and alike across languages. The word level is dominant and substitution and addition are the most common operations.

753. Hall, Christopher John. "Language Structure and Explanation: A Case from Morphology." *DAI* 48 (October 1987): 914A.

Examines the psycholinguistic and diachronic contributions to the development across language of a preference for suffixing over prefixing.

754. Hall, Malcolm Eldon. "Detecting Deception in the Voice: An Analysis of the Fundamental Frequency, Syllabic Duration, and Amplitude of the Human Voice." *DAI* 47 (March 1987): 3568A.

Audio tape recordings of polygraph examinations were analyzed for interactions of truthfulness, deception, frequency, duration, and voice amplitude.

755. Harris, Roy. "Language as Social Interaction: Integrationalism Versus Segregationalism." *LangS* 9 (October 1987): 131–143.

Compares two linguistic approaches, one treating language with nonlinguistic components of human interaction and the other treating language independently of other varieties of communication.

756. Hatfield, Deborah Helen. "Tense Marking in the Spoken English of Vietnamese Refugees." *DAI* 47 (June 1987): 4377A.

Uses a sociolinguistic approach to study language variation.

757. Higgins, Eleanor Lee. "Sociolinguistic Influences on the Structure of American Sign Language and the Maintenance of Iconicity." *DAI* 48 (October 1987): 968A.

Concludes that sociolinguistic pressure "selects for" an easy-to-teach, easy-to-learn language, which in turn favors iconic devices.

758. Hoover, Michael Lindsley. "Strategies for Processing Self-Embedded Sentences in Spanish and English." *DAI* 47 (April 1987): 4328B.

Determines that the clause as a perceptual unit varies in Spanish and English, thus influencing the rate of processing.

759. Horodeck, Richard A. "The Role of Sound in Reading and Writing Kanji." *DAI* 48 (July 1987): 117A.

The fact that meanings do not trigger Kanji when Japanese write has implications for language teaching and cognitive theories of reading and writing.

760. Horty, John Francis. "Some Aspects of Meaning in Non-Contingent Language." *DAI* 47 (June 1987): 4411A.

Argues that instead of searching for a single relation of meaning equivalence among expressions, we should expect to find several different relations of meaning congruence.

761. Hutchinson, Kathleen Mary. "The Influence of Sentence Context on Speech Recognition Skills of the Elderly." *DAI* 47 (January 1987): 2697A.

Shows experimentally that older listeners were able to use contextual clues in "everyday" sentences to recognize key words but were adversely affected by background noise.

762. Inness, Donna Kay. "An Error Analysis of the Use of Limiting, Specifying, Distinguishing, Quantifying, and Zero Determiners in the Writing of University Students of English as a Second Language." *DAI* 48 (November 1987): 1163A.

Examines the frequency for using determiners, making errors, and creating errors in the same or different categories.

763. Kasper, Robert T. "Feature Structures: A Logical Theory with Application to Language Analysis." *DAI* 48 (August 1987): 495B.

Designs and tests a system of feature structures, which are used to represent linguistic information in the processing of natural language.

764. Kelly, Michael Hugh. "On the Selection of Linguistic Options." *DAI* 47 (February 1987): 3527B.

Focuses on word order selection and concludes that speakers most typically select words possessing greatest "accessibility."

765. Kennedy, Graeme D. "Expressing Temporal Frequency in Academic English." *TESOLQ* 21 (March 1987): 69–86.

Uses computer-assisted analysis to discover how temporal frequency is expressed in the register of academic English. Recommends that such studies be used to inform ESL curriculums.

766. Kim, Changwook. "Decision Properties for Chain Code Picture Languages." *DAI* 47 (February 1987): 3429B.

Based on an investigation of picture languages, proposes a theory to account for problems in context-free decisions.

767. Kipers, Pamela S. "Gender and Topics." *LSoc* 16 (December 1987): 543–557.

Reports on research finding that women's conversations emphasize matters of home, family, and social issues while men's conversations emphasize matters of work and recreation.

768. Knight, Terry Weissman. "Transformation of Language of Design." *DAI* 47 (March 1987): 3215A.

Describes style as a rule-based "shape grammar" in a "language of design" in which stylistic changes are called "transformations."

769. Lakoff, George. *Women, Fire, and Dangerous Things: What Categories Reveal about the Mind*. Chicago: University of Chicago Press, 1987. 614 pages

A study of how human beings categorize objects and ideas. Proposes that human reason is imaginative, metaphorical, and intrinsically linked with the human body.

770. Luce, Paul A. "Neighborhoods of Words in the Mental Lexicon." *DAI* 47 (June 1987): 5078B.

Finds that individuals discriminate within memory to access words from a neighborhood of similar words.

771. Lutz, William. "Language, Appearance, and Reality: Doublespeak in 1984." *ETC* 44 (Winter 1987): 382–391.

Defines the types, sources, and consequences of today's doublespeak, noting an increasing lack of respect for language.

772. Lutz, William. "1986 Orwell and Doublespeak Awards." *QRD* 13 (January 1987): 1–5.

Reports on award winners and nominees, providing the texts that earned these distinctions.

773. Lutz, William. "Notes Toward a Description of Doublespeak (Revised)." *QRD* 13 (January 1987): 10–12.

Describes how to analyze doublespeak, classify types, and define the term.

774. Lutz, William, and Committee on Public Doublespeak. "Doublespeak Here and There." *QRD* 13 (April 1987): 1–9.

Presents examples of doublespeak found in business, education, foreign, government, medical, military, and other contexts.

775. Lutz, William, and Committee on Public Doublespeak. "Doublespeak Here and There." *QRD* 13 (October 1987): 5–12.

Presents examples of doublespeak found in business, education, foreign, government, legal, medical, military, and other contexts.

776. Lynch, Catherine M., and Mary Strauss-Noll. "Mauve Washers: Sex Differences in Freshman Writing." *EJ* 76 (January 1987): 90–94.

Describes a study "to test for certain patterns of verbal behavior which might vary with gender."

777. Macafee, Caroline. "Dialect Vocabulary as a Source of Stylistic Effects in Scottish Literature." *Lang&S* 19 (Fall 1986): 325–337.

Uses poetry by Burns, Garioch, and Mac-Diarmid to illustrate the uses of dialect in Scottish poetry. Suggests that the nonstandard nature of the language may still provide much good effect.

778. MacNeal, Edward. "How Many Passengers Are You?" *ETC* 44 (Spring 1987): 11–15.

Uses the label "passenger" to illustrate a semantic trap in English: symbolically identifying people with some part of their activities.

779. Malloy, Thomas E. "Teaching Integrative Thought: Techniques and Data." Paper presented at the CCCC Convention, Atlanta, March 1987. ERIC ED 281 195. 36 pages

Reports on the use of an "idea integration package" for writing instruction among 29 college students at a Utah university.

780. Martin, John N. *Elements of Formal Semantics: An Introduction to Logic for Students of Language.* San Diego: Academic Press, 1987. 367 pages

Intended to enable readers to evaluate ordinary research in formal semantics. Treats propositional and first-order logic separately, including for each its syntax, natural deduction proof theory, and formal semantics with Henkin-style completeness proofs.

781. Mattingly, Joseph S. "Lexical Cohesion and Text-as-Percept." *DAI* 47 (April 1987): 3749A.

Argues that "we perceive cohesive ties among specific lexical items to be meaningful principally within the context of a greater wholeness of meaning."

782. Milosky, Linda Meryl. "The Effect of Context of Resolution of Syntactic Ambiguity." *DAI* 47 (April 1987): 4329B.

Shows that students' prior knowledge establishes a context for discourse and enhances comprehension and interpretation.

783. Minor, Dennis. "Some Values of Language Study: Musen, Dumuzi, and the Sumerian Postposition." *ET* 18 (Summer 1987): 15–19.

Discusses the difference between learning a language and studying a language. Includes an examination of the Sumerian language.

784. Moerman, Michael. *Talking Culture: Ethnographic and Conversational Analysis*. Conduct and Communication Series. Philadelphia: University of Pennsylvania Press, 1987. 256 pages

A close analysis of actual Thai and American conversations. Studies the organization of language as it is actually used in social contexts.

785. Nelson, Katherine. "What's in a Name? Reply to Seidenberg and Pettito [*JEPG* 116 (September 1987)]." *JEPG* 116 (September 1987): 293–296.

Argues that children's language is very similar to the ape Kanzi's use of lexigrams at certain stages.

786. Neuner, Jerome L. "Cohesive Ties and Chains in Good and Poor Freshman Essays." *RTE* 21 (February 1987): 92–105.

Examines the relative distances between coherers and precursors, the mean length of cohesive chains, and the diversity and maturity of the vocabulary within chains.

787. Nyhart, Lynn Keller. "Morphology and the German University, 1860–1900." *DAI* 47 (April 1987): 3858A.

Traces the history of evolutionary morphology in German universities from 1860 to 1900.

788. O'Connor, Nadine. "What Nonnative Narratives Can Tell Us about Second Language Acquisition." *DAI* 48 (September 1987): 640A.

Traces the evolution of the interlanguage system of 20 Americans learning French by examining their use of tense in narratives.

789. Okurowski, Mary E. "Textual Cohesion in Modern Standard Chinese." *DAI* 47 (January 1987): 2566A.

Analyzes seven hours of Chinese radio broadcasts. Concludes that cohesion is af-

fected by "the particulars of language" and influences textual unity.

790. Onyeberechi, Sydney Emeh. "Syntactic Fluency and Cohesive Ties in College Freshman Writing." *DAI* 47 (February 1987): 2874A.

Holistically scored "high" papers showed twice as many examples of four types of syntactic constructions and five types of cohesive ties than those rated low.

791. Orilia, Francesco. "Natural Language Semantics and Guise Theory." *DAI* 47 (February 1987): 3069A.

Proposes that logical language be based on Castaneda's guise theory, according to which singular terms always denote bundles of properties.

792. Orr, Eleanor Wilson. *Twice as Less: Black English and the Performance of Black Students in Mathematics and Science*. New York: Norton, 1987. 240 pages

A linguistic explanation of low test scores, high drop out rates, and unemployability among black students. Investigates the effects of nonstandard English on learning and offers solutions to problems. Based on experience and experiments.

793. O'Seaghdha, Padraig Geroid. "The Dependence of Lexical Relatedness Effects on Syntactic Connectedness." *DAI* 47 (April 1987): 4329B.

Finds that relatedness effects exist only within syntactic sequences. Related words facilitate while unrelated words inhibit.

794. Paganini, Marcello. *Pragmatics of Literature*. Translated by Nancy Jones-Henry. Advances in Semiotics. Bloomington, Ind.: Indiana University Press, 1987. 128 pages

A translation of the work of one of the founding fathers of literary structuralism and semiotics.

795. Penfield, Joyce, ed. *Women and Language in Transition*. Ithaca, N.Y.: State University of New York Press, 1987. 224 pages

A collection of 10 essays grouped into three sections. Focuses on the role women had in altering the extent of linguistic sexism during the 1970s, on the alteration of that portion of language that serves to name women and their experiences, and on the particular problems confronted by minority women.

796. Quain, Timothy James. "Evolution of the Theory of Case Grammar: Concepts and Applications." *DAI* 47 (January 1987): 2567A.

Documents the development of the theory of case grammar and explores its possible applications for the writing classroom.

797. Riley, Kathryn Louise. "Applications of Syntax and Pragmatics to Research in Writing." *DAI* 48 (December 1987): 1450A.

Writing specialists should reevaluate the role of syntax and look at other areas of linguistics (pragmatics, sociolinguistics, and functional linguistics) when doing writing research.

798. Riordan, James Timothy, Jr. "A Nonverbal Cue to Evoke Background Knowledge during an L2 Writing Task." *DAI* 47 (June 1987): 4311A.

The experimenters' cultural bias can interfere with L2 students' responses to paratactic visual cues, but the effect can be minimized.

799. Ross, Gary. "Coherence Theory: An Interdisciplinary Study." *DAI* 47 (June 1987): 4378A.

Sees composition textbooks as uninstructive about coherence. Turns to literature, philosophy, psychology, and linguistics to discuss and judge cohesion.

800. Ryckman, Thomas Alan. "Grammar and Information: An Investigation in Linguistic Metatheory." *DAI* 47 (April 1987): 3774A.

Examines the basis of linguistic theory, focusing on the "status" and "justification" of grammars and theories of language structure.

801. Sandefur, John R. *Papers on Kriol: The Writing System and a Resource Guide.* Working Papers of the Summer Institute of Linguistics, vol. 10. Darwin, Australia: Summer Institute of Linguistics, 1984. ERIC ED 282 435. 435 pages

Prints three papers on the orthography of Australian aboriginal Kriol.

802. Savage-Rumbaugh, Sue. "Communication, Symbolic Communication, and Language: Reply to Seidenberg and Petitto [*JEPG* 116 (September 1987)]." *JEPG* 116 (September 1987): 288–292.

Describes Kanzi's training and behavior to support the interpretation that this ape uses language representationally and similarly to children.

803. Schenken, Mary Kathryn. "A Pragmatics Approach to Memory and Judgments of Indirect Request and Conversational Implicatures." *DAI* 48 (August 1987): 251A.

Suggests that indirect requests and implicatures are remembered poorly.

804. Seidenberg, Mark S., and Laura A. Petitto. "Communication, Symbolic Communication, and Language: Comment on Savage-Rumbaugh, McDonald, Sevcik, Hopkins, and Rupert [*JEPG* 115 (September 1986)]." *JEPG* 116 (September 1987): 279–287.

Offers an alternative analysis of the communication of Kanzi, a language-trained ape, drawing implications for language acquisition research.

805. Serembus, John Herman. "Absolute Comparative Probabilistic Semantics." *DAI* 48 (October 1987): 941A.

Suggests that relations between statements in formal languages can constitute a special semantics that has wide applicability.

806. Sharkey, Noel E., and Amanda J. Sharkey. "What Is the Point of Integration? The Loci of Knowledge-Based Facilitation in Sentence Processing." *JML* 26 (June 1987): 255–276.

Experiments indicate that the integration of entire sentences with prior text is facilitated by active knowledge structures.

807. Shaumyan, Sebastian. *A Semiotic Theory of Language*. Advances in Semiotics. Bloomington, Ind.: Indiana University Press, 1987. 352 pages

Separates language from psychology, developing a theory of applicative grammar used to distinguish two levels of grammar and to outline a comprehensive semiotic theory of language.

808. Sheir, Aleya A., and Mary M. Dupuis. "Developing Procedures for Assessing the Perception and Production of English Sentence Patterns by Prospective Teachers of English." *JEdR* 81 (November–December 1987): 103–108.

In Egypt, prospective teachers of English scored better on a test of sentence-pattern perception and identification than on a test of oral production.

809. Sherzer, Joel. "A Discourse-Centered Approach to Language and Culture." *AmA* 89 (June 1987): 295–309.

Argues that discourse is the concrete expression of language-culture relationships, illustrating primarily with Kuna examples. Recommends discourse analysis of myths, stories, and conversations.

810. Shopen, Timothy, ed. *Languages and Their Speakers*. Philadelphia: University of Pennsylvania Press, 1987. 310 pages

Eight essays explore how native speakers know their own languages: what is necessary to speak a particular language well, what cultural constraints affect communication, how social structure influences language, and how language influences society. A new paperback edition of a work first published in 1979.

811. Shopen, Timothy, ed. *Languages and Their Status*. Philadelphia: University of Pennsylvania Press, 1987. 340 pages

Nine essays examine the role of languages in the structure and development of communities. A new paperback edition of a work first published in 1979.

812. Shuldberg, Howard Kelly. "Syntactic and Semantic Issues in Second Language Learning." *DAI* 48 (November 1987): 1193A.

A study that "examines second language acquisition in adults in terms of formal syntactic and semantic systems."

813. Slowiaczek, Louisa M. "On the Role of Lexical Stress in Auditory Word Recognition." *DAI* 48 (November 1987): 1537B.

Finds through experiments that lexical stress, interacting with other language variables, plays an important role in auditory word recognition.

814. Spears, Monroe K. "Kipper of de Vineyards." *NYRB* 34 (7 May 1987): 38–41.

A review of *The Language of the American South* by Cleanth Brooks. Discusses Brooks's views on Black English and its function in the writing of fiction.

815. Stewart, Reed. "Mande-Speaking Peoples of West Africa: A Study of Cultural Change along Language and Environmental Continua." *DAI* 47 (February 1987): 3156A.

Discovers a unity of culture that crosses language limits within wide language families, pointing to a culture West African in extent.

816. Tarlinskaja, M. G., and L. K. Coachman. "Text-Theme-Text: Semantic Correlation between Thematically Linked Poems." *Lang&S* 19 (Fall 1986): 338–367.

Applies an algorithmic method of objective semantic analysis to seven Shakespearean sonnets on a single theme, quantifying the degree of thematic connection among poems.

817. Tawil, Nathan. "Reference and Intentionality." *DAI* 47 (May 1987): 4104A.

Considers Grice's theory of semantics, arguing that one can explain the role of word reference. Concludes that Grice's theory is defensible.

818. Taylor, M. Ean. "Functions of In-House Language: Observations on Data Collected from Some British Financial Institutions." *LSoc* 16 (March 1987): 1–6.

Applies the Whorfian hypothesis to explain how the language of banking staffs functions as social control, obscuring the reality of the money they work with.

819. Themerson, Stefan. "What's Wrong with Thinking in Terms of Classes?" *ETC* 44 (Spring 1987): 49–56.

Argues for caution in classifying because "laws of thought are difficult to apply to empirical material." Categories can mask essential qualities.

820. Troutman-Robinson, Denise Eloise. "Oral and Written Discourse: A Study of Feature Transfer." *DAI* 48 (September 1987): 641A.

Finds that, since discourse features such as direct address and basic connectives transfer from speech to writing, Black English has an impact on students' performance.

821. Turenius, Kimmo K. "On the Relationship between Text and Linguistic Structure." *DAI* 47 (February 1987): 3023A.

Indicates that a proposition's prominence "signals but does not constitute its communicative relevance" in multi-propositional sentences and the texts that include them.

822. "Verb Use Is Found to Reflect Views of Self and Others." *CHE* 33 (21 January 1987): 5.

A study of students in kindergarten through twelfth grade reveals they "use more action verbs in describing themselves" and state-of-being verbs conveying a trait to describe others.

823. Weber, Rose-Marie. "Variations in Spelling and the Special Case of Colloquial Contractions." *VLang* 20 (Autumn 1986): 413–425.

Examines the use of colloquial contractions in writing. Concludes that they offer opportunities for making speech in writing informal but do not threaten the fundamental stability and consistency of our writing system.

824. Wetterlind, Peter James. "A Speech Error Correction Algorithm for Natural Language Input Processing." *DAI* 47 (January 1987): 3004B.

Using speaker-independent phonemes, constructs a system for identifying natural language sentences.

825. Wulfeck, Beverly Briggs. "Sensitivity to Grammaticality in Agrammatical Aphasia: Processing of Word Order and Agreement Violations." *DAI* 48 (December 1987): 1802B.

Explores agrammatic aphasic subjects' sensitivity to grammatical violations. While aphasics retain some linguistic knowledge, their processing is disrupted.

826. Young, Linda Wai Ling. "Unravelling Chinese Inscrutability." *DAI* 47 (January 1987): 2640A.

Analyzes taped interchanges to document the interactive strategies that create distortions and misunderstandings between Chinese and American speakers.

827. Yuker, Harold E. "Labels Can Hurt People with Disabilities." *ETC* 44 (Spring 1987): 16–22.

Discusses solutions to disability labeling, citing the limits of applicability, the types of labels, the individuality of the disabled, and the effects of time, situation, and perceiver.

See also 47, 52, 69, 112, 120, 199, 458, 503, 556, 577, 585, 602, 613, 617, 653, 666, 674, 702, 837, 862, 870, 880, 951, 953, 954, 1184, 1194, 1258

2.9 PSYCHOLOGY

828. Baer, Sylvia. "Teaching for Creativity, Teaching for Conformity." *TETYC* 14 (December 1987): 195–204.

Reviews Amabile's findings that creativity is influenced by three sets of factors: domain skills, creative skills, and motivation. Suggests applications for English classes.

829. Bahrick, Harry P., and Elizabeth Phelps. "Retention of Spanish Vocabulary over Eight Years." *JEPL* 13 (April 1987): 344–349.

Finds that vocabulary retention is enhanced for words presented and practiced several times. Suggests that repetition is most effective over a 30-day period.

830. Baltes, Paul B. "Theoretical Review: Life-Span Development." *DP* 23 (September 1987): 611–626.

Applies perspectives associated with life-span developmental psychology to intellectual development.

831. Bartlett, James C., Morton Ann Gernsbacher, and Robert E. Till. "Remembering Left-Right Orientation of Pictures." *JEPL* 13 (January 1987): 27–35.

A study of visual memory with implications for understanding learning disorders.

832. Beatty, Michael J. "Communication Apprehension as a Determinant of Avoidance, Withdrawal, and Performance Anxiety." *ComQ* 35 (Spring 1987): 202–217.

Provides evidence suggesting that communication apprehensives avoid communication if possible and suffer considerable anxiety when forced to communicate.

833. Benoit, William L. "Argumentation and Credibility Appeals in Persuasion." *SSCJ* 52 (Winter 1987): 181–197.

Tests three means of persuasion using the cognitive response model.

834. Bereiter, Carl, and Marlene Scardamalia. *The Psychology of Written Composition.* Hillside, N.J.: Erlbaum, 1987. 413 pages

Focusing on the evolution of a writer's mental processes, the authors claim that cognitive processes vary dramatically, depending on the writer's skill. Explores the transition from immature to mature pro-cesses. The key is to subordinate simple strategies for more complex mental processes.

835. Blanchard, Harry, and Asghar Iran-Nejad. "Comprehension Processes and Eye Movement Patterns in the Reading of Surprise-Ending Stories." *DPr* 10 (January–March 1987): 127–138.

Surprising lines in stories induced more and also longer eye fixations, though without any change in mean saccade length.

836. Brooke, Robert. "Lacan, Transference, and Writing Instruction." *CE* 49 (October 1987): 679–691.

Draws connections between the instructional methods of response teaching proponents such as Elbow and Murray and Lacanian psychoanalysis.

837. Brown, Paula M., and Gary S. Dell. "Adapting Production to Comprehension: The Explicit Mention of Instruments." *CPsy* 19 (October 1987): 441–472.

Message adaptability is not necessarily related just to readers' needs. Prominant factors include the speaker's conceptual representation as well as other interpersonal and contextual factors.

838. Chisholm, Carol Lee. "The Nature of the Memory Trace Used to Support Identity Priming of the Lexicon." *DAI* 48 (December 1987): 1830B.

Investigates memory trace and derives a model of word recognition in which right-left parsing and perceptual trace aids later processing.

839. Con Davis, Robert. "Freud's Resistance to Reading and Teaching." *CE* 49 (October 1987): 621–627.

An introductory article to a double issue on psychoanalysis and pedagogy. Describes the centrality of Freud's concept of resistance to teaching.

840. Cooper, James Francis. "Brief Metaphoric Expressions in the Therapy Hour." *DAI* 48 (September 1987): 872B.

Collects and examines metaphors from 367 clients and explores the function metaphor plays in therapy.

841. Fodor, Jerry, and Zenon Pylyshyn. "Connectionism and Cognitive Architecture: A Critical Analysis." *Cognition* 28 (March 1987): 3–71.

Explores the differences between connectionist proposals for cognitive architecture and the sorts of models that have traditionally been assumed in cognitive science.

842. Fogarty, Gerard. "Timesharing in Relation to Broad Ability Domains." *Intell* 11 (July–September 1987): 207–231.

More evidence is needed before any timesharing factor can be a serious candidate for inclusion in a model of intelligence.

843. Gudykunst, William B., Seung-Mock Yang, and Tsukasa Nishida. "Cultural Differences in Self-Consciousness and Self-Monitoring." *ComR* 14 (February 1987): 7–34.

Japanese, Korean, and U.S. cultural differences in self-consciousness and self-monitoring affect both behavior and communication.

844. Herman, James F., Gay M. Cachuela, and Julia A. Heins. "Children's and Adult's Long-Term Memory for Spatial Locations over an Extended Time Period." *DP* 23 (July 1987): 509–513.

Nineteen-year-olds remember spatial-location information better than children. Perhaps they code location information in more organized ways or use environmental stimuli more effectively.

845. Intons-Peterson, Margaret Jean, and Mary M. Smyth. "The Anatomy of Repertory Memory." *JEPL* 13 (July 1987): 490–500.

Analyzes, describes, and compares the repertory or verbatim memory of experts such as actors with novices.

846. Joshua, S., and J. J. Dupen. "Taking into Account Student Conceptions in Instructional Strategy: An Example in Physics." *CI* 4 (1987): 117–135.

Shows that students' "change-resistant conceptions" remain unchanged even by disconfirming empirical evidence. The teacher's use of heuristic analogy reorganized "epistemological obstacles" to learning.

847. Kagan, Dona, and Leah Rose Pietron. "Cognitive Level and Achievement in Computer Literacy." *JPsy* 121 (July 1987): 317–327.

Cognitive level has less long-term effect on students' ability to use software than does previous computer experience.

848. Kallio, Kenneth D., and Brian L. Cutler. "Does Lexical Marking Affect Eyewitness Recall?" *JPsy* 121 (May 1987): 249–258.

The use of marked, unmarked, or neutral adjectives in question phrasing can affect witnesses' ability to recall events accurately.

849. Korhonen, Lloyd, and Cresencio Torres. "The Potential of a Language Representational System in the Instruction of Adults." *AdLBEd* 11 (1987): 32–40.

Describes the neuro-linguistic programming model of sensory-based language patterns. Presents a self-administered test to identify preferred representational patterns. Its use improves rapport.

850. Kounios, John, Allen M. Osman, and David E. Meyer. "Structure and Process in Semantic Memory: New Evidence Based on Speed-Accuracy Decomposition." *JEPG* 116 (March 1987): 3–25.

Describes a process of studying semantic memory that disentangles structure and process. Draws conclusions about how people understand language.

851. Kramer, Arthur F., and Emanuel Donchin. "Brain Potentials as Indices of Orthographic and Phonological Interaction during Word Matching." *JEPL* 13 (January 1987): 76–86.

Visually similar rhymed words are recognized much more quickly than other kinds of pairs. Orthographic and phonological aspects are part of early language.

852. Lambiotte, Judith, Donald Dansereau, Angela O'Donnell, Michael Young, Lisa Skaggs, Richard Hall, and Thomas Rocklin. "Manipulating Cooperative Scripts for Teaching and Learning." *JEdP* 79 (December 1987): 424–430.

Finds that peer teaching encourages metacognitive activities, resulting in better recall on reading tasks.

853. Lester, David. "Psychology and Literature." *Psychology* 24 (1987): 25–27.

Summarizes points of convergence in literary and psychological scholarship. Includes suicide literature, psychohistory, psychoanalytic theory, authorial creativity, and the effects of pornography on readers.

854. Lindsey, A. E., and John O. Greene. "Social Tendencies and Social Knowledge: Self Monitoring Differences in the Representation and Recall of Social Knowledge." *ComM* 54 (December 1987): 381–395.

Examines the role of individual differences in formulating interaction goals, outcome expectations, and strategies for action.

855. Mannes, Susan M., and Walter Kintsch. "Knowledge Organization and Text Organization." *CI* 4 (1987): 91–114.

Finds that study aids facilitated textual and factual recall, but not problem solving. Paradoxical "aids" that make learning difficult can hamper recall, but they facilitate problem solving.

856. Marks, William. "Retrieval Constraints on Associative Elaborations." *JEPL* 13 (April 1987): 301–309.

Investigates the relationship of sentence context to word recall. Associative elaborations assist recall.

857. Martin, Sarah H. "A Description of the Meaning-Making Strategies Reported by Proficient Readers and Writers." *DAI* 48 (December 1987): 1427A.

A study of seven twelfth graders. Describes the cognitive strategies reported by proficient readers and writers.

858. McCabe, Ann E. "Failure in Class-Inclusion Reasoning in a University Sample." *JPsy* 121 (July 1987): 351–358.

Despite Piaget's hypotheses, class-inclusional reasoning tasks are not reliable indicators of concrete operational thinking nor (perhaps) of hierarchical reasoning ability.

859. McLeod, Susan P. "Some Thoughts about Feelings: The Affective Domain and the Writing Process." *CCC* 38 (December 1987): 426–434.

Proposes Mandler's theory of emotion as a guide for research on writing anxiety, motivation, and students' beliefs about their writing abilities.

860. Medin, Douglas L., William D. Wattenmaker, and Sarah E. Hampson. "Family Resemblance, Conceptual Cohesiveness, and Category Construction." *CPsy* 19 (April 1987): 242–279.

Categories may be constructed not in terms of isolated characteristics/properties but according to a "web of relationships in which these properties participate."

861. Milner, Loreta Sue. "A Psycholinguistic Study of the Adult Life Span: Is There a Relationship between Writing and Stress across the Life Stages?" *DAI* 47 (February 1987): 2928A.

Confirms a relationship between stress and writing. Adult age categories and marker events affect the relationship between linguistic measures and stress.

862. Morgan, James L., Richard P. Meier, and Elissa L. Newport. "Structural Packaging in the Input to Language Learning: Contributions of Prosodic and Morphological Marking of Phrases to the Acquisition of Language." *CPsy* 19 (October 1987): 498–550.

Redundant cues based on prosody, function words, and concord morphology enabled students to acquire syntactic rules of a miniature language, maybe also of natural languages.

863. Morley, Donald Dean, and Kim B. Walker. "The Role of Importance, Novelty, and Plausibility in Producing Belief Change." *ComM* 54 (December 1987): 436–442.

Concludes that significant change in belief occurs only when message information is high on all three variables.

864. Morrow, Daniel G., Steven L. Greenspan, and Gordon H. Bower. "Accessibility and Situation Models in Narrative Comprehension." *JML* 26 (April 1987): 165–187.

Suggests that information accessibility depends more on described situations than on the surface organization of the narrative.

865. Nelson, Douglas L., Maria Teresa Bajo, and Jose Canas. "Prior Knowledge and Memory: The Episodic Encoding of Implicitly Activated Associates and Rhymes." *JEPL* 13 (January 1987): 54–63.

Finds that familiar concepts trigger related concepts but that words having larger numbers of related concepts are generally more difficult to recall. Rhyme influences long-term memory.

866. O'Brien, Edward J. "Antecedent Search Processes and the Structure of Text." *JEPL* 13 (April 1987): 278–290.

Studies the process whereby working memory acquires antecedents. Concludes that backward parallel search and an integrated network, not co-reference, explain behavior.

867. Petty, Richard E., John T. Cacioppo, Jeff A. Kasmer, and Curt P. Haugtvedt. "A Reply to Stiff and Boster [*ComM* 54 (September 1987)]." *ComM* 54 (September 1987): 257–263.

Focuses on continuing misperceptions of conceptual and methodological issues related to the elaboration likelihood model.

868. Petty, Richard E., Jeff A. Kasmer, Curt P. Haugtvedt, and John T. Cacioppo. "Source and Message Factors in Persuasion: A Reply to Stiff's Critique of the Elaboration Likelihood Model [*ComM* 53 (March 1986)]." *ComM* 54 (September 1987): 233–249.

"Corrects" misperceptions and misrepresentations of the model. Critiques the meta-analyses used to support Stiff's conclusions.

869. Piche, Gene L., and Duane Roen. "Social Cognition and Writing: Interpersonal Cognitive Complexity and Abstractness and the Quality of Students' Persuasive Writing." *WC* 4 (January 1987): 68–89.

Results indicated a significant relationship between interpersonal cognitive complexity and abstractness on the one hand and quality of writing, persuasiveness, appropriateness of tone, and level of persuasive strategy employed on the other hand.

870. Pinker, Steven, and Alan Prince. "On Language and Connectionism: Analysis of a Parallel Distributed Processing Model of Language Acquisition." *Cognition* 28 (March 1987): 73–193.

Finds that the shortcomings of parallel distribution processing can be attributed to connectionist architecture. Concludes that claims about the dispensability of rules in psycholinguistic explanations must be rejected.

871. Ratner, Hilary Horn, David A. Schell, Anne Crimmins, David Mittleman, and Laurie Baldinelli. "Changes in Adults' Prose Recall: Aging or Cognitive Demands?" *DP* 23 (July 1987): 521–525.

College students outperformed both out-of-college peers and older adults in text recall and study strategies, demonstrating the importance of cultural factors for memory.

872. Reder, Lynne M. "Strategy Selection in Question Answering." *CPsy* 19 (January 1987): 90–138.

Provides a "framework for understanding the role of strategy selection in question answering and has suggested what variables affect the selection process."

873. Richheit, Gert, Hans Strohner, Jochen Museler, and Eieter Nattkemper. "Recalling Oral and Written Discourse." *JEdP* 79 (December 1987): 438–444.

Differences in processing oral and written discourse are caused not by differences in processing control or by structure but by the subjects' communication experience.

874. Schacter, Daniel L. "Implicit Memory: History and Current Status." *JEPL* 13 (July 1987): 501–518.

A historical and contemporary survey of implicit memory research. Discusses theoretical explanations and future research directions.

875. Schmidt, Jan Zlotnick. "Gaining Perspective on the Self: Erik Erikson's Stages of Developmental Growth." *EngR* 38 (1987): 21–26.

Reviews Erikson's stages of development.

876. Shapiro, Michael Allan. "The Influence of Communication-Source Coded Memory Traces on World View." *DAI* 48 (October 1987): 772A.

An experimental study of memory that examines how mass media information is accumulated. Presents a model detailing how remembered events are stored and used.

877. Shimamura, Arthur P., and Larry R. Squire. "A Neuropsychological Study of Fact Memory and Source Amnesia." *JEPL* 13 (July 1987): 464–473.

Studies memory-for-content separately from memory-for-context. Procedural-declarative and episodic-semantic memory both describe the organization of the brain.

878. Slowiaczek, Louisa M., Howard C. Nusbaum, and David B. Pisoni. "Phonological Priming in Auditory Word Recognition." *JEPL* 13 (January 1987): 64–75.

Shows that both the beginnings and endings of words offer significant information in the recognition process. Contradicts existing cohort theory.

879. Stiff, James B., and Franklin J. Boster. "Cognitive Processing: Additional Thoughts and a Reply to Petty, Kasmer, Haugtvedt, and Cacioppo [*ComM* 54 (September 1987)]." *ComM* 54 (September 1987): 250–256.

Addresses the conceptual limitations of the elaboration likelihood model.

880. VanWijk, Carel, and Gerard Kempen. "A Dual System for Producing Self-Repairs in Spontaneous Speech: Evidence from Experimentally Elicited Corrections." *CPsy* 19 (October 1987): 403–440.

Validates the existence of a syntax-based correction mechanism while positing as well a "second mechanism hinging on a prosodic unit called phonological phrase."

881. Walker, Carol H. "Relative Importance of Domain Knowledge and Overall Aptitude on Acquisition of Domain-Related Information." *CI* 4 (1987): 25–42.

Suggests that domain knowledge improves performance regardless of aptitude, but low aptitude learners seemed less aware than high aptitude learners that their cognitive abilities were transferable.

882. Walker, Helen L. *Decentering: Its Place in the Writing Process.* Urbana, Ill.: ERIC/ RCS, 1986. ERIC ED 283 150. 55 pages

Studies essays written by 60 freshmen, finding a relationship between writing quality and Piaget's concept of decentering.

883. Wattenmaker, William D., and Edward J. Shoben. "Context and the Recallability of Concrete and Abstract Sentences." *JEPL* 13 (January 1987): 140–150.

Discusses the effects of context on remembering concrete versus abstract sentences.

884. Winer, Gerald, Kaye Rasnake, and David Smith. "Language Versus Logic: Responses

to Misleading Classificatory Questions."
JPsyR 16 (July 1987): 311–328.

> Examines forced-choice questions. Results
> are consistent with pragmatic theories of
> language that stress the role of context and
> intentionality as determinants of meaning.

885. Wong, Leslie Eric. "Syntactical Measures
of Cognitive Complexity with Written Samples Varying in Cultural Theme." *DAI* 48 (August 1987): 351A.

> Finds mixed results for white and nonwhite
> students writing about a neutral vignette
> and a racial vignette.

See also 133, 160, 177, 195, 208, 729, 731,
825, 887, 890, 903, 1285

2.10   EDUCATION

886. Alicea-Rodriguez, Dennis. "John Dewey
on Theory and Practice: Theory of Knowledge
and Theory of Teaching and Learning." *DAI*
48 (October 1987): 865A.

> Analyzes Dewey's theory of knowledge
> and its relationship to his theory of edu-
> cation.

887. Domjan, Michael. "Animal Learning
Comes of Age." *AmP* 42 (June 1987): 556–
564.

> Describes the current status of animal
> learning and its historical context. Con-
> cludes that this field continues to make im-
> portant contributions to understanding hu-
> man behavior.

888. Finlayson, D. S. "School Climate: An
Outmoded Metaphor?" *JCS* 19 (March–April
1987): 163–173.

> A discussion of metaphors that inhibit edu-
> cational creativity.

889. Fortune, Ron. "Learning Theory and English Studies." *BADE* 86 (Spring 1987): 12–
17.

> Examines current learning theory and dis-
> cusses how and why it should apply to
> teaching writing and literature.

890. Gagne, Ellen D., Robert D. Cutcher, and
Joella Anzelc. "The Role of Student Process-
ing of Feedback in Classroom Achievement."
CI 4 (1987): 167–186.

> Protocols suggest that students do not learn
> if they think that they cannot understand
> teacher's explanations of correct answers,
> or if they feel bad about producing errors.

891. Ghory, Ward J., and Robert L. Sinclair.
"The Reality of Marginality: Current State of
Affairs for Marginal Students." Paper pre-
sented at the American Educational Research
Association, Washington, D.C., April 1987.
ERIC ED 282 128. 32 pages

> Discusses the reality of marginal students
> in American education and explores possi-
> ble school responses.

892. Gish, Shirley. "An Oral History of Selected Twentieth-Century Teachers of Oral Interpretation of Literature." *DAI* 48 (September
1987): 513A.

> Creates and analyzes four oral histories of
> professors.

893. Hays, Janice N. "Models of Intellectual
Development and Writing: A Response to
Myra Kogen *et al.* [*JBW* 5 (Spring 1986)]."
JBW 6 (Spring 1987): 11–27.

> Addresses writing teachers' "misconcep-
> tions" of models and explains the relevance
> of models to writing instruction.

894. Heilman, Robert B. "Semicentennial Ret-
rospections: The Past as Perspective." *GR* 41
(Summer 1987): 304–314.

> "Speaks well of what went on academically
> in the olden days of the 1920s."

895. Mehan, Hugh. "Language and Power in
Organizational Process." *DPr* 10 (October-
December 1987): 291–301.

> In analyses of placement decisions by edu-
> cators, conversational structure suggests
> influences on social interaction that are

possible to describe as either *proximal* or *distal*.

896. Michaels, Sarah. "Text and Context: A New Approach to the Study of Classroom Writing." *DPr* 10 (October–December 1987): 321–346.

Combining ethnographic and linguistic analyses, a study of classroom writing and student-teacher conferences can help to clarify what goes on in writing instruction.

897. Miller, Keith D. "The Tropes of Jean Piaget." *FEN* 16 (Fall 1987): 9–11.

Analyzes tropes developed by Piaget to assert that Piaget's cognitive scheme is rhetorical rather than objective.

898. Newman, Dennis S. *English Education of Learning-Disabled Students.* Keene, N.H.: Keene State College, 1987. ERIC ED 280 024. 48 pages

Reviews the literature, examining specific teaching methodologies, study skills, and Daniel Fader's proposed English program.

899. Peters, William H., and CEE Commission on Research in Teacher Effectiveness, eds. *Effective English Teaching: Concept, Research, and Practice.* Urbana, Ill.: NCTE, 1987. 120 pages

Five articles present research on teacher effectiveness using an "organic field model of teaching English," which holds that substance, skills, and process all overlap in effective teaching. This model also stresses complex contexts in which teaching takes place. Offers suggestions for teacher development and research.

900. Pressley, Michael, Mark A. McDaniel, James E. Turnure, Eileen Wood, and Maheen Ahmad. "Generation and Precision of Elaboration: Effects on Intentional and Incidental Learning." *JEPL* 13 (April 1987): 291–300.

Demonstrates that adults learn more when they are involved with the learning task than they do when they read the material to be learned.

901. Puckett, John Lawrence. "Foxfire Reconsidered: A Critical Ethnohistory of a 20-Year Experiment in Progressive Education." *DAI* 47 (April 1987): 3652A.

Field research details both how Foxfire has fallen short of its ideals as well as how, when compared to conventional schooling, it has succeeded. Future implications discussed.

902. Reynolds, William R. "Reading Curriculum Theory: The Development of a New Hermeneutic." *DAI* 47 (May 1987): 3966A.

Suggests a method for analyzing texts about contemporary curriculum theory based on the interpretation theory of Paul Ricoeur.

903. Schuckman, Harold. "Ph.D. Recipients in Psychology and Biology: Do Those with Dissertation Advisors of the Same Sex Publish Scholarly Papers More Frequently?" *AmP* 42 (November 1987): 987–992.

Neither the sex of the advisor nor of the student appears to affect publication activity. Raises questions about the importance of role models in graduate education.

904. Small, Donald D. "Archaic Concepts: Cloakrooms, Wraps, and Compositions." Paper presented at the NCTE Convention, San Antonio, November 1986. ERIC ED 283 214. 8 pages

Suggests that English teachers discard "fussy concepts" and teach skills relevant to the real world.

905. Stewart, Sharon R. "Use of Expository Text Structure by Adolescents with Learning Disabilities." *DAI* 47 (May 1987): 4060A.

Investigates the use of text structure by learning-disabled adolescents as a reading and writing strategy.

906. Wilson, Edward, ed. "The Special Student." *ET* 18 (Spring 1987): 1–43.

Makes available as ERIC ED 283 206, a special issue with 13 essays on the "special student."

See also 839, 858, 881, 947

2.11   JOURNALISM, PUBLISHING, TELEVISION, AND RADIO

907. Balasubramanian, Siva Kumar. "The Processing of Verbal/Nonverbal Content in Television Advertisements—A Theory and Its Empirical Investigation." *DAI* 47 (March 1987): 3489A.

Constructs a model of two processes at work when an individual views advertisements: elaboration and evaluation.

908. Byrne, John Edward. "The News from Harper's Ferry: The Press as Lens and Prism for John Brown's Raid." *DAI* 47 (June 1987): 4425A.

Examines the role of the press in reporting and interpreting Brown's raid and his subsequent trial and execution.

909. Choi, Hyeon Cheol, and Samuel L. Becker. "Media Use, Issue/Image Discriminations, and Voting." *ComR* 14 (June 1987): 267–290.

Suggests that newspapers are more effective than television in helping an audience develop a distinctive picture of candidates and their positions on issues.

910. DeLoughry, Thomas J. "Personal Computers and Laser Printers Are Becoming Popular Tools for Creating Documents on Campuses." *CHE* 34 (16 September 1987): A15-A17.

Desktop publishing—designing page layouts and integrating graphics with text on personal computers—has become popular on campuses because it saves money and fosters creativity.

911. Dorfman, Ron. "The Puzzle of Objectivity: The Objective Posture." *ETC* 44 (Fall 1987): 312–315.

Argues that "objectivity" is a false aim for reporters. By being open about their biases, they may create a greater impression of trustworthiness.

912. Elliot, William R., and William L. Rosenberg. "Media Exposure and Beliefs about Science and Technology." *ComR* 14 (April 1987): 164–188.

Explores how the mass media and other factors—sex, educational level, political conservatism, and technological experience—influence some of our scientific and technological beliefs.

913. Fico, Frederick, Carrie Heeter, Stan Soffin, and Cynthia Stanley. "New Wave Gatekeeping Electronic Indexing Effects on Newspaper Reading." *ComR* 14 (June 1987): 335–351.

Explores how readers of newpapers react to an experimental newspaper format that uses topical indexes to guide readers to news stories instead of editorially determined salience cues.

914. Gandy, Oscar H., Jr., Paula W. Matabane, and John O. Omachonu. "Media Use, Reliance, and Active Participation: Exploring Student Awareness of the South African Conflict." *ComR* 14 (December 1987): 644–664.

Studies how different media affect an audience's perceptions of issues. Supports the view that intellectual interest and motivation are more important than the medium.

915. Gaunt, Phillip. "Development in Soviet Journalism." *JQ* 64 (Summer–Autumn 1987): 526–532.

Studying Soviet journalism from the public relations model is preferred to the ideologies approach that separates U.S. and Soviet journalists.

916. Kidd, Virginia. "Taking Criticism to the Streets in Print: Teaching Students to Write Criticism for Popular Consumption." Paper presented at the SCA Meeting, Chicago, November 1986. ERIC ED 278 077. 21 pages

Reports on a survey to determine if there is published scholarship that may be labelled as rhetorical criticism of the mass media.

917. Kwartowitz, Alan. "Intensionality-Extensionality and the Press: A Comparative Analysis of Selected Articles and Editorials from *The New York Times, New York Post*, and *Daily News'* Reporting of the Events in Ocean Hill-Brownsville in 1968." *DAI* 48 (December 1987): 1346A.

Compares levels of abstraction in two forms of newspaper language, bylines and editorials.

918. Levy, Mark R., and John P. Robinson. "The 'Huh?' Factor: Untangling Television News." *ETC* 44 (Spring 1987): 57–62.

Television newswriting unjustifiably assumes viewer sophistication, uses jargon without definition, and takes a secondary role to graphics and film.

919. Ludlow, Lynn. "They Commute to the World: Changes in International News Reporting." *ETC* 44 (Spring 1987): 30–41.

Historical changes in how international news is reported reveal current dangers. Information now is limited by wire services. Fewer and more poorly trained foreign correspondents duplicate rather than supplement information.

920. McCallus, Joseph Patrick. "The Rhetoric of Ethnic Journalism: The Filipino-American Press and Its Washington, D.C., Audience." *DAI* 48 (November 1987): 1289A.

Examines rhetorical strategies in ethnic newspapers directed to a particular ethnic community. Focuses on the Filipino-American press and the Marcos state visit in 1982.

921. McGucken, Emilia Nadel. "Crime News Reporting in *The New York Times*, 1900–1950: A Content Analysis." *DAI* 48 (September 1987): 752A.

Attempts to explain the historical status of crime news reporting, focusing on the concepts of power and knowledge in a disciplinary society.

922. Morris, Barry Alan. "The Communal Constraints on Parody: The Symbolic Death of Joe Bob Briggs." *QJS* 73 (November 1987): 460–473.

Examines the negative reaction to Dallas columnist Briggs's parody of "We Are the World" to determine the social constraints on humor.

923. Nicolini, Pia. "Puerto Rican Leaders' Views of English Language Media." *JQ* 64 (Summer-Autumn 1987): 597–601.

Both Mexican-Americans and Puerto Ricans are dissatisfied with the negative news about Hispanics presented in American newspapers. The number of reporters must be increased.

924. Reynolds, Christina Leah. " 'Donahue': A Rhetorical Analysis of Contemporary Television Culture." *DAI* 47 (June 1987): 4234A.

"Donahue" uses two forms of the rhetorical ritual of identification: an exemplar and significant symbols of cultural values.

925. Stanger, Gretta Guyton. "The Representation of Family Change in Social Science Journals and Women's Magazines." *DAI* 47 (June 1987): 4521A.

Examines the family-related themes of nonfiction in *Ladies' Home Journal, Redbook, Good Housekeeping, American Sociological Review*, and *Journal of Marriage and the Family*.

926. Stone, Gerald. *Examining Newspapers: What Research Reveals about America's Newspapers*. Newbury Park, Calif.: Sage, 1987. 160 pages

Reviews recent findings about newspapers and the newspaper industry. Covers news gathering, writing, editing, management, readership, and audience effects.

927. Stonecipher, Harry W., and Don Sneed. "Libel and the Opinion Writer: The Fact-

Opinion Distinction." *JQ* 64 (Summer-Autumn 1987): 491–498.

The Ollman case (1984) provides four factors in determining what constitutes opinion: the specific language used, whether or not it can be verified, the general context, and the broader context.

928. Tichenor, Phillip J., Clarice Olien, and George A. Donahue. "Effect of Use of Metro Dailies on Knowledge Gap in Small Towns." *JQ* 64 (Summer-Autumn 1987): 329–336.

Reading metropolitan dailies helped a rural populace overcome a knowledge gap between themselves and urban residents more effectively than did watching television news.

929. Welsh, Patrick. "Our Teens Are Becoming Lookworms instead of Bookworms." *TV Guide* 35 (May 1987): 2–6.

A high school English teacher expresses concern about the amount of television children watch.

930. Wolf, Rita, Tommy Thomason, and Paul La Rocque. "The Right to Know Versus the Right to Privacy: Newspaper Identification of Crime Victims." *JQ* 64 (Summer Autumn 1987): 503–507.

More and more editors are honoring the *1983 President's Victims of Crime Report*, which recommends that names and addresses of victims not be made public.

931. Zillman, Dolf, and Norbert Mundorf. "Image Effects in the Appreciation of Video Rock." *ComR* 14 (June 1987): 316–334.

Finds that incorporating sexual and/or violent images in rock videos enhanced viewers' appreciation of the music.

See also 338, 711, 948, 1608

2.12   PHILOSOPHY

932. Condit, Celeste Michelle. "Crafting Virtue: The Rhetorical Construction of Public Morality." *QJS* 73 (February 1987): 79–97.

Argues against recent calls for "privatizing" morality and makes a case for rhetoric's legitimate role in creating public moral consensus.

933. Flood, Emmet Thomas. "Philosophy and Narrative Form." *DAI* 47 (March 1987): 3448A.

Suggests that, despite the natural hostility between philosophy and narration, philosophy can be deliberately and effectively written in narrative form.

934. Grassi, Ernesto. "The Originary Quality of the Poetic and Rhetorical Word: Heidegger, Ungaretti, and Neruda." *P&R* 20 (1987): 248–260.

Argues that poetry and rhetoric, not reason, have philosophical or originating functions because metaphor unveils the rhetorical here and now of experience in history.

935. Kateb, George. "Thinking about Human Extinction (II): Emerson and Whitman." *Raritan* 6 (Winter 1987): 1–22.

Argues that "democracy is a distinctive culture," and "individuality" an ambiguous term within it.

See also 59, 108, 116, 146, 147, 157, 266, 287, 345, 769

2.13   SCIENCE AND MEDICINE

936. Anderson, Philip M., and Bonnie S. Sunstein. "Teaching the Use of Metaphor in Science Writing." Paper presented at the CCCC Convention, Atlanta, March 1987. ERIC ED 281 204. 25 pages

Studies how the use of metaphors in scientific writing assisted students ages 18 to 48 to better understand scientific subject matter.

937. Cicourel, Aaron. "Cognitive and Organizational Aspects of Medical Diagnostic Reasoning." *DPr* 10 (October–December 1987): 347–367.

Practioners formulate diagnoses within bureaucratic contexts that help define social roles. In cases of uncertainty, institutional practices influence diagnoses.

938. Erickson, Frederick, and William Rittenberg. "Topic Control and Person Control: A Thorny Problem for Foreign Physicians in Interaction with American Patients." *DPr* 10 (October–December 1987): 401–415.

Foreign physicians have difficulty in adjusting to American expectations about patient-physician relations, especially in power-sharing aspects of discourse.

939. Freeman, Sarah. "Organizational Constraints as Communicative Variables in Bureaucratic Medical Settings: A Case of Patient-Initiated Referral Talk in Independent Practice Association-Affiliated Practices." *DPr* 10 (October–December 1987): 385–400.

Contract medicine has given rise to organizational constraints typical of bureaucracies. Some constraints can affect physician-patient interactions such as referrals.

940. Gonzalez, Maria Christina. "Communication with Patients Who Are Dying: The Effects of Medical Education." *DAI* 47 (June 1987): 4231A.

Using the methods of Glaser and Strauss, this study suggests a conflict of interpersonal and medical models in communication.

941. Groce, Stephen Boggs. "Medical Interviews, Treatment Decisions, and the Social Construction of Reality: An Analysis of Doctor-Patient Communication." *DAI* 47 (April 1987): 3876A.

Analyzes the ways in which doctors and male patients interact to produce medical interviews and treatment decisions.

942. Heller, Monica, and Sarah Freeman. "First Encounters: The Role of Communication in the Medical Intake Process." *DPr* 10 (October–December 1987): 369–384.

Conversation routines serve to clarify rights, obligations, and social roles in health care systems. As such, conversation can regulate conflicting goals of patients and institutions.

943. Holmquest, Anne. "Reasoning by Sign: The Relevance of Charles Pierce's Theory of Presumption to Charles Darwin's Logic of Discovery." *DAI* 47 (January 1987): 2370A.

Applying Pierce's theory of presumption to Darwin's argument reveals his logic and discovery, helping us understand progress in scientific knowledge.

944. Huckin, Thomas. "Surprise Value in Scientific Discourse." Paper presented at the CCCC Convention, Atlanta, March 1987. ERIC ED 284 291. 17 pages

Analyzes scientific articles, noting that scientific discourse is moving to stress "surprise value," as in journalism.

945. Jenkins, Franklin Wilson. "A Taxonomy of Curricular Discourse: A Classification of Science Textbook Discourse." *DAI* 48 (November 1987): 1303A.

Analyzes six chapters of a high school chemistry textbook, sentence by sentence, to test an epistemological taxonomy for textbook discourse.

946. Linzer, Mark, Elizabeth R. DeLong, and Kenneth H. Hupart. "A Comparison of Two Formats for Teaching Critical Reading Skills in a Medical Journal Club." *JMEd* 62 (August 1987): 690–692.

Journal clubs led by faculty or senior residents can be successful, but participants' attitudes, attendance, and quantity of and approach to reading can vary.

947. Philips, Susan U. "The Social Organization of Knowledge and Its Consequences of Discourse in Bureaucratic Settings." *DPr* 10 (October–December 1987): 429–433.

Responds to the papers of Mehan, Collins, Michaels, Cicourel, Heller and Freeman, Erickson and Rittenberg, and Keller-Cohen in *Discourse Processes* 10 (October–December 1987).

948. Rabinowitz, Howard K. "Comparing the Number of Journals Available for Publication of Papers by Faculty Members in the Clinical Specialties." *JMEd* 62 (January 1987): 58–60.

The ratio of faculty to journals varies by specialty, making uncertain the use of publication quality and quantity as absolute promotion criteria.

949. Spicer, Karen-Leigh. "An Investigation of Doctor Talk in Health Crisis Situation: A Rhetorical Analysis." *DAI* 47 (January 1987): 2373A.

Finds that health crisis situations have a strong rhetorical exigence, highly involved rhetorical audiences, and a pervasive rhetorical atmosphere with the potential to influence healing.

950. Zeller, Nancy C. "A Rhetoric for Naturalistic Inquiry." *DAI* 48 (November 1987): 1333A.

Argues that fictive writing forms and strategies are more appropriate for case reporting than are conventional research reporting forms.

See also 31, 36, 56, 157, 203, 390, 428, 903, 912, 963, 989, 1584, 1608, 1687, 1772

2.14 CROSS-DISCIPLINARY STUDIES

951. Angsotinge, Geruase Tuobataabaaro. "Wisdom of the Ancestors: An Analysis of the Oral Narratives of the Dagaaba of Northern Ghana." *DAI* 47 (April 1987): 3844A.

Attempts to delineate the purpose and function of storytelling among the Dagaaba.

952. Barnes, Bernadine Ann. "The Invention of Michelangelo's *Last Judgment*." *DAI* 48 (August 1987): 235A.

Examines the process of invention and "attempts to reconstruct sixteenth-century notions of style and meaning."

953. Bennett, Marjorie Bangs. "Individual and Community Style in Personal Narratives of Storyteller Del Ringer of North Bend, Washington." *DAI* 47 (February 1987): 3152A.

Analyzes the lexical, grammatical, literary, and folkloric characteristics in narratives of 11 storytellers from Washington and Idaho.

954. Burusphat, Somsonge. "The Structure of Thai Narrative Discourse." *DAI* 47 (March 1987): 3410A.

Discusses the interrelated nature of "macrostructure, texture, constituent structure, and cultural information" in Thai narratives.

955. Coughlin, Ellen K. "Humanities and Social Sciences: The Sound of Barriers Falling." *CHE* 34 (2 September 1987): A6–7, 10,12.

Scholars in disciplines from literature to psychology are integrating their fields with other studies, especially history.

956. Fretz, Rachel Irene. "Storytelling among the Chokwe of Zaire: Narrating Skill and Listener Response." *DAI* 48 (December 1987): 1518A.

Addresses the expectations—expressive, situational, social interactional, session, and interpretive—by which listeners evaluate and respond to traditional narrating in Zaire.

957. Gallob, Karen. "An Anthropological Study of Incongruity, Play, and Identity in Mauritian Verbal Humor." *DAI* 48 (November 1987): 1245A.

Mauritian humorous texts, transcribed and translated, were "universally incongruous" and made use of narrative distancing, quotational modifications, selective characterizations, and generalized settings.

958. Gaughan, Joseph Patrick. "Narrative Tradition and Social Structure: Peasant Folktales in the Tregor, Brittany." *DAI* 47 (April 1987): 3799A.

Reports on research undertaken on the peasant social structure in Lower Brittany with the aim of restoring the area's narrative tradition to its original context.

959. Hall, Dennis R. "Mathematical Approaches to the Composing Process." Paper presented at the CCCC Convention, Atlanta, March 1987. ERIC ED 281 193. 26 pages

Discusses relationships between rhetoric and mathematics, particularly syntax and semantics, representation and problem solving.

960. Hansen, Arthur A., ed. *Fieldwork in Oral History*. Lexington, Ky.: Oral History Association, 1987. 219 pages

Twelve articles on field recording, interviewing, language use, transcript handling, and studies using oral history as a research technique. Approach is applicable to qualitative research in composition. Originally appeared in *Oral History* 15 (Spring 1987).

961. Harvey, Clodagh Margaret. "A Contemporary Perspective on Irish Traditional Storytelling in the English Language." *DAI* 48 (December 1987): 1519A.

Interviews with Irish folklorists and storytellers establish the role of folklorists as the primary audience for traditional narratives in English.

962. Maguire, Mary, and Anthony Pare, eds. *Patterns of Development*. N.p.: Canadian Council of Teachers of English (distributed by NCTE), 1985. 290 pages

An international group of writers examines language evaluation, teaching in interpretive and rhetorical communities, old ideas of theory and practice seen from current perspectives, and other language-related studies. Advocates more cooperation between researchers and classroom teachers. Bibliography.

963. Millard, David E., and Stephen J. Nagle. "Minds, Brains, and the Language Arts: A Cautionary Note." Paper presented at the CCCC Convention, New Orleans, March 1986. ERIC ED 283 221. 14 pages

Cautions that mind-brain research may not be translated directly to writing instruction.

964. Pemberton, Miriam Remage. "The Writing of Oral History: Studs Terkel's *Working* and *Hard Times*." *DAI* 48 (December 1987): 1449A.

Looks at the written representation of speech events in these books and the processes that produced them.

965. Radhayrapetian, Juliet. "Persian Folk Narrative: A Survey of Scholarship." *DAI* 48 (December 1987): 1519A.

Describes Persian folk narrative, emphasizing early data from travellers and philologists, both native and foreign. Includes selections from these studies and a selective bibliography.

966. Robbins, Bruce. "Poaching off the Disciplines." *Raritan* 6 (Spring 1987): 81–96.

Argues that "textualism" as a de-disciplined method of human sciences has not yet achieved a preeminent role as guardian of the humanities against science.

967. Shulimson, Judith Ann. "Eskimo Verbal Art and the Teachings of the Elders." *DAI* 48 (August 1987): 429A.

Verbal art is a symbolic construction of a changing tradition, but its performers do not assume control of social interaction.

968. Stewart, Kathleen Claire. "Narrative Appalachia." *DAI* 48 (August 1987): 429A.

Traces the relational logic of a "narrative culture" through a variety of story genres used in coal camps in Raleigh County, West Virginia.

969. Weiland, Steven. "History toward Rhetoric." *CE* 49 (November 1987): 816–826.

An essay review that analyzes LaCapra's study of the rhetorical practices of history as a discipline. Aligns his work with other major works of similar focus.

See also 33, 210, 568, 639, 799

3
Teacher Education, Administration, and Social Roles

3.1   TEACHER EDUCATION

970. Aber, John. "Toward Reconceptualizing Teacher Training in Composition: An Ethnographic Account and Theoretical Appraisal." *DAI* 47 (January 1987): 2488A.

A critical ethnography of participants' responses to an in-service workshop on the composing process.

971. Beckelman, Dana. "The *Me* and the *Not Me* of Academic Discourse." *FEN* 16 (Winter/Spring 1988): 2–3.

Describes the graduate school experience as limiting, misleading, dishonest. Complains about the lack of space for creativity.

972. Bissex, Glenda L., and Richard H. Bullock, eds. *Seeing for Ourselves: Case Study Research by Teachers of Writing.* Portsmouth, N.H.: Heinemann, 1987. 248 pages

Thirteen practicing classroom English teachers and graduate students demonstrate through these case studies the value of classroom-based research. Includes cases of all ages of students, first grade through adult learners. Authors are not indexed separately in this volume.

973. Boice, Robert, and Kelly A. Kelly. "Writing Viewed by Disenfranchised Groups: A Study of Women and Women's College Faculty." *WC* 4 (July 1987): 299–309.

Surveys women at universities and women's colleges on their work loads, the pressure to publish, their experience with editorial processes, and their beliefs that scholarly work will be rewarded.

974. Bolin, Frances S., and Judith McConnell Falk, eds. *Teacher Renewal: Professional Issues, Personal Choices.* New York: Teacher's College Press, 1987. 256 pages

A collection of essays written by teacher educators. Offers a rationale and strategy for engaging teachers in the policy, pedagogical, and personal issues involved in improving schools. Authors are not indexed separately in this volume.

975. Bradford, Sunny Y. "Career Development and Occupational Burnout: A Study of Selected Community College Educators." *DAI* 47 (May 1987): 3952A.

Proposes a model to explain why burnout might occur in a previously positive career. Recommends changes in educational policies.

976. Brock, Patricia Ann. "The Function and Impact of Teachers' Centres in England and Educational Improvement Centers in New Jersey on Primary Teachers." *DAI* 47 (February 1987): 3003A.

Analyzes 200 questionnaires to show differences in methods and attitudes of British and American teachers.

977. Brosnahan, Irene, Richard Coe, and Ann Johns. "Discourse Analysis of Written Texts in an Overseas Teacher Training Program." *EQ* 20 (Spring 1987): 16–25.

Describes a research project for teacher-students.

978. Bunce, Marna Louise. "A Descriptive Study of an In-Service Program Modeling the Teaching of Writing as a Process." *DAI* 47 (January 1987): 2384A.

Studies the effectiveness of an in-service program based on theories of change and growth.

979. Burden, Denise S. "Teacher Developed Writing Curriculum for Culturally Diverse Classrooms." Paper presented at the NCTE Convention, San Antonio, November 1986. ERIC ED 278 025. 17 pages

Discusses a Boston Writing Project involving graduate instruction for teachers in all subject areas to develop multicultural writing curricula.

980. Burkett, Karolyn Holm, and Dawn Holt Anderson, eds. *Taking Charge of Your Own Professional Life*. Chillicothe, Ohio: Southeastern Ohio Council of Teachers of English (distributed by NCTE), 1986. 86 pages

Eight essays urge elementary and secondary teachers to better their professional stance, including gaining the respect of administrators, attending conferences, participating in policy decisions, and using research in the classroom. Originally appeared as *Focus* (Fall 1986).

981. Burkhardt, Sally E. "Laughing While Learning." *ArEB* 29 (Spring 1987): 25–28.

Describes a Capitol Writing Project session held annually at Virginia Commonwealth University.

982. Calkins, Lucy McCormick, Shelley Harwayne, JoAnn Curtis, and Martha Horn. *A Writing Project*. New York: New York Board of Education, 1986. ERIC ED 284 267. 48 pages

Describes a program to train secondary teachers of writing.

983. Chapman, David W., and Gary Tate. "A Survey of Doctoral Programs in Rhetoric and Composition." *RR* 5 (Spring 1987): 124–186.

Briefly describes 53 programs, including faculty, requirements, core courses, recent dissertations, and numbers of students.

984. Church, Susan, and Judith Newman. "Making Connections: Using the Whole." *LArts* 64 (April 1987): 366–367.

Although teachers frequently learn about the writing process, they seem unable to see how reading and writing interconnect.

985. Clausen, Sue A. "My Treadmill." *ET* 18 (Summer 1987): 31–32.

Recounts a typical day in the life of a teacher.

986. Combies, Patricia Lee. "The Struggle to Establish a Profession: A Historical Survey of the Status of Composition Teachers, 1900–1950." *DAI* 48 (September 1987): 584A.

This study addresses the social forces facing the composition teacher in terms of promotion and tenure. Describes programs of reform.

987. Combs, Martha, ed. *National Reading and Language Arts Educators' Conference*

Yearbook. Urbana, Ill.: ERIC/RCS, 1986. ERIC ED 284 192. 46 pages

Publishes 10 papers, three concerned with writing, from the National Reading and Language Arts Educators' Conference, Kansas City, September 1986.

988. Courtland, Mary Clare, Robert Welsh, and Susan Kennedy. "A Case Study of a Teacher's Changing Perceptions of the Writing Process." *EQ* 20 (Winter 1987): 305.

Follows the professional growth of one teacher moving from a product to a process approach. Reports on the first year of a longitudinal collaborative research study.

989. Craig, G. L., and G. Page. "Teaching in Medicine: An Elective Course for Third-Year Students." *MEd* 21 (September 1987): 386–390.

Describes the course and its emphasis on written plans to reinforce teaching behaviors.

990. De Masi, Michael Francis. "Speech Communication Teachers' Self-Reports of Their Planning for Talk in the Classroom Classified and Measured against Rhetorical Standards for Planning for Persuasive Talk." *DAI* 47 (January 1987): 2370A.

A study of four speech teachers concludes that their classroom planning was not consistent with standards of current and traditional rhetorical theory.

991. Elliot, Norbert, Lee Odell, and Sally Hampton. *Beginning a Teacher-Researcher Program: The First Steps*. Urbana, Ill.: ERIC/RCS, 1986. ERIC ED 280 075. 13 pages

Reports on the effectiveness of a teacher-researcher program in the Fort Worth Independent School District to improve and access students' writing abilities.

992. Ellis, W. Geiger. "What Are You Teaching? Literature." *EJ* 76 (March 1987): 108–112.

Describes a method for recording and describing teaching behaviors in classes studying literature.

993. Farkas, David. *How to Teach Technical Editing*. Washington, D.C.: Society for Technical Communication, 1987. 52 pages

Addressed to those who teach editing or who are planning to teach editing in academic settings. Also useful for those who train editors in the workplace, experienced editors, and other nonacademic professionals.

994. Florio-Ruane, Susan. "Taking a Closer Look at Writing Conferences." Paper presented at the American Educational Research Association, San Francisco, April 1986. ERIC ED 275 003. 17 pages

Teachers who dominate talk in both classrooms and conferences need to change assumptions about instruction in order to become more effective.

995. Fox, Elizabeth. "Survival Guide to the Schools." *TWM* 19 (November–December 1987): 1–7.

Veteran teachers and writers address the problems of novice writing teachers. Solutions include preparation, organization, rapport, class discipline, spontaneity, classroom discussion, and writing.

996. Fulwiler, Toby. *Teaching with Writing: An Interdisciplinary Workshop Approach*. Upper Montclair, N.J.: Boynton/Cook, 1987. 176 pages

A detailed accounting of how an interdisciplinary writing workshop works. Extensively samples writing by teachers and students to show what can be done to foster writing in the disciplines.

997. Goswami, Dixie, and Peter R. Stillman, eds. *Reclaiming the Classroom: Teacher Research as Agency for Change*. Upper Montclair, N.J.: Boynton/Cook, 1987. 256 pages

Nineteen essays by teacher-researchers explain how teachers can become effective researchers and why they should.

998. Green, Lois Ipson. "Three Case Studies of Teachers Responding to College Students in

Individual Writing Conferences." *DAI* 48 (September 1987): 632A.

Analyzes teacher-student conferences and draws four implications for strengthening teachers' abilities to make the conferences productive.

999. Harmston, Richard Kent. "A Writing-Based, Phenomenological Approach to English Teacher Preparation." *DAI* 48 (December 1987): 1435A.

Emphasizes the need for teachers to become "learners with and for their students." We accomplish this by engaging teachers in their own theory-based practice of language teaching.

1000. Hartfield, Faye. "A Potpourri of Teaching Methods." *ET* 18 (Summer 1987): 28–30.

Looks at Hillocks's modes of writing instruction—presentational, natural process, environmental, and individualized—and then examines the instructional methods of teachers.

1001. Healy, Mary K. "The Writing Project Model: A Retrospective View." *VEB* 37 (Special 1987 Issue): 32–35.

Presents the central tenets of the Writing Project model and discusses concerns about its present and future impact on the professional growth of practicing teachers.

1002. Hennessy, Michael. "Theory before Practice in the Training of Writing Teachers." Paper presented at the CCCC Convention, New Orleans, March 1986. ERIC ED 276 031. 19 pages

Proposes a course focused on rhetorical theory for inexperienced graduate teaching assistants.

1003. Herndon, James. *Teaching and Its Discontents*. Urbana, Ill.: NCTE, 1986.

Argues that, in the imperfect system of American education, teachers must receive practical training in teaching, rather than merely theoretical instruction. A 30-minute videotape.

1004. Herrmann, Andrea W. "Teaching Teachers to Use Computers for Writing across the Curriculum." Paper presented at the CCCC Convention, Atlanta, March 1987. ERIC ED 280 032. 15 pages

Reports positive effects on 13 instructors of a course in writing with computers.

1005. Infantino, Bob. "A Look at *A Nation Prepared: Teachers for the 21st Century*." *CalE* 23 (September–October 1987): 26–27.

Discusses issues raised by the Carnegie report.

1006. Infantino, Bob. "What Teachers Should Know: NCTE Guidelines for the Preparation of Teachers of English Language Arts." *CalE* 23 (November–December 1987): 20–21.

Summarizes revised guidelines.

1007. Johnson, Martha. "Teachers as Learners, Writers, Researchers." *CalE* 23 (January–February 1987): 18–20.

Concludes that classroom research is valuable.

1008. Kretovics, Joseph R. "Schooling and the Hidden Curriculum: Empowering Teachers with Strategies for the Development of a Transformative Pedagogy." *DAI* 47 (May 1987): 3963A.

Provides a mode of inquiry to explore the political nature of pedagogy. Suggests strategies enabling teachers to act as "transforming intellectuals."

1009. Laff, Ned Scott. "Another Plain Truth about Teaching English." *BADE* 86 (Spring 1987): 48–52.

Argues that English language study is essential to teacher preparation because it alone deals with the communicative effectiveness of prescriptive grammar.

1010. Ludtke, Melissa. "Great Human Power or Magic." *Time* (14 September 1987): 76.

A description of the Bread Loaf School of English.

1011. Magrath, C. Peter, and Robert L. Egbert, eds. *Strengthening Teacher Education.* San Francisco: Jossey-Bass, 1987. 174 pages

A collection of 12 essays by educators and administrators on the issues confronting teacher educators. Defines the leadership role that higher education should take and makes specific recommendations for redesigning the curriculum and attracting good students to it.

1012. Manley, Eleanor. "Train Texas Teachers." *ET* 18 (Winter 1987): 27–29.

Argues that teachers will not and cannot teach writing as a process just because lawmakers mandate that they do so. Teachers must be trained in the writing process.

1013. Marsh, David D., Debra J. Knudsen, and Gene A. Knudsen. "Factors Influencing the Transfer of Bay Area Writing Workshop Experiences to the Classroom." Paper presented at the American Educational Research Association, Washington, D.C., April 1987. ERIC ED 282 219. 27 pages

Finds statistically significant changes in teacher behavior as the result of workshop experiences.

1014. Marsh, David D., Debra J. Knudsen, and Gene A. Knudsen. "The Role of Staff Development in Implementing the Bay Area Writing Program." *JTEd* 38 (November–December 1987): 34–39.

Implementation is linked to the intensity of the staff development, especially when the participants use theory, modeling, practice, feedback, and peer coaching.

1015. Martin, Janet. "A Retrospective on Training Teaching Assistants." *WPA* 11 (Fall 1987): 35–44.

A historical survey of trends and issues in training college teachers of English from the 1920s to the present.

1016. Michaelson, Herbert B. "How to Write and Publish a Dissertation." *JTWC* 17 (1987): 265–274.

Shows how to plan a thesis or dissertation so that it can be published in a professional journal as well as be presented for an advanced degree.

1017. Mickler, Martha Jan. "A Study of Teacher Application and Knowledge of the Components of a Research-Based Model of Spelling." *DAI* 47 (February 1987): 2873A.

Results indicate significant differences between elementary school teachers' research-based knowledge and their classroom practices.

1018. Mohr, Marian M., and Marion S. MacLean. *Working Together: A Guide for Teacher-Researchers.* Urbana, Ill.: NCTE, 1987. 144 pages

Argues for support groups among teacher-researchers to aid in developing methodology, analyzing data, and writing articles. Discusses group organization and procedures, research practices and issues, and the results of actual research. Includes a bibliography.

1019. Morris, Adrienne. "The Best Lesson." *UEJ* (1987): 16–17.

Teachers need to remember that they teach students, not just lessons. Rejecting a student hinders the educational process.

1020. Mostafa Abdel Monem, Sanad Mohammad. "English as a Foreign Language: An Identification of Multi-Disciplinary Dimensions of Nonnative Teacher Preparation in Linguistics, Literature, and Pedagogy." *DAI* 47 (June 1987): 4310A.

Focuses on the competencies American and Egyptian TESOL specialists classify as the fundamental segment of knowledge needed and sought by TEFL instructors.

1021. Mullican, James. "Preparing Teachers of English and the Language Arts: A Review Essay." *IE* 11 (Fall 1987): 29–32.

Presents an overview of *Guidelines for the Preparation of Teachers of English Language* (1986) and notes three deficiencies: it draws few differences among academic levels; it is sketchy; and it "preaches to the converted."

1022. Mulligan, Arlene. "On Teachers and Teaching: An Interview with Jimmy Britton." *CalE* 23 (May–June 1987): 6–7.

Britton traces his own development as a teacher and claims that an effective teacher is "not too teacherly."

1023. Mulligan, Arlene. "Teachers as Researchers: An Interview with Mary K. Healy." *CalE* 23 (January–February 1987): 6–8.

Discusses the role of teacher-researchers.

1024. Munby, Hugh. "Metaphor and Teacher's Knowledge." *RTE* 21 (December 1987): 377–397.

A study based on interviews with two teachers. Examines their metaphors and the way these metaphors reveal the teachers' perceptions of their professions.

1025. Nash, Tom. "By the Way, Is There Any Money in This? Encouraging Young Teachers to Publish." *EEd* 19 (December 1987): 237–243.

Sees value in having prospective teachers write for publication.

1026. Neuleib, Janice, and Irene Brosnahan. "Teaching Grammar to Writers." *JBW* 6 (Spring 1987): 28–35.

Argues that "the preparation of teachers is the crucial issue in teaching effectiveness."

1027. Nilsen, Don L. F. "The Wheat-and-Chaff Approach to Teaching Composition: Nine Steps to Becoming the Perfect Writer." *ArEB* 30 (Fall 1987): 32–36.

Uses quotations from well-known writers to illustrate each of the nine steps.

1028. Pickett, Nell Ann, and Faye Angelo. "Informal Preparation for Teaching Technical Communication Reported As More Helpful Than Formal Preparation." *SCETCJ* 20 (Fall 1987): 34.

Studies characteristics of technical communication teachers in two-year colleges.

1029. Powell, Carolyn L. "And So I Learned to Write." *IlEB* 75 (Fall 1987): 44–47.

A former student in a program directed through the Bay Area Writing Project assesses its strengths. Daily writing and constant attention created a positive attitude toward writing.

1030. Pritchard, Ruie Jane. "Effects on Student Writing of Teacher Training in the National Writing Project Model." *WC* 4 (January 1987): 51–67.

Results favored the treatment group at the junior high level while the senior high students of trained teachers achieved the highest mean score.

1031. Ray, Karen Joan. "The Impact of the Teacher's Theoretical Orientation toward Reading and Writing on the Orientation and Performance of Students with Differing Abilities." *DAI* 48 (December 1987): 1388A.

Concludes that teachers' reading and writing theories remained consistent across different ability levels. Students more readily absorbed teachers' theories if they matched their own.

1032. Rivers, William E. "Qualifications English Departments Prefer for New Teachers of Business and Technical Writing: Is It Time to Reassess Our Degree Programs?" *JBTC* 1 (January 1987): 89–99.

Reports survey information from 568 departments which indicates that degree holders who combined literature and composition study are favored in hiring. Suggests that some departments should make changes.

1033. Roche, A. John. "Engagements: Teaching and Learning." *FEN* 16 (Winter/Spring 1988): 23–28.

Presents an individual view of the education of a writing teacher.

1034. Roskelly, Hephzibah. "Active Learning to Active Teaching: A New Direction in Teacher Preparation." Paper presented at the

CCCC Convention, Atlanta, March 1987. ERIC ED 284 286. 17 pages

Describes a teacher preparation course at the University of Massachusetts at Boston.

1035. Ryan, Josephine M. "Women Teaching English to Low-Income and Minority Students: A Study of Their Perceptions and Actions." *DAI* 48 (August 1987): 298A.

Those more accepting of students deviated more from traditional grammar-based instruction.

1036. Self, Warren. "Prospective Teachers Writing to Learn Grammar." *VEB* 37 (Spring 1987): 137–142.

Prospective teachers write about grammar and language processes to acquire the rich, explicit knowledge necessary to diagnose problems and prescribe effective student activities.

1037. Simpson, Isaiah. "Training and Evaluating Teaching Assistants through Team Teaching." *FEN* 15 (Winter 1987): 4, 9–13.

Describes a different approach to working with graduate teaching assistants. The author teaches 25% of each assistant's assigned composition course.

1038. Smith, Doris. "Student Teaching: A Not So Ultimate Experience." *ET* 18 (Summer 1987): 11–14.

Discusses a survey of student teachers, their students, cooperating teachers, and the supervisors of student teachers.

1039. Spooner, Michael, and Holly O'Donnell. "From Cheap Labor to Junior Colleague: Training TAs in Composition." *EEd* 19 (May 1987): 122–126.

Offers descriptions of current approaches to training teaching assistants.

1040. Steele, James, Aviva Freedman, A. M. Beattie, Trevor Banks, James Downey, Alan McLay, and Ian Pringle. *The Teaching of Composition: A Study of the Approach to Writing Skills in Ontario Faculties of Education.* Ottawa, Canada: Carleton University Depart-ment of English, 1980. ERIC ED 277 035. 271 pages

Discusses the scope of language arts text-books, some instructional procedures, and writing textbooks approved for Ontario's secondary schools. Surveys teachers.

1041. Sullivan, Patricia. "From the Editor." *CalE* 23 (January–February 1987): 3.

Supports classroom research.

1042. Sullivan, Patricia. "Educators Support Classroom Research." *CalE* 23 (January–February 1987): 18.

Discusses the history and structure of class-room research in San Diego.

1043. Wilson, Raymond J., III. "A Continuum for Composition." *JTW* 6 (Spring 1987): 163–170.

Discusses part-to-whole and whole-to-part as designations useful for classifying instructional approaches to composition.

1044. Wiseman, Donna, and Greg Clark. "Writing Apprehension in Teachers: What Can Be Done?" *NCET* 45 (Fall 1987): 6–8.

Extended in-service instruction in process writing decreased teachers' writing apprehension and taught them an approach to their students' writing.

1045. Zambrano, Robert Peter. "Writing across the Curriculum: A Design for a Writing Institute for Deaf Educators." *DAI* 48 (July 1987): 109A.

Traces the development and design of a model that allows faculty members to maintain and improve the English of deaf students.

See also 21, 222, 899, 1048, 1147, 1217, 1225

3.2 ADMINISTRATION

1046. Beene, Lynn Dianne, and Scott P. Sanders. "Writing across the English Department." *WPA* 11 (Fall 1987): 25–34.

Describes the professional writing concentration at the University of New Mexico and its rationale for integrating the study of writing, language theory, and literary criticism into a single curriculum.

1047. Bishop, Wendy. "Toward a Definition of a Writing Program Administrator: Expanding Roles and Evolving Responsibilities." *FEN* 16 (Fall 1987): 11–14.

Reviews the theoretical and practical concerns of the writing program administrator. Includes citations from longer studies of discrete problems and methods.

1048. Bloom, Lynn Z., and Richard C. Gebhardt. "Coming of Age: The WPA Summer Workshop and Conference." *WPA* 10 (Spring 1987): 53–58.

Reports on the Council of Writing Program Administrators' fifth Summer Workshop, held in conjunction with the first WPA Summer Conference at Miami University of Ohio in 1986.

1049. Buckley, William. "Linkage Grant for the Improvement of Composition Teaching." *WPA* 10 (Spring 1987): 45–52.

Describes a year-long collaborative project between college and high school teachers in Gary, Indiana.

1050. Bullock, Richard H. "When Administration Becomes Scholarship: The Future of Writing Program Administration." *WPA* 11 (Fall 1987): 13–18.

Argues that writing program administration should be performed and regarded as a form of scholarship.

1051. "College Can Fire Teacher for Swearing at Students in Class, U.S. Court Rules." *CHE* 33 (21 January 1987): 13–14.

Fired after being warned about cursing in class, a professor argued for his rights to free speech and academic freedom, but lost in court.

1052. Eades, Vivian. "Learning to Lead from Teachers." *ET* 18 (Summer 1987): 33–34.

Discusses how the author, a supervisor and participant in a writing institute, learned from experienced teachers.

1053. Heller, Scott. "Job Conditions for Writing Instructors Called 'Fundamentally Unfair.'" *CHE* 33 (1 April 1987): 13, 16.

Participants at the 1987 CCCC convention passed a resolution decrying unfairness to writing teachers and urging that offending schools be censured.

1054. Huber, Bettina J. "English Salaries: Findings of the 1984–1985 ADE Survey." *BADE* 87 (Fall 1987): 40–49.

Reviews major national salary surveys, presents the ADE survey of salaries by rank and type of institution, and estimates salaries for 1985 through 1987.

1055. Maxwell, John C. *The Time Has Come.* Urbana, Ill.: NCTE, 1987. ERIC ED 280 054. 3 pages

Advocates altering public and administrative attitudes on class size, teacher work load, and other circumstances that impact negatively on writing instruction.

1056. Maxwell, John C. "The Time Has Come." *SLATE* 12 (April 1987).

Argues that teachers must fight at state and local levels for reduced class sizes and improved working conditions.

1057. McLeod, Susan. "Defining Writing across the Curriculum." *WPA* 11 (Fall 1987): 19–24.

Discusses the philosophical bases for writing across the curriculum programs and their various institutional manifestations.

1058. Peterson, Linda H. "The WPA's Progress. A Survey, Story, and Commentary on the Career Patterns of Writing Program Administrators." *WPA* 10 (Spring 1987): 11–18.

Presents results of a survey of past and current writing program administrators and assesses trends in the profession.

95

1059. Pfeiffer, William S. "Out of the Trenches and into the Field: Leaves of Absence for Writing Teachers." *BADE* 88 (Winter 1987): 67–70.

Describes the advantages of a year's leave in industry and explains how to benefit from a working leave.

1060. Posner, Jeanne. "Sign My Card, Please: Perspectives to Advisement." *ETC* 44 (Fall 1987): 304–306.

Shows how a school's and a faculty's attitudes toward advisement are revealed by the language used to describe advising.

1061. Quinn, Helen. "Teaching Technical Writing: A Diffusion Problem." *TWT* 14 (Winter 1987): 53–61.

Describes how members of a technical writing committee successfully disseminated a new technical writing program.

1062. Robertson, Linda R., Sharon Crowley, and Frank Lentricchia. "The Wyoming Conference Resolution Opposing Unfair Salaries and Working Conditions for Post-Secondary Teachers of Writing." *CE* 49 (March 1987): 274–280.

Presents a resolution arising spontaneously from the Wyoming Conference. The resolution proposes that CCCC institute methods for teachers of writing to take direct action against unfair practices.

1063. Robertson, Linda R., and James F. Slevin. "The Status of Composition Faculty: Resolving Reforms." *RR* 5 (Spring 1987): 190–194.

Describes the "shameful and dismal working conditions" of composition faculty that led to the Wyoming Conference Resolution, an attempt to establish professional standards for writing instructors.

1064. SLATE Steering Committee. *SLATE* 12 (March 1987).

Reports on Steering Committee meetings, new directions, state-mandated reform in Illinois, and new books from NCTE.

1065. SLATE Steering Committee. *SLATE* 12 (July 1987).

Reports on SLATE plans, presents a sample letter to parents on class size, examines the legitimacy of secular humanist charges against teachers, and discusses the Wyoming Resolution passed at the annual CCCC convention.

1066. SLATE Steering Committee. *SLATE* 12 (November 1987).

Includes reports on responding to the religious right, the listening curriculum, SLATE election results, NCTE commissions, and the Standing Committee against Censorship.

1067. Slevin, James F. "A Note on the Wyoming Resolution and ADE." *BADE* 87 (Fall 1987): 50.

Explains the origin of the resolution on working conditions and salaries of writing teachers, presents the text of the resolution, discusses the responses to it by CCCC and ADE, and urges ADE members to support it.

See also 528, 986, 1015, 1591

3.3   SUPPORT SERVICES

1068. Ackley, Elizabeth. "Beginning and Maintaining a Peer-Tutor Based Writing Center in the Secondary School." *WLN* 12 (November 1987): 3–4.

Explains that essentially the same factors must be considered when establishing a secondary school writing center as when beginning a college program.

1069. Adams, Ronald, Robert Child, Muriel Harris, and Kathleen Henriott. "Training Teachers for the Writing Lab: A Multidimensional Perspective." *WCJ* 7 (Spring–Summer 1987): 3–19.

Presents perspectives on a writing center from four points of view: a prospective tutor's, a writing teacher's, an experienced tutor's, and a director's.

1070. Allington, Richard L. "Shattered Hopes: Why Two Federal Reading Programs Have Failed to Correct Reading Failure." *Learning* 16 (July–August 1987): 60–64.

Argues that Chapter 1 and Public Law 94–142 reading programs were badly designed and did not incorporate contemporary research. Offers suggestions for change.

1071. Borko, Harold. "Getting Started in Library Expert Systems Research." *IPM* 23 (1987): 81–87.

Describes the difficulty in analyzing what a human expert does and knows and in then transferring that knowledge to a computer program.

1072. Boswell, James, Jr. "Should Community College Students Be Peer Tutors?" *WLN* 11 (April 1987): 5–6.

The experience of peer tutors at one community college suggests they can be effective.

1073. Bowers, Kim Silveira. "The Evolution of a Writing Center." *WLN* 12 (September 1987): 12–14.

Presents experiences encountered in creating a writing center.

1074. Brinkely, Ellen H. "Secondary Writing Centers: Benefits of College and Secondary Collaboration." Paper presented at the CCCC Convention, Atlanta, March 1987. ERIC ED 281 226. 11 pages

Discusses strategies for dealing with the problem of staffing high school writing centers.

1075. Cambridge, Barbara. "Defining Our Mission: New Directions for *JTW*." *JTW* 6 (Fall–Winter 1987). 195–200.

Outlines three distinctive features of the journal: "service to teachers of writing at all academic levels, emphasis on practice-as-inquiry, and commitment to scrutiny of theory."

1076. Chapman, David. "High Noon at the Writing Corral: A Tale of the West." *WLN* 12 (December 1987): 1–2.

Describes how a patient tutor can salvage and revise students' papers.

1077. Chapman, David W. "The Rogue and the Tutor: A Tale." *WLN* 11 (March 1987): 6.

Suggests that writing center directors should have faith in their tutors.

1078. Chase, Geoffrey W. "Problem Solving in the Writing Center: From Theory to Practice." *WCJ* 7 (Spring–Summer 1987): 29–35.

Describes how a seven-step problem-solving model developed by Don Koberg and Jim Bagnall applies to training peer tutors.

1079. Chiteman, Michael D. "The Writing Center and Institutional Politics: Making Connections with Administration and Faculty." *WLN* 11 (April 1987): 1–4.

Offers suggestions and strategies for getting faculty and administrators in other disciplines to be supportive of the writing center.

1080. Coleman, Karen W. "Quick Fix Versus Instruction." *WLN* 11 (May 1987).

Discusses the positive and negative features of a grammar hotline.

1081. Collins, Mark. "Oh My, I've Never Done This Sort of Thing Before!" *WLN* 12 (December 1987): 5.

A novice tutor discusses the benefits that he and his students receive from the writing center.

1082. Davis, Kevin. "Data Bases in the Writing Center: The PC as Administrative Record Keeper." *WLN* 11 (June 1987): 5–6.

Suggests the use of a data base or electronic filing system to make record keeping easier in a college resource center.

1083. DeCiccio, Albert. "Is Gentran Taking the Peer Out of Peer Tutor?" *WLN* 11 (February 1987): 1–5.

The answer appears to be "yes." Suggests a "hybrid" tutor, a mixture of the Gentran and collaborative learning styles.

1084. Devet, Bonnie. "Five Years on the Hotline: Answering the Writer's Hotline." *WLN* 12 (December 1987): 12–14.

Describes a writing center's hotline, noting types of callers and customary questions.

1085. Devet, Bonnie. "Workshops That Work." *WLN* 11 (January 1987): 13–14.

Reveals what types of topics have been successful in one writing center's open workshops.

1086. Donovan, Ronald John. "Be Your Own Publisher: The Writer's Digest Guide to Desktop Publishing Hardware." *WD* (February 1987): 26–30.

Part two of a three-part series discusses the equipment required for desktop publishing. See also articles by Andrew M. Greeley and Ronald John Donovan in *WD*, January and March 1987, respectively.

1087. Donovan, Ronald John. "You Can Be Your Own Publisher, Part III: The Writer's Digest Guide to Desktop Publishing Software." *WD* (March 1987): 34–39.

Part three of a three-part series explains what desktop publishing software is, how to shop for it, and what the best programs are. See also articles by Andrew M. Greeley and Ronald John Donovan in *WD*, January and February 1987, respectively.

1088. Dunbar-Odom, Donna. "Teaching Academic Survival Skills in the Writing Center." *IE* 11 (Fall 1987): 18–20.

Advocates helping nontraditional students become acculturated by establishing rapport, being sensitive to cultural differences, playing roles, and using polite manners.

1089. Edmonds, Ernest. "Expert Systems and Document Handling." *IPM* 23 (1987): 77–80.

Describes how human expertise is translated into computer programs that can serve as mechanical consultants for decision making.

1090. FitzRandolph, Susan. "My Internship: A Unique Learning Experience." *WLN* 11 (April 1987): 7–9.

Describes a writing intern's learning experiences during one semester in a writing center.

1091. Greeley, Andrew M. "The Writers's Digest Guide to Desktop Publishing." *WD* (January 1987): 22–27, 49.

Part one of a three-part series gives an overview of the advantages and disadvantages of desktop publishing, explaining how price, education, and ability influence its use. See also articles by Ronald John Donovan in *WD*, February and March 1987.

1092. Handlin, Oscar. "Libraries and Learning." *ASch* 56 (Spring 1987): 205–218.

Research libraries are endangered by the information explosion, but students learn most by browsing in libraries where no one tells them what to read.

1093. Harred, Larry D., and Thomas J. Russo. "Using Small Groups Effectively in the Lab: Strategies for Improving Student Self-Confidence." *WLN* 12 (September 1987): 7–10.

Illustrates strategies used to improve students' self-confidence and thus their ability to successfully engage in collaborative learning.

1094. Harris, Muriel. "Tutorial Instruction: Another Dimension Needed in Writing Programs." Paper presented at the CCCC Convention, Atlanta, March 1987. ERIC ED 281 218. 9 pages

Discusses ways in which writing center instruction differs from classroom instruction.

1095. Hicks, Joyce. "What to Consider As You Organize Your Writing Center." *IE* 10 (Spring 1987): 27–29.

Gives seven sets of questions to answer in planning a writing center. Includes a list of 11 sources to consider.

1096. Kail, Harvey, and John Trimbur. "The Politics of Peer Tutoring." *WPA* 11 (Fall 1987): 5–12.

Distinguishes between two models of peer tutoring and argues that the curriculum-based model implicates tutors in a "delivery system," while the writing center model offers a semi-autonomous space where students can empower each other through co-learning.

1097. Kari, Daven. "Revitalizing Cliches: A Workshop Strategy." *WLN* 11 (March 1987): 8–10.

Presents workshop strategies to give students useful options for working with cliches.

1098. Kilmer, Mary. "Tutor—Know Yourself." *WLN* 11 (June 1987): 13–14.

Suggests that writing center personnel should be aware of Meyers-Briggs personality types. This knowledge may help tutors work with students.

1099. Knepper, Marty. "Learning at the Learning Center: A Personal Reflection on Nine Years 'At The Lab.'" *WLN* 12 (November 1987): 13–14.

Asserts that learning centers need flexible tutors willing to meet the needs of their students.

1100. Lassner, Phyllis. "The Politics of Peer Tutoring." *WLN* 12 (September 1987): 4–6.

Discusses the dilemma peer tutors face. Are they peers or a part of the institution's system of authority?

1101. Leary, Barbara Buckett. "Interaction Place Maps: A Tool for Tutor Training." *JDEd* 10 (January 1987): 8–12.

Explains a method for helping peer tutors improve interpersonal relationships.

1102. Logan, Junius. "Literaria Bohemia Nervosa." *WLN* 12 (September 1987): 11–12.

Describes the qualities necessary for functioning as an effective writing center tutor.

1103. Magaha, Ann. "Technical Writing and Tutor Training." *WLN* 12 (December 1987): 11–12.

Asserts that collaboration between writing centers and technical writing classes can be successful.

1104. Marshall, Rick. "Word Processing and More: The Joys and Chores of a Writing Lab Computer." *WLN* 11 (June 1987): 1–4.

Discusses both the benefits and disadvantages of using computers in the writing center.

1105. McAllister, Carole, Sheila Stroup, and Charles Martin. "The Electronic Learning Laboratory: Evolving Beyond CAI." *JDEd* 10 (January 1987): 14–17.

Preliminary results of this study show measurable improvements in the writing of students who attend a microcomputer writing lab.

1106. McCallum, Paul. "Confessions of a Tutor." *WLN* 11 (June 1987): 7.

Maintains that students visiting writing centers must be shown that they can think for themselves. Offers a series of questions to help them do so.

1107. Miller, Shelly. "Dodging the Pundit: The Prevention of Pedagogy in the Writing Center." *WLN* 11 (March 1987): 1–4.

Suggests techniques that help eliminate the tutor's role confusion in the writing center.

1108. Moore, Shelee. "Robotics and English." *WLN* 11 (February 1987): 7.

Suggests that the tutor and the student define writing problems prior to attempting to solve them.

1109. Morris, Karen L. "Hats and Feathers: Roles and Attributes of Tutors." *WLN* 12 (December 1987): 10–11.

Examines the often overlapping roles of tutors and discusses character attributes and attitudes that can make a tutor effective.

1110. Neth, April. "The Writing Tutor Bicycle." *WLN* 12 (October 1987): 11–12.

Explains that tutoring, like riding a bicycle, is a skill that must be practiced and that, once learned, is rarely forgotten.

1111. Perdue, Virginia. "Writing Center Pedagogy: Developing Authority in Student Writers." *WLN* 11 (April 1987): 9–11.

Describes practices that help student writers develop authority in their writing.

1112. Petcher, Douglas. "Confessions of a Conference Goer." *FEN* 16 (Fall 1987): 19–20.

Compares the traditional conference to the traditional teacher-centered classroom. Argues for more interactive talking.

1113. Reeves, Ramona C. "The Second Language Student." *WLN* 12 (November 1987): 7–8.

Through a personal experience, a tutor learns how to help ESL students move toward becoming better writers.

1114. Roger-Hogan, Nicole. "Twenty Minutes in the Life of Bob the Tutor." *WLN* 11 (January 1987): 7–8.

Describes the approaches taken by a writing center tutor and emphasizes the need for flexibility in tutoring.

1115. Ross, Karen A. *School-College Cooperation in Teaching Composition: Programs and Possibilities*. Urbana, Ill.: ERIC/RCS, 1986. ERIC ED 275 006. 15 pages

Describes programs of institutional cooperation for strengthening secondary composition instruction in California, New York, Illinois, and Iowa.

1116. Runciman, Lex. "Should Writing Lab Conferences Be Required for Composition Students?" *WLN* 11 (May 1987): 12–14.

According to students surveyed, the answer is "yes."

1117. Ryan, A. Leigh Keller. "An Investigation and Description of Some Relationships between Tutorial Assistance in a Writing Center and the Writing Apprehension of Freshman Composition Students." *DAI* 47 (February 1987): 2930A.

Students' writing apprehension decreased significantly with tutoring in a process-oriented conference-centered approach.

1118. Schmidt, Deborah A. "The Tutor's Corner." *WLN* 11 (March 1987): 7.

Explains how word processors can assist both tutors and students in the writing center.

1119. Schwartz, Helen J. "Planning and Running a Computer Lab for Writing: A Survival Manual." *BADE* 86 (Spring 1987): 43–47.

Provides guidelines and advice for planning and running a computer lab. Covers institutional support, materials, policies, and administration.

1120. Scott, Paulette. "Tutor-Student Conferences: Theories and Strategies." *WLN* 12 (November 1987): 8–12.

Reviews tutoring textbooks and conference styles. Illustrates how writing conferences can help both tutors and students.

1121. Seckendorf, Margaret Hess. "Writing Center Conferences: An Analysis." *DAI* 47 (February 1987): 3024A.

Concludes that differences between undergraduates and tutors in defining writing causes a "dissonance" that must be resolved for successful conferences.

1122. Selfe, Cynthia L. "Creating a Computer-Supported Writing Lab: Sharing Stories and Creative Vision." *CC* 4 (April 1987): 44–65.

Describes how to set up and run a college computer lab to support a writing program.

1123. Sickbert, Virginia. "For Next Year." *WLN* 11 (May 1987): 5.

An experienced writing center tutor suggests how new tutors can help students.

1124. Slattery, Pat. "Technology in the Writing Center: Do We Need It?" *WLN* 11 (May 1987): 6–7.

Twelve writing center directors interviewed suggest that technology is needed to complement individualized instruction.

1125. Smith, Frank R. "The Etiquette of Submitting an Article for Publication." *JTWC* 17 (1987): 207–214.

Describes the procedures followed in screening and editing an article for publication in a professional journal and guides authors in preparing acceptable materials.

1126. Spaeth, Elizabeth A. "What Do Tutors Learn When They Are Not Tutoring?" *WLN* 12 (December 1987): 2–4.

Presents learning activities for tutors that connect their writing center duties with their intellectual development.

1127. Stave, Anna M. "Client Perceptions of a University Writing Center." Paper presented at the CCCC Convention, Atlanta, March 1987. ERIC ED 284 225. 17 pages

Reports on a survey of writing center clients. Most did not believe that they were good writers but were pleased with their conferences.

1128. Strickland, Bill. "The Writer's Digest Guide to Writer's Conferences, Workshops, and Seminars." *WD* (May 1987): 32–46.

A state-by-state guide to over 400 gatherings that teach writing and provide contacts with editors, publishers, journalists, photographers, authors, dramatists, poets, and business or technical writers.

1129. Sweeney, Sharon. "Networking Computers at the Learning Center." *WLN* 11 (May 1987): 8–9.

Discusses the problems and possibilities of networking computers at a learning or writing center.

1130. Taufen, Phyllis M. "What Do You Do When the Budget Is Zero?" *WLN* 11 (May 1987): 1–3.

Discusses the success of one underfinanced writing center.

1131. Taylor, David. "Invasion of the Gremlins." *WLN* 12 (November 1987): 1–3.

Presents an example of a self-test designed to encourage students to go to the writing center for help.

1132. Trimbur, John. "Peer Tutoring: A Contradiction in Terms?" *WCJ* 7 (Spring–Summer 1987): 21–28.

Raises questions about the role of the peer tutor. Presents two models of tutor training—apprentice and co-learner—and emphasizes the latter in initial training stages.

1133. Wilson, April. "First Impressions." *WLN* 12 (December 1987): 5–6.

Illustrates how first impressions between a tutor and student can often be inaccurate.

1134. Wolcott, Willa. "Establishing Writing Center Workshops." *WCJ* 7 (Spring–Summer 1987): 45–49.

Explains a six-step process for presenting workshops on writing topics for interested students.

1135. Wolterbeek, Marc. "Resisting and Accepting Writing Centers: A Personal View." *WLN* 11 (January 1987): 10–11.

Concludes that resistance by English department faculty members is simply a "fear of the unknown." They do not understand writing centers.

1136. Yarmove, Jay. "Interlock: A Proposal for a 'Cosmopolitan' Writing Lab." *WLN* 11 (June 1987): 8–9.

Proposes a writing center staffed with faculty from various disciplines who are also knowledgeable about the principles of writing.

1137. Young, Virginia Hudson. "Exploiting the Writing-Speaking Relationship in the

Writing Center." *WLN* 12 (October 1987): 1–5.

Describes how tutors can help students transfer their informal speaking voice to a more appropriate, formal writing voice.

See also 1049, 1575

3.4   ROLE IN SOCIETY

1138. Allen, Diane. "Public Communication: Speaking Out for Teachers of English." *SLATE* 12 (October 1987).

Describes how to build public support for the teaching of English through positive individual statements and an affiliate communication committee. Includes bibliography.

1139. Cain, William E. "Education and Social Change." *CE* 49 (January 1987): 83–88.

An essay review of two books. Examines the political dimensions of educational reform as viewed by two American social democrats.

1140. Conway, Jill K. "Politics, Pedagogy, and Gender." *Daedalus* 116 (Fall 1987): 137–153.

A historical, statistical description of feminization in nineteenth-century American secondary education. Coding schools as "female" prevents demanding, competitive curricula and adequate financial support.

1141. Glass, Mary Lee. "Education and Politics: Strange Bedfellows Indeed." *CalE* 23 (November–December 1987): 12–13, 27.

Argues that teachers must be involved in politics.

1142. Glenn, Charles L. "Textbook Controversies: A Disaster for Public Schools?" *PhiDK* 68 (February 1987): 451–455.

Examines charges of censorship and countercharges of insensitivity to minority values. Recommends "common sense and flexibility."

1143. Heller, Scott. "English Teachers Favor Emphasis on How to Read, Write, Think, Rather Than on Becoming Familiar with Specific Literary Works." *CHE* 33 (5 August 1987): 9–10.

A three-week conference of elementary through college English teachers rejected arguments favoring a single focus for learning such as "cultural literacy."

1144. Heller, Scott. "Scholars Ponder How to Teach English to Students of a Television Generation." *CHE* 33 (1 July 1987): 9, 11.

Reports on the Coalition of English Association's meeting to rethink the teaching of English.

1145. Joyce, John J. "The English Coalition Meeting: A Report." *CEAF* 17 (1987): 1–3.

Reports on the agenda and recommendations of the English Coalition meeting of July 1987.

1146. Lane, Ken. "An Interview with Gerald Hayward, Sacramento PACE Director." *CalE* 23 (September–October 1987): 24–25.

The Director of Policy Analysis for California Education, a research center, discusses legislative actions, bilingual education, and class size.

1147. Lane, Ken. "Teaching Conditions and the Commission on Teacher Credentialing." *CalE* 23 (November–December 1987): 10–11.

Surveys prospects for educational reform in California, particularly in class size and funding.

1148. Lane, Kenneth S. "The Conditions for Educational Reform." *CalE* 23 (January–February 1987): 28–29.

Urges a "reform-from-within" model.

1149. Lane, Kenneth S. "Many School Problems, Few Funding Solutions." *CalE* 23 (May–June 1987): 28–29.

Reports legislative actions.

1150. Lane, Kenneth S. "The Outlook for Education in California." *CalE* 23 (March–April 1987): 28–29.

Summarizes legislative issues relating to education, including limits on state spending, rising expenses, and reform movements.

1151. McHugh, Nancy. "Education and Politics: The English Coalition Conference." *CalE* 23 (November–December 1987): 6–7, 21.

Reports on issues raised at the conference.

1152. Mooney, Carolyn J. "Sophocles in Randolph County: North Carolina State University's Unusual Extension Program." *CHE* 34 (25 November 1987): A12-A13, A16.

Humanities professors at North Carolina State University teach extension courses on such topics as creative writing, art history, and the Constitution, to appreciative, small town residents.

1153. Page, Ernest R. "An Afternoon with Senator Gary Hart." *CalE* 23 (May–June 1987): 12–14.

State senator Hart discusses class size, support systems, financing the California Writing Project, minority teachers, and other educational issues.

1154. Peterson, Robert Dean, and Donald E. Miller. "Educating in 'Post-Industrial' Society." *JT* 22 (Spring 1987): 30–33.

In a world where the only constant is change, improving communication skills and a sense of self are of paramount importance.

1155. Poteet, Ralph A. "Is Legislation Enough to Reform Education?" *ET* 18 (Winter 1987): 14–17.

Discusses the implications of Texas House Bill 72, which brought about much change in the state's educational system.

1156. Shor, Ira, and Paulo Freire. *A Pedagogy for Liberation: Dialogues on Transforming Education.* South Hadley, Mass.: Bergin & Garvey, 1987. 224 pages

Discusses the problems of educational systems in relation to those of the larger society and argues for liberating the classroom from its traditional constraints. The teacher's role is crucial in empowering students to think critically about themselves and their relation to society.

1157. Simich-Dudgeon, Carmen, ed. *Issues of Parent Involvement and Literacy: Proceedings of the Symposium Held at Trinity College, Washington, D. C., June 1986.* Urbana, Ill.: ERIC/RCS, 1986. ERIC ED 275 206. 19 pages

A collection of 19 papers from a collaborative project between Trinity College and Arlington, Virginia, Public Schools. Focuses on parent involvement in bilingual, limited English, refugee, and adult education.

1158. Stevens, Larry P., and William E. Piland. "Adult Illiteracy and the Role of the Community College." *CCR* 15 (Winter 1987): 48–54.

Suggests that community colleges adopt the role of "middle man" in organizing, facilitating, and orchestrating a broadly based community-wide effort to increase adult literacy.

1159. Willinsky, John. "The Promise of Copyright in the Classroom: Pedagogy and Politics." *EQ* 20 (Fall 1987): 231–242.

Discusses the Canadian laws governing the duplication of copyrighted material for classroom use.

See also 85, 1065, 1789

4
Curriculum

4.1 GENERAL DISCUSSIONS

1160. Armistead, L. Pendleton, David M. Moore, and Daniel E. Vogler. "Selected General Education Influences Affecting Degree Completion for Community College Occupational Students." *CCR* 15 (Winter 1987): 55–59.

Based on the views of graduates and leavers, this study concludes that general education continues to present problems for colleges committed to increasing occupational enrollment.

1161. Beach, Richard. "Differences in Autobiographical Narratives of English Teachers, College Freshman, and Seventh Graders." *CCC* 38 (February 1987): 56–69.

Compares narratives of adolescents and teachers, relating the differences to social cognition. Discusses implications for teachers.

1162. Beene, Lynn Dianne. "Writing Assignments: What We Know We Don't Know."

Paper presented at the CCCC Convention, Atlanta, March 1987. ERIC ED 280 085. 16 pages

Explores how the phrasing of writing assignments influences what students write.

1163. Berry, Elvera B. "Undergraduate Education: A Burkean Perspective." *DAI* 48 (August 1987): 313A.

Uses Burke's linguistic, rhetorical, and literary theories to reconceptualize academic disciplines.

1164. Bertch, Julie. "Integrating Thinking Strategies and Activities into Writing Assignments." *ArEB* 30 (Fall 1987): 18–20.

Argues that written assignments in response to readings can enhance critical thinking. Provides an outline of summarizing activities.

1165. Betheu, Edward E. "Sentence-Combining: An Innovative Approach to the Development of Writing Skills." *NCET* 45 (Fall 1987): 22–27.

An overview of the reasoning and research on sentence-combining's effect on reading comprehension, composition skills, punctuation, syntactic fluency, syntactic maturity, and overall writing quality.

1166. Blackinton, Pat. "Ordinary Folks, Extraordinary Stories: A Guide to Conducting Interviews and Writing Personality Profiles." *UEJ* (1987): 42–47.

Discusses benefits to students from interviewing and being interviewed. Presents a guideline for student interviewers and suggestions for writing openings and endings.

1167. Brown, T. K., III. "As Far As You Using Proper English, Just Lay Back, Your Not Alone." *TETYC* 14 (May 1987): 106–116.

A catalog of improprieties in contemporary usage.

1168. Byrd, Vicki. "A Novel Approach." *ET* 18 (Summer 1987): 35–38.

Discusses 16 steps to help students write literature instead of writing about literature. Uses *Johnny Tremain* as an example.

1169. Cambridge, Barbara L. "Equal Opportunity Writing Classrooms: Accommodating Interactional Differences between Genders in the Writing Classroom." *WI* 7 (Fall 1987): 30–39.

Cites research showing gender differences in classroom interactions. Suggests activities and a model for writing teachers that promote equal participation and enhanced learning.

1170. Christiansen, Mark A. "Writing a Linguistic Autobiography." *VEB* 37 (Spring 1987): 119–121.

Enumerates and organizes a series of questions that prompt students' linguistic autobiographies for language and composition study.

1171. Collins, Allan, John Seely Brown, and Susan E. Newman. *Cognitive Apprenticeship: Teaching the Craft of Reading, Writing, and*

Mathematics. Center for the Study of Reading Technical Report, no. 402. Urbana, Ill.: University of Illinois, 1987. ERIC ED 284 181. 37 pages

Suggests an "apprenticeship" model of literacy transmission, noting that school instruction is now only abstractly related to real needs.

1172. Corcoran, Bill, and Emrys Evans. *Readers, Texts, Teachers*. Upper Montclair, N.J.: Boynton/Cook, 1987. 272 pages

Twelve chapters intended to help teachers implement reader-response theory in their classes. Offers detailed examples of how and why the theory works.

1173. Cross, Eli. "CAWmputer Encouragement for Student Writers." *TETYC* 14 (May 1987): 146–149.

A humorous essay about a computer program that offers students encouragement.

1174. Daniel, Carter A. "If Men and Women in Business Are Ignorant of Literature, It's Our Fault." *CHE* 34 (2 September 1987): B1–B2.

Argues that English teachers caused the popularity of their courses to decline by acting imperiously, especially to non-English majors, and by teaching narrowly designed classes.

1175. Davis, Diana. "*English Teaching:* An International Exchange." *JCS* 19 (May–June 1987): 291–292.

A review of James Britton's *English Teaching*. Argues that this compilation of essays celebrates what Britton believes best in English teaching and "provides an excellent exemplar of the dissemination of ideas across oceans."

1176. Davis, Kevin. "The Role of Peer Tutoring: Steps to Describing a Three-Dimensional Model." Paper presented at the CCCC Convention, Atlanta, March 1987. ERIC ED 280 033. 16 pages

Advocates developing a three-dimensional model of tutoring that incorporates theory and research so that tutors may better understand the tutoring process.

1177. Devlin, Frank. "The Student as Questioner: Reversing the Equation." *EngR* 38 (1987): 2–7.

Explores the goals for a process-centered writing course.

1178. DiPardo, Anne, and Sarah Warshauer Freedman. *Historical Overview: Groups in the Writing Classroom.* CSW Report, no. 4. Berkeley, Calif.: CSW, 1987. ERIC ED 282 229. 21 pages

Traces the use of peer groups in writing classrooms, noting how language theory supports such collaboration.

1179. Dodd, Anne Wescott. "A Writing Log Helps Teachers Help Students." *TETYC* 14 (February 1987): 27–31.

Student logs noting dates and times that they worked on writing with comments on their processes helped the instructor plan course activities.

1180. Dolgin, Steven Alfred. "Creative Writing and the Composing Process: The Role of Creative Writing in the English Curriculum." *DAI* 48 (September 1987): 585A.

Concludes that the objectives of critical thinking, reading, and writing may be achieved through a course in creative writing.

1181. Dragga, Sam. "Building Speaking-Writing Bridges." *ET* 18 (Summer 1987): 5–10.

Discusses four differences between speaking and writing and suggests seven ways to build bridges "across this cognitive, linguistic, and stylistic disparity."

1182. Dunn, Ann Hill, and Michael F. Graves. "Intensive Vocabulary Instruction as a Prewriting Technique." *RRQ* 22 (Summer 1987): 311–330.

Teaching a related set of words to students before they write an essay improves the essay's quality.

1183. Duran, Robert L., and Walter R. Zakahi. "Communication Performance and Communication Satisfaction: What Do We Teach Our Students?" *ComEd* 36 (January 1987): 13–22.

Identifies what speech communication skills should be taught. Suggests that students are not sufficiently self-reflective of their communicative performance.

1184. Farr, Marcia, and Harvey Daniels. *Language Diversity and Writing Instruction.* Urbana, Ill.: NCTE, ERIC/RS, ERIC/UD, and the Institute of Urban and Minority Education, 1986. 99 pages

Surveys research on language variation, which demonstrates that all dialects have inherent integrity and that dialects can interfere with writing standard English. Presents 15 recommendations for teaching linguistically diverse students in grades seven through college.

1185. Fletcher, J. B. [pseud.]. "Deadline Dodgers: An Empirical Study, of Sorts." *TETYC* 14 (May 1987): 117–120.

A humorous essay on why students fail to turn work in on time.

1186. Fox, Thomas Allen. "The Social Uses of Language in the Classroom." *DAI* 47 (February 1987): 2926A.

Argues for the conscious use of students' social backgrounds in teaching. Uses case studies to show that students' reading and writing enacts values derived from social experience.

1187. Fraser, David A. "Identifying Effective Memory Strategies: A Human Experiment in Information Science." *DAI* 47 (January 1987): 2350A.

Concludes that visualization, when used in connection with writing, is the most effective retention strategy for students.

1188. Fulwiler, Toby, ed. *The Journal Book.* Upper Montclair, N.J.: Boynton/Cook, 1987. 352 pages

Thirty-nine articles by writing teachers and researchers explore the use of student journals, detailing implications, applications, theory, and practice. Gives examples from many grades and disciplines.

1189. Gambell, Trevor J., and Carolle Debert. "Writing: Making Meaning in an Art Form." *EQ* 20 (Summer 1987): 157–162.

Reconsiders the act of writing as the creation of a work of art. Suggests ways in which a new approach might affect the teaching of writing.

1190. Gentry, Brian. "Using Imitation to Teach Writing." *UEJ* (1987): 48–51.

Argues that imitation is a natural method of learning. Suggests using samples of both professional writing and the teacher's writing as models for students.

1191. George, Diana. "Teaching Writing as a Way of Knowing: Roland Barthes and Structures of Interpretation." *CollT* 35 (Spring 1987): 62–66.

Discusses Barthes as an aid to teachers helping students think about and interpret their writing topics.

1192. Gere, Anne Ruggles. *Writing Groups: History, Theory, and Implications.* Studies in Writing and Rhetoric. Carbondale, Ill.: Southern Illinois University Press, 1987. 128 pages

Traces the history of writing groups in America, examining their theoretical foundations and challenging the concept of writing as individual performance.

1193. Gladis, Stephen D. "Owners Versus Renters Theory." *ArEB* 30 (Fall 1987): 37–40.

Describes the benefits possible when students become responsible for their own writing. Suggests that teachers give up some control of the classroom to encourage this responsibility.

1194. Gould, Christopher. "Josephine Turck Baker, *Correct English*, and the Ancestry of Pop Grammar." *EJ* 76 (January 1987): 22–27.

Traces the history of "correct" English usage in the twentieth century and discusses the effects these changes have had on today's "innovations" in teaching writing.

1195. Gozzi, Joan Daniels. "Magazine Mania Gets Kids Writing and Thinking." *Learning* 16 (September 1987): 41–50.

Presents teaching activities to help students read, understand, and write about the contents of magazines.

1196. Greer, Martin Glenn. "Enhancing Creative Writing: Effects of Fantasy and Motivational Orientation." *DAI* 47 (March 1987): 3366A.

Results indicate higher levels of creativity in the experimental group after introducing mediating techniques.

1197. Gruner, Charles R. "Why Johnny Can't Operationalize: A Question of Nailing Down Meaning." *ETC* 44 (Summer 1987): 155–159.

Calls for teaching students to "operationalize," to solve problems successfully in a practical, workable, enforceable manner through the use of general semantics instruction.

1198. Haltiner, Maurine E. "Multifoliate Rose: Creative Editing." *UEJ* (1987): 69–74.

Gives suggestions for incorporating recursive editing practice in writing units to improve revision skills. Sample texts included.

1199. Hansford, B. C., and J. A. Hattie. "Perceptions of Communicator Style and Self-Concept." *ComR* 14 (April 1987): 189–203.

Students who perceived themselves as relaxed and attentive, with little communication apprehension and with a positive communication image, believed themselves to have a high self-concept.

1200. Harris, Muriel. "The Ins and Outs of Conferencing." *WI* 6 (Winter 1987): 87–96.

Urges an end to problem-solution writing conferences. Advocates instead a "coaching" approach that includes setting goals, being flexible, and doing more listening and questioning.

1201. Heller, Scott. "A New Wave of Curricular Reform: Connections between Disciplines." *CHE* 34 (2 September 1987): A28–30, 34.

An increasing number of colleges require multi-disciplinary "general education" courses, primarily in the humanities and social sciences.

1202. Hise, Jesse. "Intuitive Writing." *ArEB* 29 (Spring 1987): 5–7.

Suggests setting time limits to produce intuitive writing.

1203. Hoffman, Gary. "Toward Literate Writing: Back to Basics But Not Back to Boring." *CurrR* 27 (September–October 1987).

Describes an approach to teaching writing that emphasizes creative choices, rules that work, strategic structures, and the use of exciting examples.

1204. Hurst, Mary Jane. "Teaching Students to Write More Effective Sentences." *ArEB* 29 (Spring 1987): 17–21.

Describes how grammatical, semantic, and stylistic work on sentences can be used to improve writing.

1205. Infantino, Bob. "Developing a Core Curriculum in Literature: An Undesirable Idea." Paper presented at the NCTE Convention, San Antonio, November 1986. ERIC ED 279 007. 13 pages

Argues that establishing a core curriculum for literature study is narrow and elitist unless it promotes independent, critical thinking and diversity.

1206. Jobst, Jack. "Word Processing: Two Ethical Concerns." *JTWC* 17 (1987): 1–8.

Describes two possible abuses of computers used for word processing: the plagiarism of someone else's work and censorship prompted by editing or revision programs.

1207. Johnson, Craig E. "An Introduction to Powerful and Powerless Talk in the Classroom." *ComEd* 36 (April 1987): 167–172.

Reviews the literature on powerful/powerless talk and suggest ways to use the findings in the speech classroom.

1208. Karolides, Nicholas J., ed. "Reading/Writing: Theories and Practice." *WiEJ* 26 (October 1983): 1–36.

Seven articles examine recent theories about the relationship between reading and writing. Also available as ERIC ED 278 995.

1209. Karolides, Nicholas J., ed. "Visual Literacy/Process Writing." *WiEJ* 27 (October 1984): 1–36.

Six articles provide a rationale for a process approach to composition instruction and techniques for improving students' awareness of visual arts. Also available as ERIC ED 278 998.

1210. Karolides, Nicholas J., ed. "Writing Anxiety." *WiEJ* 24 (April 1982): 1–36.

Six articles investigate characteristics of writing apprehension and techniques to eliminate it. Also available as ERIC ED 278 991.

1211. Karolides, Nicholas J., and Laura Quinn, eds. "Curriculum Development." *WiEJ* 29 (October 1986): 1–36.

Nine articles provide administrators and teachers with suggestions for curriculum development at all levels. Also available as ERIC ED 280 026.

1212. Kellogg, E. W., III. "Speaking in E-Prime: An Experimental Method for Integrating General Semantics into Daily Life." *ETC* 44 (Summer 1987): 118–128.

Argues that teaching students to distinguish among uses of *is* in their prose helps clarify thinking and enhances creativity, problem solving, and interpersonal communication.

1213. Kirby, Susan C. "Self-Evaluation: A Way to Improve Teaching and Learning." *TETYC* 14 (February 1987): 41–46.

Self-evaluation techniques and instruments help students revise their work. They arc also useful during writing.

1214. Kort, Melissa Sue. "The Politics of Literacy: Issues Facing a Two-Year College." *TETYC* 14 (October 1987): 174–180.

Argues that creating separate reading and writing courses for vocational students violates the spirit of community colleges.

1215. Kurth, Anita. "Writing as Performance and the Need for Applause." *TETYC* 14 (February 1987): 22–26.

Discusses writing as an act of public performance, compared to visual arts, public speaking, and athletics. Students need praise and sympathy with understanding their often uncomfortable situations.

1216. Lueders, Edward. "The Human Animal: Instinct with Language." *UEJ* (1987): 3–12.

Suggests that English teachers allow students to write about sciences, especially natural sciences. Uniting sciences and humanities is something civilization must do.

1217. Lundy, Eileen T. "The Status of the Profession: Who Is in Control?" *ET* 18 (Winter 1987): 8–13.

Reports the consensus of NCTE's Commission on Curriculum in the areas of curriculum control, teacher education, and writing and literature instruction.

1218. Martin, Nancy. "Writing: What Still Needs to Be Done?" *VEB* 37 (Special 1987 Issue): 50–54.

Unassessed journal writing and practical, public writing can enhance personal understanding. Topics should be chosen by the individual and read by the teacher and students.

1219. Marting, Janet. "The Power of the Past. Inquiries into the Old Pedagogy." Paper presented at the CCCC Convention, Atlanta, March 1987. ERIC ED 280 071. 13 pages

Discusses the longevity of traditional models of writing instruction.

1220. Meeks, Lynn Langer. "Damn the Noise and Full Pen Ahead." *UEJ* (1987): 13–15.

Argues that in-class student writing provides learning reinforcement through peer interactions, gives students a perspective on writing processes, and helps them gain editing skills.

1221. Menefee, Emory. "Becoming Optimally Human: An Approach toward Critical Thinking." *ETC* 44 (Winter 1987): 335–338.

Advocates a general semantics approach to teaching critical thinking. Students need to learn "fluency of moving among abstraction levels" as a first step in problem solving.

1222. Meyers, Chet. *Teaching Students to Think Critically: A Guide for Faculty in All Disciplines*. San Francisco: Jossey-Bass, 1987. 146 pages

Shows teachers how to develop the necessary skills for teaching serious, critical thought in their courses. Nine chapters examine what critical thinking is, how it can be taught, and why it should be part of every course.

1223. Miller, Carol, and Michael A. Benedict. "Developing a Writing Program at Fox Chapel." *PCTEB* 54 (November 1986): 12–21.

Details the development of a unified writing program that trains teachers using research in writing as its foundation.

1224. Mortensen, Peter. "Analyzing Conference Conversation: A Writer Learns to Talk about Writing." Paper presented at the CCCC Convention, Atlanta, March 1987. ERIC ED 281 246. 22 pages

Examines a writing conference for ways in which the teacher and student negotiate for meaning. A partial transcript and linguistic analysis are appended.

1225. Mottram, Richard A., and Marie-Dominique Schock. "France and America Meet at the Lectern: An Experiment in Team Teaching." *ET* 18 (Spring 1987): 22–25.

Describes the team-teaching experience of a native of France with a Ph.D. in French and an American with a Ph.D. in English.

1226. Nella, O. J. [pseud]. "Have You Ever Noticed That Andy Rooney Always Finds Topics for HIS Papers?" *TETYC* 14 (May 1987): 134–136.

A humorous essay on using questions to generate writing topics.

1227. Nilsen, Alleen, Ken Donelson, Don Nilsen, and Marie Donelson. "Humor for Developing Thinking Skills." *ETC* 44 (Spring 1987): 63–75.

Humor reveals gaps in a student's experience and multiple viewpoints; teaches careful observation, selection, and the making of meaning; and shows how to relate ideas.

1228. Nugent, Susan Monroe, ed. "Synthesize, Synthesize, Synthesize." *Leaflet* 86 (Winter 1987).

Contains eight articles discussing the value of and methods for teaching synthesis in the writing classroom. Also available as ERIC ED 281 212.

1229. Oliver-Bello, Blanche Louise. "An Examination of Selected Teaching Strategies to Test Their Effectiveness in the Teaching of Writing." *DAI* 47 (March 1987): 3343A.

Experimental strategies favorably affected writing development but showed little influence on writing apprehension.

1230. Oyler, Kathryn. "Using Film to Write." *UEJ* (1987): 61–64.

Describes a method of integrating film and television with writing instruction. Students write novelizations of films, film scripts, and episodes for television shows.

1231. Peyton, Joy Kreeft. "Literacy through Written Instruction." *Passage* 2 (Spring 1986): 24–29.

Discusses how dialogue journals work to promote student-centered writing activities that encourage the natural development of literacy skills. Also available as ERIC ED 273 097.

1232. Pope, Mike. "The Finger of the Moon." *EJ* 76 (February 1987): 78–80.

Poses questions about an educational system that teaches students "linguistics, descriptions of language," but tells students "they are being taught reading and writing."

1233. Quest, Zeba. "Comfort Zone." *ET* 18 (Summer 1987): 42–43.

Advocates using contemporary music as a way of establishing a good first impression in the English class.

1234. Raum, Elizabeth. "The Magic of Conferences." *WLN* 11 (March 1987): 11–13.

The writing conference is an effective method of helping students become responsible for their writing.

1235. Reither, James A. "What Do We Mean by 'Collaborative Writing' (and What Difference Might It Make)?" Paper presented at the CCCC Convention, Atlanta, March 1987. ERIC ED 280 084. 12 pages

Finds value in defining collaborative writing as the process of gathering information to contribute to a group project.

1236. Roen, Duane. "Learning to Bunt/Learning to Write." *JBC* 24 (Winter 1987): 65–72.

Effective writing teaching, like effective baseball coaching, involves showing the novice exactly how to do the task on the pressure-free practice field.

1237. Roen, Duane H. "Writing Assignments That Work." *JTW* 6 (Spring 1987): 31–40.

Examines five features of successful writing assignments in elementary, secondary, and college courses.

1238. Roth, Robert G. "Addressing Unknown Readers: The Expanded Other Meets the Self." Paper presented at the CCCC Convention, Atlanta, March 1987. ERIC ED 281 203. 11 pages

Students should be encouraged to recognize that when writers write for an unknown audience their sense of audience evolves during revisions.

1239. Sanders, Donald A., and Judith A. Sanders. "Capturing the Magic of Metaphor." *Learning* 15 (February 1987): 37–39.

Describes seven steps for using metaphor as a teaching tool to improve student reading and writing.

1240. Schuster, Charles I., comp. *Trends and Issues in English Instruction, 1987.* Urbana. Ill.: NCTE, 1987. ERIC ED 281 200. 22 pages

Prepared by the directors of seven NCTE commissions, this report summarizes current trends in the teaching of English.

1241. Schuster, Edgar H. "Students against the Text: An Opportunity for Divergent Thinking in the Classroom." *PCTEB* 55 (April 1987): 3–12.

Outlines strategies for using textbooks' "inescapable deficiencies" as a pedagogical device.

1242. Shook, Ronald. *The Odd Couple: How We Teach and How They Learn.* Urbana, Ill.: ERIC/RCS, 1982. ERIC ED 281 198. 12 pages

Argues that writing instructors can best facilitate the growth of student writers by increasing writing practice and making it cross disciplinary.

1243. Shor, Ira, ed. *Friere for the Classroom: A Sourcebook for Liberatory Teaching.* Upper Montclair, N.J.: Boynton/Cook, 1987. 256 pages

An anthology of essays collected from professional journals and written by teachers using Freire's methods in their classrooms.

1244. Shurbutt, Sylvia Bailey. "Student Peer Evaluation: A Practical Approach." *ArEB* 29 (Spring 1987): 22–24.

Presents suggestions for helping students develop the skills necessary to work successfully in peer evaluation groups. Includes a sample peer evaluation checklist.

1245. Staton, Jana, Joy Kreeft Peyton, and Shelley Gutstein, eds. *Dialogue* 3 (December 1985–December 1986): 1–50.

Four issues of this journal, available as ERIC ED 279 202, focus on second and native language teaching. Discusses employing journals in reading and writing classes.

1246. Stewart, Donald C. "Some Thoughts on Arrangement." *JAC* 7 (1987): 92–100.

We teach arrangement as the imposition of preexisting forms, a method that conflicts both with the flexibility of classical rhetoric and with liberating classroom philosophies.

1247. Strackbein, Deanna, and Montague Tillman. "The Joy of Journals—With Reservations." *JR* 31 (October 1987): 28–33.

Describes the advantages and disadvantages of using journals.

1248. Strong, William. *Creative Approaches to Sentence Combining.* Theory and Research into Practice. Urbana, Ill.: NCTE, ERIC/RCS, 1986. 85 pages

Argues that sentence combining serves many more purposes than previously thought for improving syntactic fluency, decision making, analysis and synthesis, as well as for teaching content. Describes many approaches and gives guidelines for creating effective exercises.

1249. Suhor, Charles. "Two Problems in the Teaching of English." *Trends and Issues in Education* 3 (January 1987): 73–99.

Focuses on the problems of selecting literature and learning grammar. Abstracted as ERIC ED 281 901 but available as ERIC ED 281 897.

1250. Troyka, Lynn Quitman. "Help Me Help You." *ET* 18 (Spring 1987): 4–7.

Teaching at various levels, the author has tried to adapt her methods to the individual student and to appreciate differences in learning styles.

1251. Walborn, Eric D. *"Imitatio* Revisited: Its Theoretical and Practical Implications into the Twenty-First Century." Paper presented at the CCCC Convention, Atlanta, March 1987. ERIC ED 281 202. 12 pages

Argues that imitation is an effective tool in student-centered writing instruction. Explains that imitation does not violate the tenets of the new rhetoric.

1252. Walker, Laurie. "Grammar as a Hostage to Ideology." Paper presented at the Canadian Society for the Study of Education, Hamilton, Canada, June 1987. ERIC ED 284 253. 26 pages

Argues that those who favor teaching grammar can be treated as "fundamentalists," believing that textbooks contain the holy word, as with the Bible or Koran.

1253. Walshe, R. D. "The Learning Power of Writing." *EJ* 76 (October 1987): 22–27.

Argues that writing, although commonly undervalued as a mere tool of expression, is "learning at its best. . . a thinking-out, a discovery procedure."

1254. Weiser, Irwin. "Better Writing through Rhetorically Based Assignments." *JTW* 6 (Spring 1987): 41–48.

Advocates developing assignments that "require students to explore the relationship among writer, reader, subject, and language."

1255. Wells, M. Cyrene. "Show Students How to Bring Writing to Life by Adding Detail." *Learning* 16 (October 1987): 40–41.

Encourages students to revise by adding specific detail to texts.

1256. Westergard, Brent. "Creating Characters for Stories." *UEJ* (1987): 65–68.

Describes a writing unit stressing character development, which may be useful in motivating students to write short stories.

1257. White, Edward M., and Linda G. Polin. *Research in Effective Teaching of Writing, Volumes I and II: Final Project Report.* Washington, D.C.: NIE, 1986. ERIC ED 275 007. 604 pages

Analyzes the comparative effectiveness of postsecondary writing programs at 19 California state universities.

See also 124, 891, 1733

4.2 HIGHER EDUCATION

4.2.1 DEVELOPMENTAL WRITING

1258. Anderson, Kristine F. "Using a Spelling Survey to Develop Basic Writers' Linguistic Awareness: A Response to Ann B. Dobie [*JBW* 5 (Fall 1986)]." *JBW* 6 (Fall 1987): 72–78.

Argues that effective spelling instruction must be based on current research recognizing "English orthography as a complex but highly regular writing system."

1259. Baxter, Barbara. "Basic Writing: Breaking through the Barriers of Apathy and Fear." *SCETCJ* 20 (Fall 1987): 4–6.

Addresses the needs of basic writers.

1260. Boserra, Wendy Colby. "Effects of Word Processors upon the Writing Processes of Basic Writers." *DAI* 48 (July 1987): 34A.

Students devoted time and energy to revising and editing on word processors, but they did not do more prewriting than usual.

1261. Brown, Stuart, Zita Ignham, and Duane H. Roen. "Reading-Writing Connections: College Freshmen Basic Writers' Apprehension and Achievement." Paper presented at the CCCC Convention, New Orleans, March 1986. ERIC ED 274 965. 18 pages

Confidence in writing is enhanced by understanding the connection between reading and writing and by equipping students with composing strategies.

1262. Coats, Sandra. "Teaching the Use of Computers." *JDEd* 10 (January 1987): 2–5.

Presents a three-step method of teaching the logical relationships underlying connectors by focusing on coordinate and subordinate sentences within paragraph structures.

1263. Coleman, Eve B. *An Ethnographic Description of the Development of Basic Writers' Revision Skills.* Urbana, Ill.: ERIC/RCS, 1984. ERIC ED 283 151. 42 pages

Studies the learning logs of five basic writing students, finding that revision skill improves with monitoring.

1264. Coleman, Eve B. "Response Groups as a Source of Data for Classroom-Based Research." Paper presented at the CCCC Convention, Atlanta, March 1987. ERIC ED 281 192. 21 pages

Peer response groups in a basic college writing class facilitated greater understanding of student growth.

1265. Curtis, Marcia S., and Sara L. Stelzner. "A Questioning Voice: Instructors and Basic Writers Interact." *JBW* 6 (Spring 1987): 55–64.

Presents a procedure and rationale for using "one-on-one workshops" to help students become "strong writers" and "strong readers of their own texts."

1266. Dean, Sharon L. "Cognitive Development through Synthesis." *Leaflet* 86 (Winter 1987): 2–7.

Gives examples of writing assignments that require both simple and complex synthesis.

1267. Doby, Francine S. "Integrating Summary Writing with Reading Comprehension: Rhetorical Forms." *DAI* 47 (February 1987): 2926A.

Summary writing by underprepared college freshmen enhanced their reading comprehension.

1268. Duffey, Suellynn Kay. "Basic Writers: Case Studies of Revision and Concept Formation." *DAI* 48 (November 1987): 1136A.

Demonstrates how revision and thinking interact. Students use personal experience essays to develop such processes as abstracting, generalizing, inferring, and synthesizing.

1269. Etchison, Craig. *A Comparative Study of the Quality and Syntax of Compositions by First-Year College Students Using Handwriting and Word Processing.* Urbana, Ill.: ERIC/RCS, 1984. ERIC ED 282 215. 33 pages

Studies 200 freshmen enrolled in process-centered classrooms, finding that those using computers achieved significantly greater gains in writing quality and in words produced.

1270. Ganz, Alice. "Finding the Writer in a Learning-Disabled Child." *EngR* 38 (1987): 2–3.

Discusses ways to teaching learning-disabled children how to write.

1271. George, Sharon. "The Importance of Reading in Writing." *ET* 18 (Summer 1987): 46–47.

Discusses how to use adolescent novels to teach reading and writing simultaneously.

1272. Gilbert, Janet R. "Patterns and Possibilities for Basic Writers." *JBW* 6 (Fall 1987): 37–52.

Reviews research on the lexicogrammar of spoken and written texts, lists focal points of instruction, shows pattern use in case studies, and describes "Lexigram" for analyzing patterns.

1273. Gorrell, Donna. "Freedom to Write—Through Imitation." *JBW* 6 (Fall 1987): 53–59.

Argues that teaching imitation to basic writers is an effective way of "teaching form and sense of language while encouraging . . . creativity."

1274. Gould, Christopher. "Literature in the Basic Writing Course: A Bibliographic Survey." *CE* 49 (September 1987): 558–574.

Argues for the place of literature in basic writing courses and provides a bibliographic and survey discussion of available sources.

1275. Hayes, Christopher C. "Teaching Basic Reading to Basic Writers." *JR* 31 (November 1987): 100–108.

Finds that a course integrating reading and writing activities improved students' reading skills.

1276. Horning, Alice S. "The Trouble with Writing Is the Trouble with Reading." *JBW* 6 (Spring 1987): 36–47.

Presents two case studies suggesting that specific syntax and semantic difficulties in writing are related to reading problems in syntax and comprehension among basic writers.

1277. Hunter, Paul, and Nadine Pearce. "Basic Writers: The Writing Process and Written Products." *TETYC* 14 (December 1987): 252–264.

Argues that properly structured assignments reduce "premature" editing. Basic writers can be helped in moving from reflexive to extensive writing.

1278. Iovino, Suzanne F. "The Effect of Dominant Hemisphere Processing Modes and Notetaking Strategy on the Comprehension and Retention of Academically Underprepared College Readers." *DAI* 48 (September 1987): 617A.

Concludes that outlining aided academically underprepared college readers to achieve greater immediate comprehension, while networking improved students' abilities to retain information over time.

1279. Jaskulek, Margaret. "A Comparison Study of College Essays Composed at Two Levels of Proficiency to Determine Which Features of Written English Characterize Success at Each Level." *DAI* 47 (February 1987): 2987A.

Establishes features that differentiate remedial and developmental writers. Most important are essay and paragraph unity and organization, thesis demonstration, and development.

1280. Jolly, Peggy. "Meeting the Challenge of Developmental Writers." *TETYC* 14 (February 1987): 32–40.

Argues that academically disadvantaged students operate at low levels of developmental cognition. Teachers must diagnose individual problems and teach inductively. Writing should be taught as process and evaluated objectively.

1281. Larson, Deborah Aldrich. "Snow White and Language Awareness." *JTW* 6 (Spring 1987): 171–179.

Uses drama in a writing workshop to demonstrate appropriate shifts in dialect. Students learned about tone, style, word choice, and sentence revision.

1282. Lavanna, Elizabeth M. "A Self-Paced Approach to Improved Basic Communication Skills (Workbook)." *DAI* 48 (December 1987): 1344A.

College communication students using a remedial workbook scored significantly higher on a standardized test of language skills than those who did not.

1283. Lesnick, Henry. "Avoiding Failure: Achieving Success for College Students with Dyslexia-Related Problems—A Developmental Language Program." *CJCJ* 57 (June–July 1987): 42–44.

Recommends screening for dyslexia among low-skilled readers and writers. Suggests appropriate instructional strategies for language problems.

1284. LoPresti, Gene Frank. "Four Basic Skills Students: A Naturalistic Study of Reading/Writing Models They Bring to College." *DAI* 48 (September 1987): 585A.

Describes how complex variables interact to create individual and unpredictable models of reading and writing for poor readers and writers.

1285. Martinez, Joseph G. R., and Nancy C. Martinez. "Reconsidering Cognition and the Basic Writer: A Response to Myra Kogen [*JBW* 5 (Spring 1986)]." *JBW* 6 (Fall 1987): 79–82.

Argues that cognitive theory may be of limited use in basic writing research. Disputes evidence that basic writers are cognitively immature.

1286. McAllister, Carole, and Richard Louth. "The Effect of Word Processing on the Revision of Basic Writers." Paper presented at the CCCC Convention, Atlanta, March 1987. ERIC ED 281 232. 25 pages

Reports on a study of 100 basic writers, finding that word processing raised the quality of their revising.

1287. McKoski, Martin M., and Lynne C. Hahn. "Basic Forms, Basic Writers." *JDEd* 11 (November 1987): 6–12.

Profiles three types of basic writers and suggests strategies for teaching basic conventions that differentiate speech from writing.

1288. Moberg, Goran George. "Remedial Writing on Computers: Evaluation by Students and Faculty of a Pilot Project, Fall 1985." *CC* 4 (August 1987): 35–51.

Describes the genesis of a program of word processing used in remedial classes. Includes questionnaire responses by students and faculty comments.

1289. Moss, Robert F. "Plumbing the Surfaces: The Value of Frivolous Subjects in Developmental English." *EngR* 38 (1987): 17–20.

Explores how using contemporary soap operas and comedies encourages student learning in writing courses.

1290. Moss, Robert F. "Using Current Events in Basic Writing." *JGE* 38 (1987): 301–315.

Describes and gives examples of news stories used in a developmental writing course at Hunter College. Suggests using topics of greatest interest to students.

1291. Moss, Robert F. "Using Television News in Basic Writing Classes." *JBW* 6 (Spring 1987): 65–77.

Recommends using broadcast journalism "as the pedagogical framework" for coursework designed to improve students' analytical and critical abilities.

1292. Moxley, Joseph M. "The Uninvolved = Poor Writers." *CollT* 35 (Winter 1987): 16–18.

Presents five case studies showing a range of college students' attitudes toward writing. Suggests implications for understanding the perceptions of inexperienced writers.

1293. Neverow-Turk, Vara S., and David F. Turk. "Teaching Utopian Literature: Applying Mikhail Bakhtin's Theories in the Writing Class." Paper presented at the NCTE Convention, San Antonio, November 1986. ERIC ED 279 009. 19 pages

Applies concepts of Bakhtin when assigning research papers to inexperienced student writers.

1294. Noguchi, Rei R. "Transformational-Generative Syntax and the Teaching of Sentence Mechanics." *JBW* 6 (Fall 1987): 26–36.

Shows how students can use tag-formation and yes-no question rules to correct mechanical errors.

1295. Oram, Virginia White. "Tutoring the Remedial College Student." *ArEB* 29 (Spring 1987): 8–9.

Explains the need for tutoring and gives suggestions for conducting sessions.

1296. Porter, Albert H. "Analysis of Gender and Age-Based Disparities in Basic Skills Proficiencies of Community College Freshmen and in Longitudinal Outcomes for Those Remediated in English and Mathematics." *DAI* 47 (February 1987): 2863A.

A study of 2178 students showed that remediation reversed significant disadvantages in English preparation.

1297. Posey, Evelyn Joyce. "The Writer's Tool: A Study of Microcomputer Word Processing to Improve the Writing of Basic Writers." *DAI* 48 (July 1987): 39A.

Students using word processing were more motivated to write and generated more drafts than students who did not use microcomputers. However, word processing did not improve writing abilities or increase revision.

1298. Rainey, Kenneth T. "Misdirection in the Relation between Writing and Cognitive Development." Paper presented at the CCCC Convention, Atlanta, March 1987. ERIC ED 281 213. 20 pages

A writing exercise developed at Memphis State University encouraged students to compare a reader's response with an author's intentions for a given text.

1299. Roueche, John E., George A. Baker, III, and Suanne D. Roueche. "Open Door or Revolving Door? Open Access and the Community College." *CJCJ* 57 (April–May 1987): 22–26.

Asserts that the promise of open access will not bring about true opportunity unless literacy teaching is improved and the curriculum reshaped.

1300. Rubin, Donald L., and William M. Dodd. *Talking into Writing: Exercises for Basic Writers.* Urbana, Ill.: NCTE, ERIC/RCS, 1987. 63 pages

Argues that too much emphasis is placed on grammar. Recommends using oral communication exercises from an oral-based culture that depends heavily on dialogue rather than the extended monologues required in writing assignments. Discusses role-switching, peer questioning, "topic sculpting," and forensic discussion. Covers writing across the curriculum.

1301. Rubin, Lois. "A Tagmemic Approach to Writing about Literature." *EngR* 38 (1987): 13–17.

Explores the cognitive and affective benefits of using tagmemics in remedial writing courses.

1302. Schor, Sandra. "An Alternative to Revising: The Proleptic Grasp." *JBW* 6 (Spring 1987): 48–54.

Presents a procedure and rationale for engaging students in "the writing of the parts [of essays] always strengthened by the crisscrossing supports of the partially seen whole."

1303. Sessions, Jill L. "Teaching Basic Writers to Use Word Processing: Problems and Promises." *CAC* 1 (Spring 1987): 190–195.

Suggests that having basic writers maintain an interactive journal is fun but ultimately does not improve writing.

1304. Snyder, William C. "Ideas in Practice: A Sentence-Revising Format for Basic Writers." *JDEd* 11 (September 1987): 20–22.

Describes Diagnosis and Revision with Clues (DRWC), a method for developing students' abilities to practice effective revision.

1305. Tighe, Mary Ann. "Reducing Writing Apprehension in English Classes." Paper presented at the NCTE Spring Conference, Louisville, March 1987. ERIC ED 281 196. 18 pages

Reports on a study of how a process writing course reduced writing apprehension for 13 of 16 students at an Alabama university.

1306. Timmons, Theresa Cullen. "Marking Errors: A Simple Strategy." *TETYC* 14 (February 1987): 18–21.

Using highlighters created marked improvement in developmental students' ability to proofread their work. Describes a dictation technique.

1307. Trimmer, Joseph F. "Basic Skills, Basic Writing, Basic Research." *JBW* 6 (Spring 1987): 3–9.

Summarizes a survey of basic writing programs in U.S. colleges and universities and discusses interviews with editors choosing basic writing textbooks for major publishers.

1308. Villanueva, Victor. "Intonation, Mazes, and Other Oral Influences on the Revision Decisions of Traditional and Basic Writers in Freshman College Composition Courses." *DAI* 47 (February 1987): 2931A.

Analyzes transcriptions of peer editing sessions. Breakdowns in the flow of speech reveal the inability of basic writers to integrate oral and literal strategies.

1309. Weiser, Irwin. "Developing a Basic Writing Program: Addressing Error Individually." *ArEB* 29 (Spring 1987): 42–47.

This program stresses rhetorical skills in class and assigns students individualized grammar and mechanics work to complete during tutoring sessions.

1310. Whitt, Lena Massey. "The Effects of Sentence-Combining Instruction on the Growth of Syntactic Fluency in Adult Basic Writers." *DAI* 48 (November 1987): 1139A.

Concludes that "even though verbal fluency increases, syntactic growth does not necessarily follow." A specific method addressing sentence structure problems must be a major objective of instruction.

1311. Wilhoit, Stephen. "Discourse-Based Interviews and Student Punctuation Strategies." *IE* 11 (Fall 1987): 24–26.

Urges making students' tacit knowledge explicit and giving additional instruction on an individual basis.

1312. Wolcott, Willa, and Dianne Buhr. "Attitude as It Affects Developmental Writers' Essays." *JBW* 6 (Fall 1987): 3–15.

Summarizes an empirical study indicating that "writing improvement seems linked to positive writing attitudes." Discusses the study's implications for basic writing instruction.

See also 7, 94, 425, 893, 1026, 1335, 1347, 1368, 1372, 1383, 1395, 1410, 1636, 1672, 1677, 1762

4.2.2 FRESHMAN COMPOSITION

1313. Anson, Chris M. *Exploring the Dimensions of Purpose in College Writing*. Urbana, Ill.: ERIC/RCS, 1985. ERIC ED 274 964. 31 pages

Interviews with four freshman writers about their performances on tasks varied for audience, mode, and focus show two tendencies, either "rhetorically limited" or "rhetorically flexible" purposes.

1314. Benesch, Sarah. "Word Processing in English as a Second Language: A Case Study of Three Nonnative College Students." Paper presented at the CCCC Convention, Atlanta, March 1987. ERIC ED 218 383. 11 pages

Studies the effects of microcomputers on the writing processes of three nonnative college students. Data include drafts, journals, interviews, field notes, and videotapes.

1315. Blake, Robert W. "Reading Literature: Integrating Close Reading, Responding, and Writing—A Model for Teaching." *EngR* 38 (1987): 25–29.

Examines the importance of teaching literature with writing.

1316. Brooke, Robert. "Underlife and Writing Instruction." *CCC* 38 (May 1987): 141–153.

Relates writing instruction to Goffman's social theory. Claims that instruction should be a disruptive form of underlife that empowers students to assume roles other than contained ones.

1317. Brown, Carol Smullen. "A Tutorial Procedure for Enhancing the Reading Comprehension of College Students." *DAI* 47 (April 1987): 3719A.

Reports on case studies of five students. Think-aloud reading protocols yielded information about thinking processes while reading.

1318. Buckley, William K. "The Rise of the Corporate Mind in Composition Teaching." Paper presented at the International Conference on the Teaching of English, Ottawa, May 1986. ERIC ED 280 069. 13 pages

Discusses how universities have abandoned literature for skill-oriented writing. By making students more employable, they have abandoned critical thinking.

1319. Burley, Anne, and Deborah Shaller. "Summaries in the Composition Class." *MarylandEJ* 21 (Spring 1987): 43–50.

Students write summaries of readings to learn careful reading and to draw attention to a writer's strategies. Provides context and examples.

1320. Clark, John. "Hopeless Case: *Hopefully* on a Roll." *IE* 10 (Spring 1987): 17.

Condemns the meaningless use of *hopefully*.

1321. Coe, Richard M. "Public Doublespeak— Let's Stop It." *EQ* 19 (Fall 1986): 236–238.

Presents suggestions for working in the classroom to eradicate doublespeak.

1322. Comprone, Joseph J. "The Function of Text in a Dialogic Writing Course." Paper presented at the Kentucky Philological Association, Louisville, March 1987. ERIC ED 284 239. 29 pages

Uses Bakhtin, Burke, Hirsch, and Iser to sketch a dialogic model of transmitting literacy at the college level.

1323. Corder, Jim W. "Occasion and Need in Writing: An Annotated Essay." *FEN* 16 (Winter–Spring 1988): 3–4, 10.

Suggests that occasion and need might supply a new taxonomy for types of composition courses.

1324. Coulter, Catherine Ann. "Writing with Word Processors: Effects on Cognitive Development, Revision, and Writing Quality." *DAI* 47 (January 1987): 2551A.

A study of 62 college freshmen determined that word processing had no effect on writ-

ing quality or revision strategies, but some possible effect on cognitive development.

1325. Cramer, Carmen. "The Trinity Turned Wholly: A Transactional Analysis of Communication with Suggestions for Adulthood." *FEN* 16 (Winter/Spring 1988): 19–23.

Explains voice and audience problems in composition courses in terms of immature child/parent communication. Suggests that students have difficulty "speaking" a self.

1326. Dean, Robert L. "Cognitive, Pedagogic, and Financial Implications of Word Processing in a Freshman English Program: A Report on Two Years of a Longitudinal Study." Paper presented at the Association for Institutional Research, Orlando, June 1986. ERIC ED 280 384. 22 pages

Reports on two years of microcomputer application in a college freshman English program. Studies six instructors and six control and experimental sections.

1327. Dean, Robert L. "Preparing for Educational Technologies: An Empirical Evaluation of the Cognitive, Pedagogical, and Financial Implications of Electronic Text Processing in a University Freshman English Composition Process." *DAI* 48 (November 1987): 1124A.

Concludes that the experimental method did not significantly improve writing skills and was "more consumptive of human and capital resources."

1328. Devet, Bonnie. "Bringing Back More Figures of Speech into Composition." *JTW* 6 (Fall–Winter 1987): 293–304.

Traces the history of figurative language in teaching composition. Advocates teaching nine rhetorical devices: anaphora, epistrophe, climax, anadiplosis, rhetorical questions, polysyndeton, asyndeton, antimetabole, and puns.

1329. Draheim, Marilyn Elaine. "A Study of the Effects of Directed Reading-Thinking Activity and Conceptual Mapping Instruction on Reading and Writing Exposition." *DAI* 47 (January 1987): 2489A.

Compares traditional instructional approaches with directed reading-thinking activities and conceptual mapping instruction to study their effects on college students' abilities to recall high level ideas and to improve holistic scores.

1330. Ebner, Emanuel C. "Alternatell." *ETC* 44 (Summer 1987): 171–173.

Presents a procedure that reassembles known observations by reordering or supplementing information. This helps students see multiple explanations of an event without taking an adversarial stance.

1331. Gardner, Ruth, and Jo McGinnis. *Computers in College Composition: A Comparative Study of Ten Schools.* Urbana, Ill.: ERIC/RCS, 1986. ERIC ED 284 241. 131 pages

In 14 chapters, reports on a survey of 10 college composition programs using computers.

1332. Gaskins, Jake. "Teaching as Parenting: or, 'More Die of Heartbreak.' "*FEN* 16 (Winter/Spring 1988): 16–19.

Explores the idea that composition classes using inquiry and natural process methods assist students to mature.

1333. Griffin, Susan. "The Internal Voice of Invention: Shaftesbury's Soliloquy." Paper presented at the CCCC Convention, Atlanta, March 1987. ERIC ED 282 249. 10 pages

Shaftesbury's diaries offer a suggestion for writers: talk to yourself.

1334. Groden, Suzy, Eleanor Kutz, and Vivian Zamel. "Students as Ethnographers: Investigating Language Use as a Way to Learn to Use the Language." *WI* 6 (Spring–Summer 1987): 132–140.

Describes an experiment in which college students investigated the ways language is used in their everyday lives and wrote letters to one of the researchers about their findings.

1335. Haas, Teri Sinclair. "A Case Study of Peer Tutor's Writing Conferences with Stu-

dents: Tutors' Roles and Conversations about Composing." *DAI* 47 (June 1987): 4309A.

Describes the focus and subjects of conferences between students and peer tutors. Also analyzes the mutable roles of each member of the dyad.

1336. Hale, Helena. *What's Happening in Freshman Composition in the California Two-Year Colleges: 48 Interviews.* Urbana, Ill.: ERIC/RCS, 1980. ERIC ED 275 350. 150 pages

Summarizes interviews conducted in 1979 and 1980 with 48 freshman composition teachers at 11 two-year colleges.

1337. Hansen, Kristine. "Relationships between Expert and Novice Performance in Disciplinary Writing and Reading." Paper presented at the CCCC Convention, Atlanta, March 1987. ERIC ED 283 220. 14 pages

Describes a freshman course designed to explore the discourse conventions of various disciplines.

1338. Harkins, Patrick. "What Makes Writing Good? An Assignment That Clarifies Values." *IE* 11 (Winter 1987): 15–18.

Students write and argue for their own theories of what makes writing good.

1339. Hawisher, Gail E. "The Effects of Word Processing on the Revision Strategies of College Freshmen." *RTE* 21 (May 1987): 145–159.

Advanced college freshmen did not revise more extensively and successfully with a computer than with pen and typewriter.

1340. Hernadi, Paul. "The Aims of Discourse Revisited: Reading and Writing beyond Genre." *BADE* 88 (Winter 1987): 27–29.

Sees value and genre as key coordinates of all texts. Finds that similarities of aim—to instruct, to delight, to move—link texts composed with texts studied.

1341. Hood, Michael D. "Teaching Freshman Composition: The Language of Oppression Versus the Language of Liberation." Paper presented at the CCCC Convention, New Orleans, March 1986. ERIC ED 278 045. 20 pages

> Condemns mechanical literacy and favors critical literacy. Discusses the advantages of teaching critical literacy.

1342. Hulce, Jim. "Dewriting: Breaking into Writing." *ExEx* 32 (Spring 1987): 7–9.

> Presents an exercise in which students strip details and descriptions from a passage and then "remodel" the work.

1343. Hynes, Peter. "Writing across the Official Languages: Bilingualism and Rhetoric in the Canadian College." *EQ* 20 (Spring 1987): 52–61.

> Addresses the challenge of teaching both English and French composition in Canadian universities, focusing on divergences between the rhetorical theories involved.

1344. Jelinek, Carol. "Discussion and Separation: Useful Techniques during the Writing Conference." *EngR* 38 (1987): 22–25.

> Discusses goals for teacher-student writing conferences.

1345. Jenkins, Ruth. "Responding to Student Writing: Written Dialogues on Writing and Revision." *WI* 6 (Winter 1987): 82–86.

> Describes an experiment in which students wrote responses about the "most surprising and beneficial" teacher's comments on their final papers.

1346. Jeremiah, Milford A. "Using Television News and Documentaries for Writing Instruction." Paper presented at the CCCC Convention, Atlanta, March 1987. ERIC ED 280 031. 13 pages

> Discusses the use of television news and documentaries in high school and college essay writing instruction.

1347. Karbach, Joan. "Using Toulmin's Model of Argumentation." *JTW* 6 (Spring 1987): 81–92.

> Reviews the structure of warrants, grounds, and claims. The model is effec-tive because of its flexibility, value as a heuristic, and focus on audience.

1348. Kari, Daven M. "A Cliche a Day Keeps the Gray Away." *TETYC* 14 (December 1987): 265–270.

> An author at play in the fields of the Word makes a case for cliches, including techniques for creative modification.

1349. Karis, William. "*TWI* Resource File: Contrasting Proofreading and Revision." *WI* 6 (Winter 1987): 97.

> Describes a class activity: first students mark mechanical errors in an "intentionally mangled" text, then rewrite a passage with serious content errors and discuss the difference.

1350. Keller, Robert D. "Robert Frost and the Teaching of Summary, Synthesis, Critical Analysis, and Research." *Leaflet* 86 (Winter 1987): 38–44.

> Describes a course that uses Frost's poetry to stimulate students' thinking and writing.

1351. Kern, Alfred. "BASIC Writing: The Student as Programmer." *BADE* 86 (Spring 1987): 4–7.

> Argues that students who write computer programs actively engage in thinking and problem solving and learn to be better writers.

1352. Lang, Frederick K. "Power and Light without Electricity." *FEN* 15 (Winter 1987): 2–4.

> A description of a composition course that uses literature and whole texts.

1353. Lieberman, David. "The Significance of Significance in Structure." Paper presented at the CCCC Convention, Atlanta, March 1987. ERIC ED 284 290. 13 pages

> Argues that instruction in coherence is not as effective as stressing personal significance.

1354. Liebman-Kleine, JoAnne. "The Student as Researcher: An Ethnographic Study of

Contrastive Rhetoric." Paper presented at the CCCC Convention, Atlanta, March 1987. ERIC ED 281 194. 37 pages

Students in two freshman composition classes, one ESL and one native, studied cultural differences and similarities in the production of discourse.

1355. Little, Sherry Burgus. "The Computer as Audience: Using Homer, a Text-Analysis Program." *CC* 4 (April 1987): 106–120.

Describes the experience of using Homer with students and shows examples of Homer's comments on student papers.

1356. Logsdon, Loren. "To Make a Virtue of Necessity: A Creative Way to Teach Sentences." *IlEB* 74 (Spring 1987): 44–51.

Describes a method for studying sentences in a complete writing context. Forty or 50 sentences to be edited tell a story. Gives samples.

1357. Lott, Clarinda Harriss. "Alternative Shapes in Expository Writing." Paper presented at the CCCC Convention, Atlanta, March 1987. ERIC ED 282 248. 9 pages

Advocates personal writing and experimentation in structure, arguing that conventional forms reflect "male" concepts of order.

1358. Lovejoy, Kim B. "The Gricean Model: A Revising Rubric." *JTW* 6 (Spring 1987): 9–18.

Four conversational maxims—quantity, quality, relation, and manner—force attention on audience as part of a cooperative principle useful in revising.

1359. Lynn, Steven. "Philosophies of Grading." *JDEd* 10 (January 1987): 26–27.

Discusses four common philosophies of grading writing and suggests an "ideal" orientation to strive for.

1360. Malachowski, Ann Marie. "Individualized Assignments Combine Writing and Learning." *EngR* 38 (1987): 7–11.

Presents a variety of developmentally based writing assignments.

1361. Marcus, Stephen. "Getting On-Line: Computers and Writing Instruction." *CJCJ* 58 (October–November 1987): 38–39.

Presents advice for changing faculty and student attitudes toward word processing.

1362. Marsella, Joy, and Roger Whitlock. "An English Department Reexamines Itself: Becoming a Department of Literacy." Paper presented at the CCCC Convention, New Orleans, March 1986. ERIC ED 276 042. 14 pages

Proposes an example of departmental curricular change suited to teaching and research on literacy.

1363. Marshall, Thomas. "A Comment on 'The Content of Classroom Writing' [*CE* 48 (September 1986)]." *CE* 49 (November 1987): 834–836.

Argues that Perelman's emphasis on freshman composition as introduction to institutional discourse is limited and should emphasize writing more as self-discovery and social activity.

1364. Martin, Gyde Christine. "Teaching Aesthetic Reading: One More Argument for Literature in the Writing Class." *FEN* 16 (Fall 1987): 17–19.

Describes aesthetic reading (as opposed to reading for content) as a task similar to process writing. Suggests that it should be part of the composition class.

1365. McBride Robinson, Cecelia A. "Peer and Traditional Instruction: A Comparison of the Effectiveness of Peer Tutoring/Editing and Traditional Instruction on the Writing Abilities of Freshman Composition Students." *DAI* 48 (August 1987): 295A.

Pre- and posttest gain scores indicated no treatment differences. However, differences between sexes did exist.

1366. McCullough, Elaine. "Mastery of the English Language; or, Through the Looking

Glass and Back Again." *EngR* 38 (1987): 15–17.

Explores the importance of grammatical errors in student writing.

1367. McGavran, James Holt, Jr. "The Wordsworths and the Writing Process: Towards an Androgynous Rhetoric." *CEAF* 17 (1987): 5–10.

Works by the Wordsworths are useful examples of the writing process and of the ideal of androgyny.

1368. Miller, Peter. "The Class Newsletter." *TWM* 18 (January–February 1987): 8–11.

Presents the class newsletter as a way of teaching developmental writing and freshman composition. Includes numerous examples.

1369. Mullican, James. "Hopefully, Hopefully Isn't Completely Hopeless." *IE* 11 (Winter 1987): 26–27.

Reacts to an article [*IE* 10 (Spring 1987)] disdaining *hopefully* as a sentence modifier. Advocates attention to more meaningful concerns than questions of divided usage.

1370. Mullins, Carolyn J. "On Teaching Writing with PCs." *CAC* 1 (Spring 1987): 172–184.

Reports on the growth, problems, and advantages of the campus-wide microcomputer writing program at Virginia Polytechnic Institute.

1371. Neil, Lynn Riley. "Imitation: Playing with Language." *ExEx* 32 (Spring 1987): 3–5.

Presents an imitation exercise.

1372. Nielson, Christopher. "Language, Politics, Power: Teaching the Pledge of Allegiance." *IE* 11 (Winter 1987): 9–11.

Narrates four steps for teaching concrete diction, the value of close reading, and notions about values, America, and the power of language.

1373. Page, Miriam Dempsey. "Thick Description and a Rhetoric of Inquiry: Freshmen and Their Major Fields." Paper presented at the CCCC Convention, Atlanta, March 1987. ERIC ED 279 020. 20 pages

Discusses a freshman research course in which students investigate their major fields of study or special areas of interest.

1374. Page, Miriam Dempsey. "Thick Description and a Rhetoric of Inquiry: Freshmen and Their Major Fields." *WI* 6 (Spring–Summer 1987): 141–150.

Describes a five-step process in which students explore the complexities and layers of meanings in their major fields, using Clifford Geertz's conception of "thick description."

1375. Perelman, Les. "Les Perelman Responds [to Marshall, *CE* 49 (November 1987)]." *CE* 49 (November 1987): 836–837.

Argues that his purpose is to empower students by analyzing the social context of their discourse.

1376. Pfaffenberger, Bryan. "Word Processing and Text Revision: Interpreting the Empirical Evidence." *CAC* 1 (Winter 1987): 105–118.

Examines the historical development of sequentially displaying information on the computer screen. Suggests that this sequentiality discourages revision.

1377. Porter, James E., and Richard N. Ramsey. "A Philosophy of Composition for a Writing Program: Articulating Composition as a Liberal Art." *JTW* 6 (Spring 1987): 133–154.

Presents an example of a composition instructor's handbook designed to establish coherence in a university writing program.

1378. Porter, Jeffrey. "The Reasonable Reader: Knowledge and Inquiry in Freshman English." *CE* 49 (March 1987): 332–344.

Outlines the role of the enthymeme in students' probing of texts.

1379. Purdy, Dwight. "Dwight Purdy Responds [to Sledd, Reagan, and Clarke, *CE*

49 (September 1987)]." *CE* 49 (September 1987): 593–596.

Responds to criticisms of his article.

1380. Pytlik, Betty P., and David Bergdahl. "Sequenced Writing Assignments." *ExEx* 33 (Fall 1987): 3–5.

Presents a sequence of eight assignments focusing on the family and progressively distancing writers from their subject and audience.

1381. Reid, Louann. "Collaborative Learning: Bridging the Gap between Speaking and Writing." Paper presented at the NCTE Convention, San Antonio, November 1986. ERIC ED 279 000. 17 pages

Outlines seven elements of a classroom climate that contributes to more effective collaborative learning.

1382. Roderick, John M., and Sandra Katz. "Using the Computer to Teach Composition: A Strategy." *Leaflet* 86 (Fall 1987): 13–19.

Describes a pre-college English course that used Multi-mate and the Writing Is Thinking program to help students write for a history course.

1383. Rosen, Joan G. "Problem Solving and Reflective Thinking: John Dewey, Linda Flower, Richard Young." *JTW* 6 (Spring 1987): 69–78.

Finds that Dewey, Flower, and Young advance mutual conclusions: help students solve problems; "become familiar with their own minds and hearts"; have courage for confrontation; and draw conclusions "with integrity, individuality, and imagination."

1384. Rosenthal, Joyce W. "Integrating Word Processing into Freshman Composition." *CAC* 1 (Winter 1987): 119–125.

Reports that having students in freshman English classes write with word processors results in longer, more substantive essays and fewer mechanical errors.

1385. Roth, Audrey J. "Keeping Current: Teaching the New MLA Style." *FlaEJ* 23 (Fall 1987): 31–33.

Points out that in order to keep up with what is current in the profession, English teachers should teach current MLA parenthetical documentation.

1386. Ruszkiewicz, John J. "Assuming Success: The Student Writer as Apprentice." *FEN* 15 (Winter 1987): 13–15.

Discusses reasons for giving students more control in composition courses.

1387. Saunders, Pearl I. *Computer-Assisted Writing Instruction in Public Community Colleges*. Urbana, Ill.: ERIC/RCS, 1986. ERIC ED 274 989. 45 pages

A survey of CAI in community college writing programs shows a lack of interest and support for computers despite access to them.

1388. Saxton, Ruth O. "From the Impersonal to the Personal: A Cognitive Rationale for a Freshman Writing Syllabus." Paper presented at the CCCC Convention, Atlanta, March 1987. ERIC ED 284 285. 12 pages

Offers a rationale for a course at a California women's college in which reading–writing assignments lead to personal writing.

1389. Scheiber, H. J. "Toward a Text-Based Pedagogy in the Freshman Composition Course—With Two Process-Oriented Writing Tasks." *FEN* 15 (Winter 1987): 15–18.

Assumes that the purpose of freshman composition is to instruct in terms of texts and academic tasks. Offers assignments based on whole texts from disciplines.

1390. Schmittauer, Janet Elaine. "Words into Bytes: An Analysis of the Initial Drafting Behaviors of Freshman Composition Students in a Curriculum Focusing on Contemporary American Poetry." *DAI* 48 (November 1987): 1107A.

Describes initial drafting behaviors. Lists 19 reasons for using contemporary American poetry in freshman composition.

1391. Schultz, John. "Locked Apart, Brought Together: The Power of the Speech-Writing Relationship." Paper presented at the CCCC Convention, New Orleans, March 1986. ERIC ED 274 983. 28 pages

Offers several activities using the power of speech to improve college composition.

1392. Schwartz, Mimi. "Developing the Self through Writing." *JTW* 6 (Fall–Winter 1987): 247–258.

Advocates personal writing and rewriting as tools for personal and intellectual growth. Discusses two case studies.

1393. Schwertman, Kathryn. "The Mystery of Misconnecting Agendas." Paper presented at the CCCC Convention, Atlanta, March 1987. ERIC ED 283 212. 15 pages

Suggests that teachers may assume too authoritarian a role in writing conferences.

1394. Shimabukuro, James Norio. "The Effect of Alternate Instructional Sequences on Student Imitation of Model Essay Subjects." *DAI* 47 (June 1987): 4282A.

This study placed 143 college freshmen in TopicFirst, ModelFirst, and NoModel composing gorups. Notes major differences between the ModelFirst and NoModel groups, but negligible differences when comparing other groups.

1395. Shook, Ronald. "If I Were King." *JTW* 6 (Spring 1987): 181–188.

Advocates conferencing, eliminating textbooks, subordinating grammar instruction, and eliminating writing classes so that writing faculty can teach in content classes. Includes an annotated bibliography.

1396. Shurbutt, S. Bailey. "Integration of Classroom Computer Use and the Peer Evaluation Process: Increasing the Level of Composition Proficiency through Student Revision." *WCJ* 8 (Fall–Winter 1987): 35–42.

Explains a rationale and describes a procedure for integrating collaborative writing strategies with computers in college composition courses.

1397. Singleton, Carl. "We Can Never Teach Students to Write If They Can't Use Standard Grammar." *CHE* 33 (20 May 1987): 40–41.

Argues that students cannot express themselves because they lack knowledge of English grammar, punctuation, and usage.

1398. Sledd, James, Sally Reagan, and Reginald D. Clarke. "A Comment on 'Social Construction, Language, and the Authority of Knowledge' and 'A Polemical History of Freshman Composition in Our Time' [*CE* 48 (December 1986)]." *CE* 49 (September 1987): 585–593.

Three letters respond to Bruffee's and Purdy's articles, citing several differences of opinion.

1399. Soven, Margot. "The Conversation Model: A Paradigm for Connecting Freshman Composition to the Disciplines." Paper presented at the CCCC Convention, New Orleans, March 1986. ERIC ED 276 036. 15 pages

Examines Bazerman's model of writing across the curriculum. Includes sample assignments.

1400. Stark, Merritt W., Jr. "Teaching Freshman Composition Using a Word Processor." *CAC* 1 (Winter 1987): 132–137.

Reviews the pros and cons of teaching writing with a word processor.

1401. Stine, Linda J. "Answers and More Questions: A Survey of Computer Use in Composition Instruction." *EQ* 20 (Spring 1987): 26–37.

Reports on a survey to determine what equipment and methods college writing teachers used. Finds little consensus although using computers was generally a positive experience.

1402. Stone, Tom. "Ars Poetica." *JTW* 6 (Spring 1987): 109–115.

> "An allegorical disclaimer of classical syllogistic reasoning."

1403. Stracke, J. Richard, and Sara Snow. "Speaking, Writing, and Performance: An Integrated Approach to the Word." Paper presented at the NCTE Convention, San Antonio, November 1986. ERIC ED 280 018. 11 pages

> Discusses four class projects based on the belief that students and teachers must be conscious of the world.

1404. Strickland, James. "Computer-Tutors and the Freshman Writer: A Protocol Study." Paper presented at the New York Learning Skills Association, Rochester, N.Y., April 1987. ERIC ED 283 198. 22 pages

> A case study of one freshman using a computer invention heuristic.

1405. Summerfield, Judith Fishman. "Narrative Compositions: An Exploration of Narrative in the Teaching of College Composition." *DAI* 47 (February 1987): 2931A.

> Describes the theory and practice of a composition course in which narrative generated all reading and writing assignments. Discusses narrative as both social act and verbal construct.

1406. Swift, Patricia Worrell. "The Effect of Peer Review with Self-Evaluation on Freshman Writing Performance, Retention, and Attitude at Broward Community College." *DAI* 47 (April 1987): 3653A.

> Studies the effects of combining peer review with self-evaluation. Conclusions suggest a need for increased attention to writing process in classrooms.

1407. Teich, Nathaniel. "Rogerian Problem Solving and the Rhetoric of Argumentation." *JAC* 7 (1987): 52–61.

> Denies the existence of Rogerian rhetoric but proposes Rogerian principles to supplement the teaching of policy arguments.

1408. Teichman, Milton, and Marilyn Poris. *Word Processing in the Classroom: Its Effects on Freshman Writers.* Urbana, Ill.: ERIC/RCS, 1985. ERIC ED 276 062. 59 pages

> Using word processing significantly enhanced the writing of college students, reduced writing apprehension, and improved recognition of standard English.

1409. Ulmer, Gregory L. "Textshop for Psychoanalysis: On Deprogramming Freshman Platonists." *CE* 49 (November 1987): 756–770.

> Describes a workshop methodology based on surrealism.

1410. Walker, Carolyn P., and David Elias. "Writing Conference Talk: Factors Associated with High- and Low-Rated Writing Conferences." *RTE* 21 (October 1987): 266–285.

> Concludes that writing conferences are successful when focused on the student, the student's writing, and criteria for success in writing.

1411. Walter, James F. "Reading, the Imagination, and Writing." *BADE* 86 (Spring 1987): 29–33.

> Calls for critical reading of literature as the foundation for an integrated literature and writing curriculum and as a valid response to the cultural crisis.

1412. Ware, Elaine. "Proofreading: A Review of the Literature and Suggestions for Teaching Techniques." *MarylandEJ* 21 (Spring 1987): 63–70.

> Advocates methods that include proofreading as a systematic part of writing, that slow the proofreader down, and that limit the number of steps without oversimplifying.

1413. White, Lana. "A Centuries-Old Dialectic." *JTW* 6 (Spring 1987): 189–193.

> Two vignettes and an expository section highlight the "mechanic" and "organic" views of form in writing.

1414. Whitlock, Roger. "Making Writing Groups Work: Modifying Elbow's Teacherless Writing Group for the Classroom, 1977–1987." Paper presented at the CCCC Convention, Atlanta, March 1987. ERIC ED 284 284. 9 pages

Offers suggestions for structuring peer feedback in composition courses.

1415. Wilcox, Lance. "Time Lines in the Composing of Narratives: A Graphic Aid to Organization." *WI* 6 (Spring–Summer 1987): 162–173.

Illustrates the use of a horizontal time line with vertical lines of varying lengths to help students organize narrative essays.

1416. Willey, R. J. "Audience Awareness: Methods and Madness." Paper presented at the CCCC Convention, New Orleans, March 1986. ERIC ED 276 007. 24 pages

Presents methods for teaching audience awareness.

1417. Young, Thomas. "Writing and Riding." *IE* 11 (Fall 1987): 22–23.

Argues that both writing and riding are skills that need practice, analysis, and experts to emulate.

1418. Zeiger, William. "A Dialectical Model for College Composition." *FEN* 16 (Fall 1987): 14–16.

Proposes a dialectical model for freshman essay writing that stimulates students to incorporate opposing viewpoints into their thinking.

See also 43, 265, 321, 435, 716, 882, 889, 1117, 1311, 1419, 1431, 1463, 1473, 1542, 1588, 1598, 1600, 1640, 1660, 1674, 1689, 1700, 1729, 1742

4.2.3 ADVANCED COMPOSITION

1419. Cambridge, Barbara. "What Do Students Talk about When They Talk about Writing?" *IE* 11 (Winter 1987): 4–8.

Advocates pedagogical changes based on students' analysis of their own writing.

1420. Holley, Marie Frances Bruno. "I. Rationale for a Woman-Centered Composition Course; II. *The Man Who Made Teeth.*" *DAI* 47 (June 1987): 4310A.

Part one proposes a women-only writing workshop and describes the resulting creative freedom. Part two is a collection of original short stories.

1421. Mulderig, Gerald. "Defining Advanced Composition." *JTW* 6 (Spring 1987): 117–125.

Defines advanced composition as "a course in understanding audience and rhetorical situation," which receive little attention in freshman composition courses.

1422. Ronald, Kate. "The Politics of Teaching Professional Writing." *JAC* 7 (1987): 23–30.

Explores the contradiction between teaching writing as a way of knowing and as a job skill. Argues for including writing in professional courses.

1423. Stay, Byron L. "Satire in the Creative Writing Classroom." *MarylandEJ* 21 (Fall 1987): 10–15.

Recommends that creative writing classes begin with satire because it emphasizes credibility, minimizes the need for character development, limits subjects and stances, and prevents excessive ego involvement on the part of the writer.

1424. Waxman, Barbara. "Catching the Runaway Train: Computers and the Advanced Composition Class." *CAC* 1 (Spring 1987): 208–213.

Celebrates the advantages of computer-assisted composition and suggests ways to integrate CAI with sound composition instruction.

1425. Welch, Kathleen E. "Autobiography and Advanced College Writing." Paper presented at the CCCC Convention, Atlanta, March 1987. ERIC ED 281 229. 14 pages

Advocates including autobiography in a college writing course that draws on students' oral abilities to produce writing.

See also 37, 1319, 1328, 1351, 1402, 1407

4.2.4 BUSINESS COMMUNICATION

1426. Barbour, Dennis H. "Process in the Business Writing Classrooms: One Teacher's Approach." *JBC* 24 (Winter 1987): 61–64.

Describes how the author came to shift to a two-part process approach to teaching business case reports.

1427. Bednar, Anita S. "Communication Needs of Recent Graduates." *ABCAB* 50 (December 1987): 22–23.

Presents results of a survey of recent graduates about the oral, written, and interpersonal communication their current positions require.

1428. Blyler, Nancy Roundy. "Process-Based Pedagogy in Professional Writing." *JBC* 24 (Winter 1987): 51–60.

Discusses process pedagogy in business communication, first theoretically, then by describing the course, sample tasks, and materials.

1429. Bowman, Joel P., and Bernadine P. Branchaw. "Business Communication: Its Process and Product." *JBC* 24 (Winter 1987): 23–25.

Claims that writing processes are individualized and cannot be forced on writers. Finds the process approach another in a sequence of panaceas.

1430. Bracher, Peter. "Process, Pedagogy, and Business Writing." *JBC* 24 (Winter 1987): 43–50.

The process approach to writing usually stresses personal and expressive writing, focusing on discovery, but business writing, which is transactional and rhetorical, does not suit the process approach.

1431. Carter, Ron. "The Vocational Interview." *IE* 10 (Spring 1987): 18–22.

Describes seven steps for doing a factual interview. Includes 41 interview questions, 14 hints for conducting the interview, and 6 ways of evaluating a rough draft.

1432. Christian, Rod. "An Editing Process That Works." *ABCAB* 50 (September 1987): 27–28.

Describes a method of teaching students to edit letters in a business communication class. Gives examples.

1433. Cole, David. "The Familiar Letter in Business Writing Courses." *IE* 11 (Fall 1987): 5–9.

Familiar letters allow students to transfer goodwill, audience awareness, humor, specificity, politeness, and dramatization to business letters.

1434. Connor, Jennifer J. "Technical Writing Kits: Their Origins, Functions, and Contexts." *JTWC* 17 (1987): 231–242.

Argues that kits for producing buzz words are probably anonymous in origin, have become a part of organizational folklore, and seem intended to satirize purveyors of gobbledygook.

1435. Cullinan, Mary. "Developing Business Writing Skills through Group Activity." *ABCAB* 50 (March 1987): 21–23.

Describes the goals and methods of group exercises to revise poorly written business correspondence.

1436. Forsberg, L. Lee. "Who's Out There Anyway? Bringing Awareness of Multiple Audiences into the Business Writing Class." *JBTC* 1 (September 1987): 45–69.

Offers a nonlinear, multilevel, interactive conceptual model of the business writing process on which students can base task analysis in case study assignments.

1437. Freed, Richard C., and Glenn J. Broadhead. "Using High-Affect Goals in Teaching Proposal Writing." *JAC* 7 (1987): 131–138.

Identifies six affective goals that can be used to guide sentence revisions for technical and business proposals.

1438. Gilsdorf, Jeannette W. "More Process: A Luxury? An Illusion? A Millstone?" *JBC* 24 (Winter 1987): 27–28.

Argues that business communication courses should not teach the classical writing process because of a lack of time, differences among writers, and the power of word processors.

1439. Griffin, C. W. "Headfirst: Two Introductory Assignments." *ABCAB* 50 (December 1987): 17–18.

Describes assignments introducing business writing students to types of business documents and the processes of writing them.

1440. Halden-Sullivan, Judith. "Business Basics: Using a Cognitive Approach in the Business Communication Class." *ABCAB* 50 (December 1987): 11–15.

Discusses the "cognitive competencies" that are essential to effective business thinking and should therefore be challenged in the classroom.

1441. Iandoli, Ce Ce. "Twenty Spring Rolls and One Plastic Rose: Teaching Business Writing to America's New Immigrants." *ABCAB* 50 (June 1987): 16–18.

Describes six dilemmas the author finds in business writing classes with a large proportion of foreign-born students.

1442. Jacobi, Martin J. "Using the Enthymeme as a Heuristic in Professional Writing Courses." *JAC* 7 (1987): 41–51.

Explains how to teach students to use an enthymeme to provide both rhetorical logic and structure for the persuasive business letter.

1443. Johnson, Cheryl E. "An Analysis of Written Communication Performed by Corporate Managers with Access to a Computer and Recommendations for Business Communica-

tion Course Offerings in Community Colleges in the U.S." *DAI* 47 (March 1987): 3287A.

Argues for including business communication and computer courses in target curricula because of increased emphasis on writing skills in management.

1444. Kent, Thomas. "Genre Theory in the Area of Business Writing." *TWT* 14 (Spring 1987): 232–242.

Concepts derived from contemporary genre theory can help business writing courses and textbooks move away from current formulaic approaches toward a more reader-centered one.

1445. Kent, Thomas. "Schema Theory and Technical Communication." *JTWC* 17 (1987): 243–252.

Teachers may employ research from cognitive psychology to show students why following certain writing guidelines helps readers better process information.

1446. Kotler, Janet, and Dona Hickey. "Let's Call the Whole Thing Off." *JBC* 24 (Winter 1987): 13–16.

Argues that the process-product controversy is not about the classroom but about research methods. Process researchers err in thinking that behavior reveals cognitive processes.

1447. Lehman, Carol M. "Business Communications Students Demonstrate Realistic Business Practices." *ABCAB* 50 (December 1987): 19–21.

Describes a group term assignment with written and oral components and an emphasis on realistic business roles.

1448. Lipson, Carol. "Teaching Students to 'Read' Culture in the Workplace: Reply to Gerald Parsons [*TWT* 14 (Spring 1987)]." *TWT* 14 (Spring 1987): 267–270.

Finds faulty the assumptions behind Parson's response to her article on the cultural context of technical communication.

1449. Loomis, Betty H., and Dorothy C. Wilkinson. "Peers Versus Peers in a Peerless Learning Experience." *ABCAB* 50 (March 1987): 19–20.

Describes a classroom group exercise in organizing a business report and in using graphics and headings for emphasis and readability.

1450. Maik, Thomas A. "Word Processing in the Business Writing Classroom: Applications and Reactions." *ABCAB* 50 (December 1987): 4–6.

Describes the use and benefits of word processing in a business writing course.

1451. McIssac, Claudia Mon Pere. "Improving Student Summaries through Sequencing." *ABCAB* 50 (September 1987): 17–20.

Describes techniques for teaching summary writing in a business writing course.

1452. Mendelson, Michael. "Business Prose and the Nature of the Plain Style." *JBC* 24 (Spring 1987): 3–18.

The prose style advocated in prominent business textbooks is too narrow. Proposes an expanded version of the plain style based on Greek rhetoric, clarity, conciseness.

1453. Moore, Patrick. "The Raw and the Cooked: Using More Realistic Cases in Business and Technical Writing Courses." *JBTC* 1 (September 1987): 91–97.

Argues that most case studies assume factors that actual writers must elicit and develop. Urges teachers to give students experience with dynamic, untidy, "raw" cases. Offers sample assignments.

1454. Morgan, Meg, Nancy Allen, Teresa Moore, Dianne Atkinson, and Craig Snow. "Collaborative Writing in the Classroom." *ABCAB* 50 (September 1987): 20–26.

Describes a collaborative report project in a business writing class. Topics covered include sequencing assignments, forming groups, and evaluating performance.

1455. Murphy, Herta A. "Process Versus Product in Freshman Composition and Business Communication Textbooks and in Our Teaching." *JBC* 24 (Winter 1987): 79–88.

Examining eight best-selling business writing textbooks and teachers' practices shows that process is already being taught in business writing.

1456. Neeld, Elizabeth Cowan. "A Report on Writing in Business." *VEB* 37 (Special 1987 Issue): 125–131.

Presents examples of business writing that transcend stereotypes of bland prose. Asks that writing and business communication courses match that complexity.

1457. Ober, Scot. "The Status of Postsecondary Business Communication Instruction: 1986 Versus 1982." *JBC* 24 (Summer 1987): 49–60.

Replicates a 1982 survey of 356 institutions. Found major differences in instruction.

1458. Olander, Karen W. "My Favorite Assignment: Reference Report." *ABCAB* 50 (December 1987): 16.

Describes a final reference report assignment in a business and technical writing class.

1459. Parry, Sally E. "Using Foreign Investment to Structure Assignments for a Business Communications Class." *ABCAB* 50 (June 1987): 28–30.

Describes a series of assignments in which students write from the perspective of actual American companies with foreign investments.

1460. Parsons, Gerald M. "The Elusiveness of Workplace Culture: Response to 'Technical Communication: The Cultural Context' [*IWI* 13 (Fall 1986)]." *TWT* 14 (Spring 1987): 265–266.

Finds that Carol Lipson's analysis of and pedagogical advice about corporate cultures are "too simplistic and even naive."

1461. Pearson, Patricia. "Turning On to Word Processing." *ABCAB* 50 (June 1987): 19–23.

Explains how to select a word processor for writing classes. Outlines its benefits and explains how to use it in the classroom.

1462. Pomerenke, Paula J. "Process: More Than a Fad for the Business Writer." *JBC* 24 (Winter 1987): 37–39.

Explains and defends using the process approach, which includes audience analysis, heuristics, and peer revision.

1463. Roy, Emil. "Freshman Composition with a Business Focus." *TETYC* 14 (December 1987): 285–293.

Describes a course focused on *Death of a Salesman*.

1464. Seymour, Tom. "Writing a Funding Proposal." *ABCAB* 50 (June 1987): 30–32.

Describes an assignment in which students write proposals for funding and submit them to management.

1465. Shelby, Annette. "Note on Process." *JBC* 24 (Winter 1987): 21.

Discusses three reasons why business communication teachers do not use recent developments in composition pedagogy.

1466. Stephenson, William. "A Real-Life Basic for Reports in Business and Technical Writing." *TETYC* 14 (December 1987): 271–272.

An instructor's file folder of newspaper clippings is a useful resource for students.

1467. Varner, Iris I. "Internationalizing Business Communication Courses." *ABCAB* 50 (December 1987): 7–11.

Presents a rationale and steps for integrating international aspects in a business communication course. Gives sample course units.

1468. Warburton, T. L. "The ABCs of Group Communication: A Primer for Effective Group Performance." *JTWC* 17 (1987): 303–315.

Shows how three basic principles of effective group performance can teach students to perform successfully in groups.

1469. Waxler, Robert P. "On Process." *JBC* 24 (Winter 1987): 41–42.

Argues that business textbooks mainly teach writing-as-product through models, contrary to the real nature of business, where language makes meaning.

1470. Yontz, Ruth. "Providing a Rationale for the Process Approach." *JBC* 24 (Winter 1987): 17–19.

Providing a rationale for requiring extended writing, using the work of Murray and Elbow, helps students.

See also 118, 205, 507, 521, 523, 529, 530, 533, 689, 1032, 1479, 1619, 1626, 1674

4.2.5 SCIENTIFIC AND TECHNICAL COMMUNICATION

1471. Allen, Jo, and Sherry Southard. " 'But I Did Proofread!' Teaching Technical Communication Students to Revise Stylistically." *TWT* 14 (Spring 1987): 170–173.

Suggests guidelines for stylistic revision.

1472. Anderson, W. Steve. "Designing an Applied Writing M.A. within a Traditional English Department." Paper presented at the CCCC Convention, Atlanta, March 1987. ERIC ED 280 056. 12 pages

Describes the M.A. in Technical and Expository Writing Program implemented at the University of Arkansas at Little Rock.

1473. Bishop, Wendy. "Developing Community in the Writing Classroom with a Note Card Introduction Method." *ExEx* 32 (Spring 1987): 33–36.

Presents an exercise for the first day of class. Students fill out cards, interview each other, and introduce each other to the class.

1474. Bradford, Annette Norris. "Writing Training Information: A Comparison of

Books, On-Line Tutors, and Videotapes." *JTWC* 17 (1987): 115–127.

Compares three types of training media for technical writers who may have to write such material.

1475. Braun, Miriam, and Judith Rosenhouse. "Breaking Communication and Linguistic Barriers: Designing a Course of Technical Writing in Hebrew." *JTWC* 17 (1987): 79–92.

Describes problems encountered and solved when designing such a course.

1476. Butler, Douglas R. "Government Projects and Teaching the Technical Proposal." *TWT* 14 (Winter 1987): 44–51.

Describes a four-week unit intended to help students write convincing technical proposals.

1477. Christian, Barbara. "Using the Entire Manual: A Proposal for the Integrated Presentation of Technical Writing Information." *JTWC* 17 (1987): 145–156.

Describes assignments that help technical writing teachers incorporate in a one-semester writing course the many topics covered in a modern technical writing textbook.

1478. Corey, Jim, and M. Jimmie Killingsworth. "The Internship Report." *TWT* 14 (Spring 1987): 133–141.

Recommends a four-part structure for reports written on internships in technical and professional communication. Such reports include an introduction, a narrative section, an analysis and evaluation section, and an appendix.

1479. Curry, Jerome. "The Instruction-Writing Assignment: Making It Work." *ABCAB* 50 (September 1987): 29–30.

Describes a method of teaching students to write a set of instructions in a technical writing class.

1480. Ellery, Celia. "Using U.S. Government Documents in the Technical Writing Classroom." *JBTC* 1 (September 1987): 98–104.

Explains how to locate, obtain, and use government documents.

1481. Fitschen, Ken. "Teaching Layout: Letting the Students See for Themselves." *TWT* 14 (Winter 1987): 90–96.

Describes a sequence of assignments that enables students to understand the importance of a document's layout.

1482. Foeman, Anita K., and Gary Pressley. "Ethnic Culture and Corporate Culture: Using Black Styles in Organizations." *ComQ* 35 (Fall 1987): 293–307.

Examines the positive impact black organizational members can make on the workplace as a result of their unique linguistic and rhetorical strategies.

1483. Fry, Robert B., Jr. "The Purposes and Audiences of Software Writing in Large-Scale Technical Projects." *DAI* 47 (March 1987): 3433A.

Examines discourse traits of software writing using a Kinneavy model. Concludes that software writers demonstrate "consistent purposes" and show audience consideration.

1484. Gabbard, Jo Anne. "Specialists in Technical Communication Lead Participants in Week of Study at Summer Institute." *SCETCJ* 20 (Fall 1987): 28–33.

Describes the 1987 Institute in Technical Communication.

1485. Gilbertsen, Michael, and M. Jimmie Killingsworth. "Behavioral Talk-Write as a Method for Teaching Technical Editing." *JBTC* 1 (January 1987): 108–114.

Explains how two-student "talk-edit" teams can embody basic behavioral principles in a process-oriented workshop application of Zoellner's pedagogy.

1486. Glassman, Steve. "The Technical Writer as Playwright." *TWT* 14 (Winter 1987): 118–119.

Description-of-process skits teach students to describe processes with more clarity and detail than ordinarily.

1487. Hall, Dean G., and Bonnie A. Nelson. "Initiating Students into Professionalism: Teaching the Letter of Inquiry." *TWT* 14 (Winter 1987): 86–89.

Describes the benefits of this type of assignment in technical writing classes.

1488. Hall, Dean G., and Bonnie A. Nelson. "Integrating Professional Ethics into the Technical Writing Course." *JTWC* 17 (1987): 45–62.

Argues that teachers of technical writing should teach their students to appreciate the ethical "consequences of their recommendations." Provides one successful method for accomplishing this.

1489. Henson, Leigh. "Preparing Students to Write in Major-Field Courses: A Faculty Questionnaire for Data-Based Instructional Design." *TWT* 14 (Winter 1987): 108–110.

Describes a questionnaire designed to elicit faculty attitudes about student writing.

1490. Jacobson, Thomas L. "Metaphors and Stopping Behavior in Reading of Technical Material." *DAI* 47 (June 1987): 4222A.

Finds that using metaphors in technical writing reduced readers' stopping and enhanced comprehension for some.

1491. Kelly, Rebecca, and Carol M. Barnum. "A Foot in Both Camps: Academe and Workplace." *TWT* 14 (Winter 1987): 77–85.

Describes the work experience of two technical writing teachers, shows how such experiences can carry over into the classroom, and suggests ways interested instructors can gain similar experience.

1492. Killingsworth, M. Jimmie, and Scott P. Sanders. "Portfolios for Majors in Professional Communication." *TWT* 14 (Spring 1987): 166–169.

Suggests principles for developing a portfolio of "writing and art work samples"

for majors in technical communication and professional writing.

1493. Kohl, Herbert. "On Science Writing." *TWM* 18 (May–June 1987): 10–11.

Excerpted remarks from Kohl's lecture on the art of scientific writing, in which he tells how to slant writing toward various audiences and publications.

1494. MacKenzie, Raymond, and Nancy MacKenzie. "The Use of a Public Relations Course in Training Technical Communicators." *TWT* 14 (Spring 1987): 158–165.

Argues that including a public relations course in a technical writing curriculum helps students understand the field and introduces them to business theories and organizational policies.

1495. Mendelson, Michael. "Teaching the Abstract as an Introduction to Technical Writing." *TWT* 14 (Winter 1987): 1–10.

Requiring beginning technical writing students to condense a technical article into an abstract allows them to focus on important aspects of the writing process.

1496. Mullins, Carolyn J. "Grading Comments on Technical Writing Assignments." *TWT* 14 (Spring 1987): 178–185.

Describes a system for coding typical comments teachers make while grading student papers.

1497. Nelson, Ronald J. "Beyond the Basic Technical Writing Course: A Status Report, Part II." *TWT* 14 (Winter 1987): 62–67.

Provides catalog descriptions for various types of technical writing courses offered at different universities.

1498. Olds, Barbara. "Beyond the Casebook: Teaching Technical Communication through 'Real Life' Projects." *TWT* 14 (Winter 1987): 11–17.

As a capstone to a four-course sequence in technical communications, engineering students work as a team, solving a real client's problem and writing relevant documents.

1499. Olds, Barbara. "Technical Writing across the Curriculum: Epics." Paper presented at the CCCC Convention, Atlanta, March 1987. ERIC ED 283 170. 12 pages

Describes the Engineering Practices Introductory Course Sequence at the Colorado School of Mines.

1500. Painter, Carolyn M. "An Alternative Technical Report: The Interview Report." *TWT* 14 (Winter 1987): 111–113.

Describes the formats for and the benefits of interview report assignments.

1501. Pemberton, Carol A. "Making Technical Writing Practical for Freshmen and Sophomores." *TWT* 14 (Winter 1987): 20–27.

Builds "a practical course in technical writing. . . around major projects that the students themselves design."

1502. Pieper, Gail W. "The Scoop on Good Humor." *TWT* 14 (Spring 1987): 174–177.

Argues that humor can be used in computer training manuals to reduce the apprehension of beginners learning a new system.

1503. *Proceedings of the Thirty-Fourth International Technical Communication Conference.* Washington, D.C.: Society for Technical Communication, 1987.

A collection of 199 papers presented in Denver, May 1987. Subjects include advanced technology applications; management and professional development; research, education, and training; visual communication; and writing and editing. Authors are not indexed separately in this volume.

1504. Richardson, Malcolm. "A Memo-Writing Assignment to Freeze the Blood." *TWT* 14 (Winter 1987): 97–98.

Uses a classroom memo to "reflect the frustrations and pressures of writing at work."

1505. Robbins, Richard. "Helping to Make Reports Real: A Brainstorming Aid for Assignments in Technical Communication." *TWT* 14 (Winter 1987): 99–102.

Presents a matrix that enables students to analyze quickly the major components of any technical writing assignment.

1506. Roberts, David D. "Three Needs in Technical Writing: Findings from Student Diagnostics." *TWT* 14 (Spring 1987): 186–191.

Technical writing students need to know how valuable strong communication skills are, how to write in teams, and when to use graphics.

1507. Roesler, Glenn R. "Of Fallacies, Ferris Wheels, and Figurative Language: Metaphor in Science and Technical Writing." *JTW* 6 (Fall–Winter 1987): 281–291.

Argues that disciplinary conventions should not obviate the benefits of metaphor: innovative conceptualization, communication with an audience, and breaking down barriers.

1508. St. John, Maggie Jo. "Writing Processes of Spanish Scientists Publishing in English." *ESP* 6 (1987): 113–120.

Provides a contrastive analysis of differences in the approach to writing Spanish scientists take. Suggests that revision is mainly at the sentence rather than the global level.

1509. Santelmann, Patricia. "Teaching Technical Writing: How to Focus on Process." *TWT* 14 (Winter 1987): 103–107.

Describes a classroom sequence that requires students to "solve a problem for which there is no clear-cut solution" and to communicate their results in writing.

1510. Sawyer, Thomas M. "Argument." *JTWC* 17 (1987): 253–263.

Shows how principles common to nearly all textbooks on debate can be "applied to the writing of persuasive proposals and problem-solving engineering reports."

1511. Scheiber, H. J. "From Prose to Peer Editor: Teaching Engineers (and Others) to Write and Communicate." *JTWC* 17 (1987): 385–395.

Describes a method for helping engineers and other professionals turn writer-centered documents, which are needlessly repetitive, excessively detailed, and chronologically organized, into reader-centered documents.

1512. Skelton, Terrance M. "The In-House Course as a Research Tool for Technical Communication." *TWT* 14 (Winter 1987): 29–42.

Describes the pedagogical and research implications of a short course based on the sentence-level application of syntactic and semantic principles.

1513. Stohrer, Freda F. "Technical Writing 1987: Galloping Off in at Least Two Directions." Paper presented at the CCCC Convention, Atlanta, March 1987. ERIC ED 283 215. 12 pages

Contrasts the college technical writing course with corporate training programs.

1514. Sullivan, Dale. "The Computer as a Two-Way Medium in the Technical Writing Classroom." *TWT* 14 (Spring 1987): 143–150.

Describes a technical writing course in which students spent "about 80 percent of class time writing and rewriting their papers" on Zenith microcomputers.

1515. Sullivan, Frances J., ed. *Basic Technical Writing*. Anthology Series, no. 7. Washington, D.C.: Society for Technical Communication, 1987. 52 pages

An anthology of 25 papers presented at the International Technical Communication Conference. For beginning technical writers. Authors are not indexed separately in this volume.

1516. Tessman, Rita Mae. "Problems of Objectivity: Vague Writing in the Physical Sciences." *DAI* 47 (February 1987): 3019A.

Argues that scientists and editors would probably produce better results if they paid more attention to conceptual control and coherence and less attention to the mechanics of sentences.

1517. Topf, Mel A. "Job Application Correspondence: Integral to the Technical Communication Course." *TWT* 14 (Winter 1987): 114–117.

The case method teaches students how to write job application correspondence.

1518. Valetta, Clement L., and Robert A. Paoletti. "A Structural Heuristic and Writing: Language and DNA upon a Blue Guitar." *JTWC* 17 (1987): 215–229.

Demonstrates how a heuristic based on tagmemics can be used to "organize subjects descriptively and functionally, explore alternative arrangements, and discover new cross-discipline parallels."

1519. Vaughn, Jeanette W., and Nancy Darsey. "Negative Behavior Factors in the Employment Interview: Interviewer Opinions and Observations." *TWT* 14 (Spring 1987): 208–218.

Describes the negative behaviors on-campus interviewers noted most frequently among students in job interviews.

1520. Weinstein, Edith K. "Using Technical Articles to Teach Technical Report Writing." *TWT* 14 (Spring 1987): 151–157.

Students study journal articles by asking questions that focus on comprehension, unity, coherence, definitions, illustrations, and documentation.

1521. Young, Gene. "Student Editing Internships in Low-Industry Geographical Areas." Paper presented at the CCCC Convention, Atlanta, March 1987. ERIC ED 280 030. 12 pages

Describes Morehead State University's technical writing internship program. Includes suggestions for implementing internships.

1522. Youra, Steven. "Rewriting the Engineering Curriculum: Professionalism and Professional Communication." *JTWC* 17 (1987): 407–416.

Describes some ways in which writing activities have been and can be incorporated into the engineering curriculum.

See also 27, 145, 216, 285, 495, 507, 519, 542, 993, 1028, 1103, 1445, 1453, 1458, 1466, 1468, 1661, 1689

4.2.6 WRITING IN LITERATURE COURSES

1523. Crow, Edith. "Shaping the Self: Using Steppingstones and Autobiography to Create and Discover Archetypes in 'An Illustrious Monarchy.' " Paper presented at the CCCC Convention, Detroit, March 1983. ERIC ED 278 016. 17 pages

Shows how diary journals define archetypal patterns in writers' lives, which then awaken interest in significant metaphors in literature.

1524. Doubler, Janet M. "Literature and Composition: A Problem-Solving Approach to a Thematic Literature Course." *DAI* 48 (September 1987): 585A.

Demonstrates the effects of exigency on the processes of reading and writing and the mutual effects of reading and writing on one another.

1525. Dowling, H. Fil, Jr. "Using Journals to Help Students Learn Literature." *WAC* 5 (December 1987): 6–9.

Delineates a method for using the journal in an American literature survey course. Presents such topics as observation, interpretation, and reaction.

1526. Goldberg, Marilyn. "Piaget's Structuralism and the Teaching of Literature." *JGE* 38 (1987): 272–287.

Advocates an integration of Piagetian methodologies of assimilation, accommodation, and conducive learning environments in literature courses.

1527. Haefner, Joel. "On First Seeing a Copy of Keats's Life-Mask." *EJ* 76 (April 1987): 45–49.

Analyzes the variety of discourse aims that students used in an in-class freewriting assignment prompted by Keats's life-mask.

1528. Hoberman, Ruth. "Writing Stories and Writing Skills." Paper presented at the CCCC Convention, New Orleans, March 1986. ERIC ED 277 031. 11 pages

Illustrates how students learn about short stories by writing them and analyzing each other's works.

1529. Lang, Frederick K. "Between Writers." *FEN* 16 (Winter/Spring 1987): 10–16.

Presents assignments for a literature course that helped inexperienced student writers learn the work of experienced writers by participating in text constructing activities.

1530. Mullican, James C. "The Grammar, Rhetoric, and Symbolic of a Poem." *ExEx* 33 (Fall 1987): 29–32.

Applies Kenneth Burke's distinctions among grammar, rhetoric, and symbolic to May Swenson's "Questions."

1531. O'Sullivan, Maurice J. "The Group Journal." *JGE* 38 (1987): 288–300.

Describes a group novel-writing project and an open class journal used in a literature class. Both were used as a means of class dialogue.

1532. Reilly, Jill M., and Richard W. Beach. "The Effects of Prewriting on Literary Interpretation." Paper presented at the American Educational Research Association, San Francisco, April 1986. ERIC ED 276 058. 26 pages

Guided writing results in superior interpretive essays about characters and setting in short stories when compared to non-guided prewriting assignments.

1533. Root, Robert L., Jr. "Writing in the Dark: Composing Criticism." *JTW* 6 (Fall–Winter 1987): 203–210.

Analyzes the processes of three drama critics, finding that "the key to criticism is connections made in context." Criticism is "a reading act and then a writing act."

1534. Van DeWeghe, Richard. "Making and Remaking Meaning: Developing Literacy Responses through Purposeful, Informal Writing." *EQ* 20 (Spring 1987): 38–51.

Discusses five ways whereby students develop their understanding of literature through writing: generating meaning hypotheses, creating heuristic moments, overcoming difficulties with reading, finding meaning through analogy, and finding meaningful problems.

1535. Viera, Carroll. "A Collaborative Approach to Required Literature Courses." *ExEx* 33 (Fall 1987): 33–37.

Outlines a sophomore survey course in which students collaboratively prepare and teach units on the authors studied.

1536. Wentworth, Michael. "Writing in the Literature Class." *JTW* 6 (Spring 1987): 155–162.

Advocates flexibility in the number, type, and sequence of written responses to texts.

1537. Williams, William. "The Right Stuff: What Do We Teach When We Teach Literature?" *EngR* 38 (1987): 14–16.

Discusses the importance of Russian formalism, Marxist theory, and literature.

1538. Zavatsky, Bill, Mary Logue, Bernadette Mayer, Gary Lenhart, Alan Ziegler, Geof Hewitt, Ron Padgett, and Anne Waldman. "Poetic Forms: A New Look." *TWM* 19 (September–October 1987): 1–6.

Presents selections of traditional and modern poetic forms and techniques: form definition, summaries of histories, and quoted good examples. Gives suggestions on the use of each form.

See also 1266, 1350, 1352, 1367

4.2.7 COMMUNICATION IN OTHER DISCIPLINES

1539. Allen, Michael S. "Fishing on the Wooster Review: A Look at a Student Interpretive

Community." Paper presented at the CCCC Convention, Atlanta, March 1987. ERIC ED 280 052. 17 pages

Reports on the formation and operation of a student-formed interpretive community, the editorial board of the *Wooster Review,* a student literary magazine.

1540. Allen, Robert. "Critical Thinking and Science Teaching." *JCST* 17 (November 1987): 139–140.

Identifies and describes nine "key references" for developing instruction to improve critical thinking skills.

1541. Ambron, Joanna. "Writing to Improve Learning in Biology." *JCST* 16 (February 1987): 263–266.

Journal entries and microthemes can help students relate classroom material to their own experience.

1542. Ambrose, Susan Adele. "How Historians Think: A Writing across the Curriculum Course for Freshmen at the University Level." *DAI* 47 (April 1987): 3848A.

Describes a freshman course combining English and history at Carnegie Mellon University.

1543. Anderson, Kristine F. "Interview with Robert Jones, Michigan Tech." *WAC* 4 (May 1987): 5–6.

Robert Jones discusses qualities of successful writing across the curriculum programs in general and at Michigan Technological University.

1544. Bailey, Ben E. "The Making of a Believer." *SCETCJ* 20 (Fall 1987): 7–9.

Describes a writing across the curriculum program at Tougaloo College.

1545. Barnes, Linda Laube, and Isaiah Smithson. *Writing across the Curriculum: Papers from the Annual Composition Conference.* Urbana, Ill.: ERIC/RCS, 1986. ERIC ED 277 004. 57 pages

A collection of seven essays that discuss radical pedagogy, student-centered curricula, and two extensive projects involving students in research.

1546. Bishop, Wendy. "Planning for a Writing across the Curriculum Program." *EngR* 38 (1987): 18–21.

Reviews the theory behind writing across the curriculum programs and discusses university programs.

1547. Burton, Gerald Lee. "Essay Writing in College Mathematics and Its Effect on Achievement." *DAI* 47 (January 1987): 2492A.

A study measuring the effect of essay writing on learning mathematical skills, problem solving, and retention. Essay writing did not affect math achievement but prompted greater retention.

1548. Clines, Ray. "Expressive Writing in the Content Areas." *OrE* 9 (Spring 1987): 11–13.

Describes a writing across the curriculum course for education majors. Includes examples of assignments in different disciplines.

1549. Comprone, Joseph. "The New Rhetoric: A Way of Connecting Community and Discourse Conventions in Writing across the Disciplines Courses." Paper presented at the CCCC Convention, Atlanta, March 1987. ERIC ED 279 019. 10 pages

Concepts of warrants and universal audience serve a balancing function for English professors establishing writing across the curriculum programs.

1550. Davis, David J. "Eight Faculty Members Talk about Student Writing." *CollT* 35 (Winter 1987): 31–35.

Reports on attitudes toward writing across the curriculum and the changes implemented. Maintains that the institutional context, especially the role of administration, is crucial to success.

1551. Duke, Charles R. *Integrating Reading, Writing, and Thinking Skills into the Music*

Class. Urbana, Ill.: ERIC/RCS, 1984. ERIC ED 278 029. 13 pages

Illustrates exercises for both musicians and listeners to foster skills in identifying theme and purpose. Shows how journal writing is also an aid to critical reading.

1552. Duke, Charles R. "Integrating Reading, Writing, and Thinking Skills into the Music Class." *JR* 31 (November 1987): 152–159.

Argues that integrating reading, writing, and thinking helps students become more thoughtful musicians and readers.

1553. Duquin, Lorene Hanley. "Shaping Your Article Ideas to Sell." *WD* (January 1987): 37–40.

A freelance writer explains a four-step system for writing successful query letters and proposals to popular and professional publications.

1554. Ede, Lisa. "The Case for Collaboration." Paper presented at the CCCC Convention, Atlanta, March 1987. ERIC ED 282 212. 12 pages

Argues for collaborative learning, but notes the difficulty of implementing it in the competitive environment of college.

1555. Foos, K. Michael. "Abstracts Can Enhance Writing Skills." *JCST* 16 (February 1987): 254–255.

Writing weekly annotated abstracts of assigned readings helps students hone critical thinking and writing skills as well as gain familiarity with the professional literature.

1556. Freedman, Aviva. "Dimensions of the Composing Process." Paper presented at the CCCC Convention, Atlanta, March 1987. ERIC ED 283 197. 22 pages

Reports on case studies of six undergraduates writing across the curriculum, noting a range of composing processes.

1557. Friday, Robert, and Bernard F. Beranek. *Report on a Pilot Project Which Combined Speech Communication and English Compo-*

sition Instruction. Pittsburgh: Duquesne University, 1984. ERIC ED 279 046. 22 pages

Describes a course at Duquesne University that integrates composition and speech communication. Students write essays, do oral readings, and participate in discussion groups.

1558. Fulwiler, Toby. "The Politics of Writing across the Curriculum." Paper presented at the NCTE Convention, San Antonio, November 1986. ERIC ED 276 061. 10 pages

As an educational reform movement, writing across the curriculum programs have caused a noticeable change among students, faculty, and their institutions.

1559. Fulwiler, Toby. "Writing across the Curriculum: Implications for Teaching Literature." *BADE* 88 (Winter 1987): 35–40.

Explains how writing across the curriculum developed and what its premises are. Compares practices with the traditional teaching of literature and finds them essential to effective education.

1560. Gates, Rosemary L. "*Aitita kairos:* Classical Rhetoric in the Writing across the Curriculum Program." Paper presented at the CCCC Convention, New Orleans, April 1986. ERIC ED 274 974. 25 pages

Applies Aristotelian distinctions to writing across the curriculum.

1561. Grow, Gerald. "Teaching Writing through Negative Examples." *JTW* 6 (Fall–Winter 1987): 239–244.

Presents exercises for writing negative magazine articles: the worst grammar, terrible words, the worst possible article, and the awful two-page spread.

1562. Hemmeter, Thomas, and David Conners. "Research Papers in Economics: A Collaborative Approach." *JAC* 7 (1987): 81–91.

Proposes a "research-based pedagogy" for teaching writing in an advanced course in industrial organization. Notes that the research paradigm in economics parallels the writing process.

1563. Kelly, Kathleen A. *Writing across the Curriculum: What the Literature Tells Us*. Urbana, Ill.: ERIC/RCS, 1985. ERIC ED 274 975. 20 pages

Summarizes common program elements, student requirements, faculty involvement, and administrative or institutional support.

1564. Konopak, Bonnie C., Michael A. Martin, and Sarah H. Martin. "Reading and Writing: Aids to Learning in the Content Areas." *JR* 31 (November 1987): 109–117.

Argues that writing can help students understand course material.

1565. Larew, Karl G. "Student Blunders as Teaching Tools." *MarylandEJ* 21 (Fall 1987): 49–52.

Uses pseudohistory (collections of student blunders) to teach proofreading skills in a world history class. Presents methods and one collection: Luther was a Pheasant.

1566. Larsen, Richard B. "Computerized Writing across the Curriculum." *WAC* 5 (December 1987): 5–6.

Describes how computers may assist student writers in gathering, organizing, and presenting specific data in written form for courses across the curriculum.

1567. Lopate, Kay L. "The Organization of College Lectures in Selected Introductory Level Courses." *DAI* 48 (October 1987): 887A.

Examines whether lecture material can be analyzed in the same way as textual material in social science and humanities courses.

1568. Lotto, Edward, Lucy Bednar, and Richard Gaughan. "Moving away from the Text: Tutoring Writing in Government, History, and Computer Science." *PCTEB* 55 (April 1987): 13–21.

Describes the assumptions, curricula, and support services for junior writing-intensive courses designed to familiarize students with writing in their majors.

1569. MacDonald, Susan Peck. "Problem Definition in Academic Writing." *CE* 49 (March 1987): 315–331.

Describes and analyzes the use of problem definition techniques in the writing models of different academic disciplines.

1570. Madigan, Chris. "Writing as a Means, Not an End." *JCST* 16 (February 1987): 245–249.

Science teachers should have students write to master course material. Discusses successes, teachers' concerns, and handling the paper load.

1571. Maher, J. "Editorial: English as an International Language of Medicine." *MEd* 21 (July 1987): 283–284.

Argues for the use of English as an international medium for textbooks and professional journals. Encourages ESL instruction in medical schools and hospitals.

1572. McCarthy, Lucille Parkinson. *A Stranger in Strange Lands: An Ethnographic Study of a College Student Writing in Two Academic Contexts*. Urbana, Ill.: ERIC/RCS, 1985. ERIC ED 284 278. 31 pages

Observes one student in a biology and a poetry course, stressing the social context in which writing is created.

1573. McCartney, Hunter P. "Applying Fiction Conflict Situations to Analysis of News Stories." *JQ* 64 (Spring 1987): 163–170.

Plot situations used in literary works were present in the angles for 97 major news stories. Indignation was the emotion provoked in the reader most often.

1574. McIntosh, William J. "The Expanded Syllabus as an Aid for the Underprepared Science Student." *JCST* 17 (November 1987): 137–138.

Using an expanded syllabus containing clear behavioral objectives and information on reading and writing strategies has improved student attitudes and achievement.

1575. Mertens, Thomas R. "Reflections on Writing and Reviewing Grant Proposals." *JCST* 16 (February 1987): 267–269.

A grant evaluator provides general recommendations for writing successful grants and emphasizes the need to follow the granting agency's instructions.

1576. Miller, George A. *Explanatory Skills*. Cambridge, Mass.: National Academy of Education, 1986. ERIC ED 279 688. 33 pages

Advocates science instruction that develops higher-order cognitive skills. Encourages testing by means of interviews, free response tests, and thinking protocols.

1577. Morgan, Lorraine, Bill Friar, and Jean Kutner. "Pushing the Write Button: Writing across the Curriculum." Paper presented at the CCCC Convention, Atlanta, March 1987. ERIC ED 280 028. 12 pages

Outlines a two-semester introductory writing-intensive course in the human biology program at Stanford University. Confirms that participating students improved writing performance.

1578. Myers, Richard L. "From Cultural Experience to Conceptualization." *JCST* 16 (February 1987): 270–272.

Using a "cultural experience" method that incorporates writing, discussion, and research helps minority students build bridges between their perspectives and academic perspectives.

1579. Naeraa, N. "On Making Laboratory Report Work More Meaningful through Criterion-Based Evaluation." *MEd* 21 (May 1987): 199–296.

A syllabus and lab manual providing more explicit criteria for composing and evaluating laboratory reports have yielded positive results.

1580. Osborne, Philip Barry. "Writing the 'Art-of-Living' Article." *WD* (April 1987): 20–25.

A *Reader's Digest* editor explains the "widest-open market for new writers" and shows how to write inspirational or self-help narratives, essays, and articles.

1581. Papay, Joseph L. "Plato, Prose, and Poetry: Reading Philosophic Masters—On Language—And Teaching Literacy Today." *WAC* 5 (December 1987): 9–12.

Discusses the past—what Plato says about writing—and explains what students can learn about writing, speaking, listening, and reading in a philosophy course.

1582. Parsigian, Elise Keoleian. "News Reporting: Method in the Midst of Chaos." *JQ* 64 (Winter 1987): 721–730.

Forty-eight reporters followed eight sequential steps in reporting news stories. Order exists even in the prewriting stage.

1583. Phillips, Jack J. "Eleven Reasons Why Engineering Technology Students Should Improve Writing Skills." *WAC* 4 (May 1987): 7–9.

Discusses 11 practical reasons why writing will be important to engineering students after they graduate.

1584. Powell, Gerald F., and Alice Anne O'Donell. "Medical Students' and Residents' Data Analysis in Patient Progress Notes." *JMEd* 62 (July 1987): 606–607.

Written progress notes reflect an inability of students to analyze data and to tie it to a proposed treatment plan.

1585. Rooth, Tom. "The 20-Minute Grammarian." *BADE* 86 (Spring 1987): 55–57.

Describes the effects of having a teaching assistant lecture briefly on writing and offer drop-in tutoring in a senior marketing course.

1586. Rothney, John. "Developing the Twentieth-Century World History Course: A Case Study at Ohio State." *HT* 20 (August 1987): 465–486.

Discusses an experimental history course in which one of the alternative strategies used was group work.

1587. Ruiz, Vicki L. "Teaching Chicano/American History: Goals and Methods." *HT* 20 (February 1987): 167–177.

Outlines such assignments as interviewing Mexican-Americans and writing simple quantitive research papers, useful in teaching students Chicano/American history.

1588. Russell, Nick. "Retro-Writing." *ExEx* 33 (Fall 1987): 7–10.

Presents an exercise in which students rewrite published prose into "ordinary" writing to identify what elements of style made the original effective.

1589. Sauers, Frances W. "Menage a Trois: Reading, Writing, and Rhetoric." *CollT* 35 (Winter 1987): 23–25.

Advocates incorporating rhetoric in the form of oral presentations into writing classes.

1590. Schwartz, Stephen W. " 'Dear Journal': Out of the Mouths of Babes." Paper presented at the CCCC Convention, Atlanta, March 1987. ERIC ED 283 171. 8 pages

Describes the functions of a learning journal in a college orientation course.

1591. Sellers, Jim. "If Your Yarn Elicits Yawns, Learn to Give a Speech that Sparkles." *ASBJ* 174 (April 1987): 40–41.

Offers 15 suggestions for composing an effective speech about education issues.

1592. Sharp, Julie Ervin. "Expressive Summary Writing to Learn College Biology." *DAI* 48 (September 1987): 586A.

Writing expressive summaries helped students learn biology better initially and sustained this learning advantage.

1593. Shawl, Stephen J. "Satisfying All the Students Most of the Time." *JCST* 16 (March–April 1987): 447–452.

A multi-option syllabus combined with peer tutoring and collaborative learning strategies allows an introductory course to meet the needs of different student populations.

1594. Sipple, Jo-Ann M. "Proposing, Preparing, and Prototyping: Three Ps of Writing across the Curriculum Programs That Last." *WAC* 4 (May 1987): 3–5.

The second part of an essay dealing with four requirements of a successful writing across the curriculum program. Part I [*WAC* 4 (December 1986)] discusses planning such a program.

1595. Smithson, Isaiah, and Paul Sorrentino. "Writing across the Curriculum: An Assessment." *JTW* 6 (Fall–Winter 1987): 325–342.

Discusses the effects, after five years, of a writing across the curriculum program at Virginia Polytechnic Institute. Finds that professors, at personal risk, still use writing to teach and that students retain a positive attitude toward writing.

1596. So, Clement Y. K. "The Summit as War: How Journalists Use Metaphors." *JQ* 64 (Summer–Autumn 1987): 623–626.

Noncompetitive, nonhostile metaphors should have been used to describe the summit and to encourage cooperation.

1597. Stanley, Linda, and David Shimkin. "The Triadic Journal: The Purposes and Processes of Journal Writing across the College Curriculum." *WAC* 5 (December 1987): 2–4.

Discusses roles students may assume in using journals in academic courses across the curriculum.

1598. Stotsky, Sandra. "Civic Writing: An Exploratory Study." Paper presented at the National Reading Conference, Austin, Tex. December 1986. ERIC ED 279 017. 24 pages

Condones exploring the purpose and audiences of civic writing as well as its potential to motivate personal and moral development. Examines two pieces of such writing.

1599. Strauss, Michael J., and Toby Fulwiler. "Interactive Writing and Learning Chemistry." *JCST* 16 (February 1987): 256–262.

Students submit questions in a large lecture section, which the instructor discusses in the next class. This "feedback loop" promotes greater attention, better understanding, and improved learning.

1600. Stygall, Gail. "Toulmin and the Ethics of Argument Fields: Teaching Writing and Argument." *JTW* 6 (Spring 1987): 93–108.

Considers the limits of formal logic. Discusses the negotiability of data between disciplines through the analysis of warrants, backing, and claims.

1601. Surlin, Stuart H. "Value System Changes by Students as a Result of Media Ethics Course." *JQ* 64 (Summer–Autumn 1987): 564–568.

Students came to realize that expressing an ethical opinion is natural and normal, not exceeding "courageous."

1602. Taylor, William M. *Political Science 202: International Relations Writing Assignments.* Los Angeles: ERIC/JC, 1987. ERIC ED 284 711. 50 pages

Offers a rationale for five writing assignments given in a community college political science course.

1603. Wallace, David Adams, and Mervin Pasch. "The Past as Experience: A Qualitative Assessment of National History Day." *HT* 20 (February 1987): 179–194.

The National History Contest provides students with ways to develop reading and writing skills as they "learn history in an 'active way.'"

1604. Wallace, Ray. "Writing across the Curriculum: A Faculty Survey." *WLN* 11 (January 1987): 8–10.

A survey of professors across the curriculum reveals "content quality, development of ideas, and overall paper organization" to be the most valued writing skills.

1605. Wilson, James C. "Teaching Journalism to English Majors." *CollT* 35 (Spring 1987): 59–60.

Presents three assignments to teach journalistic writing without the resources of journalism school. A report of a lecture, a personality profile, and an oral history.

1606. Wolfe, Rosemary F. "Writing across the Curriculum through Supplemental Instruction: An Approach to Writing Essay Exams." *MarylandEJ* 21 (Fall 1987): 43–48.

Paid "model students" supplemented classroom instruction by modeling skills needed for success and by conducting review sessions. Nineteen participants had significantly more success than 22 nonparticipants.

1607. Woolever, Kristin R. "The Dramatic Elements of Legal Writing: The Role of Audience." Paper presented at the CCCC Convention, New Orleans, March 1986. ERIC ED 278 027. 12 pages

Illustrates the importance of audience, purpose, and tone for effective writing in four types of legal communication.

1608. Zeidner, M. A. "Responsibility in Reporting Medical News." *JBTC* 1 (January 1987): 129–132.

Argues that medical reporting is uncritical and uninformative, more promotional than precise.

See also 14, 990, 1046, 1057, 1337, 1346, 1373, 1374, 1399, 1744, 1782

4.3 ADULT EDUCATION

1609. Bean, Rita M., and Rhonda S. Johnson. "The Pittsburgh Adult Competency Program: A Model for Effective Literacy Programming." *AdLBEd* 11 (1987): 1–12.

Describes an adult literacy program stressing reading and math. Student journals record reflections on learning experiences and provide the basis for individual student-teacher conferences.

1610. Courage, Richard. "Teaching Writing to Academically Underprepared Adult Students: The School of New Resources Experience." Paper presented at the CCCC Convention, New Orleans, March 1986. ERIC ED 276 060. 13 pages

Describes the goals of a student-centered program of writing instruction for adults over 21 pursuing a B.A. degree.

1611. Cuellar, Sylvia. "Creating a Classroom Newsletter: From Theory to Practice." *AdLBEd* 9 (1985): 1–5.

Recommends using a classroom newsletter to involve teachers and students in the learning process. Also available as ERIC ED 272 740.

1612. Ford, Arthur. "Word Processing in the Continuing Education Composition Class." *CAC* 1 (Spring 1987): 161–169.

Describes experiences teaching continuing education students to use full-immersion word-processing software.

1613. Garcia, Victoria Lynn. "Adult Education and Political Development: Case Study Based on the Nicaraguan Literacy Campaign and Adult Education Program." *DAI* 48 (July 1987): 210A.

Examines the relationship between participating in adult basic education and factors related to political development in Nicaragua.

1614. Gorrell, Donna. "Writing across the Curriculum in Adult Basic Education." Paper presented at the CCCC Convention, Atlanta, March 1987. ERIC ED 281 217. 11 pages

Assigning freewriting exercises prior to practicing the formal characteristics of discourse has value in an adult basic education class.

1615. Hardiman, Wintonnette Joyce. "The Ancient Egyptian Autobiographical Tradition and Its Pedagogical Value to the Urban Adult Learner." *DAI* 48 (September 1987): 750A.

Describes the ancient Egyptian autobiographical tradition, demonstrating its value in a contemporary urban adult teaching situation.

1616. Herrera, Rosa Maria Torres. "Adults' Cognitive Styles and Rate of Learning: A Study of Military Personnel in a Basic Skills Program." *DAI* 48 (December 1987): 1379A.

Tests for field dependent and independent learning styles were administered to 114 people enrolled in the Army's Basic Skills Education Program. Finds no statistically significant differences in rates of learning.

1617. Kolenbrander, Ronald W. "Adult Literacy, the Reagan Administration, and the Corporate Response: A Policy Study." *DAI* 47 (May 1987): 3944A.

Examines the components of the Reagan administration's policy toward adult literacy and ascertains the role of the private sector in assisting adult illiterates.

1618. Lytle, Susan L., Thomas W. Marmor, and Faith H. Penner. "Literacy Theory in Practice: Assessing Reading and Writing of Low-Literate Adults." Paper presented at the American Educational Research Association, San Francisco, April 1986. ERIC ED 278 675. 65 pages

Reports the preliminary results of an investigation exploring the influences of literacy instruction on 76 adults in Philadelphia.

1619. McCarron, William E., and Terry L. Bangs. "Teaching Writing outside the Classroom." *ABCAB* 50 (December 1987): 1–3.

Offers 10 practical suggestions for a successful business writing short course taught outside the university.

1620. Mei, Dolores M., James T. Langlois, Philip Herr, and Doris Innis. *Adult Basic Education 1985–1986: End-of-Year Report.* New York: New York City Board of Education, 1987. ERIC ED 284 028. 35 pages

Describes an adult education program serving 39,000 students, about half immigrants.

1621. Millard, Thomas L. "Active Learning: The Equilibrium between Student Writing and Critical Thinking." Paper presented at the Regional Conference on University Teaching, Las Cruces, N.M., January 1986. ERIC ED 281 227. 12 pages

When graduate students at Montclair State College were encouraged to write for publication, their confidence as writers grew.

1622. Nazareth, Peter. "Adventures in International Writing." *WLT* 61 (Summer 1987): 382–387.

Relates experiences as a participant in the International Writing Program at the University of Iowa. Discusses how international authors have fared and been funded.

1623. Nieh, Hualing, and Paul Engle. "The World Comes to Iowa (and Its International Writing Program)." *WLT* 61 (Summer 1987): 367–372.

International Writing Program, now in its twentieth year, is described by its co-founders, who have published 36 books to help fund the program.

1624. Pomerenke, Paula J., and JoAnna Stephens Mink. "The Needs of Adult Learners in Composition." *TETYC* 14 (October 1987): 205–210.

Examines the problems of mixed adult and pre-adult classes and the characteristics of older students.

1625. Safman, Phyllis C. "Illiterate Women: New Approaches for New Lives." Paper presented at the Annual Conference of the American Association for Adult and Continuing Education, Hollywood, Fla., October 1986. ERIC ED 275 856. 17 pages

Reviews national efforts to address illiteracy among women.

1626. Scheiber, H. J. "Consciousness Raising and Collaboration: The One-Day Professional Writing Seminar." *ABCAB* 50 (September 1987): 30–33.

Describes a one-day business writing seminar that focuses on raising participants' consciousness about successful communication practices and collaborative methods.

1627. Sherrill, Sharon L. "Teaching Writing to Adults: Synthesis of Research and a Report on Current Practice in the North Carolina Community College System." *DAI* 48 (November 1987): 1090A.

Instructors viewed adult learners as being better than traditional-age learners. Instructors were not trained in adult education and taught writing the same way to all ages.

1628. Tingle, Mark. "Literacy Development and the Working-Class Student." *WI* 7 (Fall 1987): 21–27.

Describes resistance to literacy instruction in a class composed of members of the California Conservation Corps. The use of group work reduced this resistance.

1629. Trivisonno, Ann. "Freirean Literacy and the Liberal Arts: Empowering the Returning Adult." Paper presented at the CCCC Convention, Atlanta, March 1987. ERIC ED 284 245. 11 pages

Uses the work of Paulo Freire to explain a sequence of assignments in Humanities Focus on Life, a course for adults returning to school.

1630. Ward, Annita Marie. *Comparative Literacy Attainment Behaviors of Nonliterate Adults and Preliterate and Early Literate Children.* Urbana, Ill.: ERIC/RCS, 1986. ERIC ED 284 184. 13 pages

Tests illiterate adults and children at grades two and kindergarten, finding that illiterate adults lack some of the metacognitive skills of second-grade children.

See also 20, 283, 443, 701, 1152, 1193, 1648, 1757

4.4   ENGLISH AS A SECOND LANGUAGE

1631. Al-Braik, Mubarek S. "Investigation of the Successful Attributes of English as a Second Language of Saudi Arabian Students Studying in the United States of America." *DAI* 47 (May 1987): 4005A.

Supports previous findings that learner attitudinal variables play an important role in learning foreign languages.

1632. Anakasiri, Sontaya. "Indicators of Quality in Second Language Written Communication." *DAI* 48 (September 1987): 583A.

Confirms that text length is not a predictor of quality writing, but subordination, cohesion, and substitution forms are related to quality.

1633. Arndt, Valerie. "Six Writers in Search of Texts: A Protocol-Based Study of L1 and L2 Writing." *ELT* 41 (1987): 257–267.

Discusses the findings of case studies comparing the composing activities of six Chinese students in L1 and L2. Suggests implications for teaching.

1634. Bang, Hwa-Ja Park. "The Effect of Using Class Discussion as a Prewriting Activity in Teaching Composition to ESL Students." *DAI* 47 (May 1987): 4005A.

Concludes that the improvement in writing performance shown by students can be attributed to their experiences in class discussion.

1635. Barkho, Leon Y. "Interlanguage across Academic Contexts." *ESP* 6 (1987): 157–161.

Examines four essay examination papers from Iraqi university students. Concludes that groups vary according to their motivation and their readiness for an ESP course.

1636. Blanton, Linda Lonon. "Reshaping ESL Students' Perceptions of Writing." *ELT* 41 (April 1987): 112–118.

Outlines a writing program using a variety of methods to help reduce anxiety and increase writing proficiency.

1637. Campbell, Elizabeth, and Kristine Webb. "Tutoring Techniques for Students in the Oral Tradition." *WLN* 12 (October 1987): 5–9.

Presents methods for helping ESL students or students who speak nonstandard English improve their writing.

1638. Carrell, Patricia L., and Pamela Floyd. "Effects on ESL Reading of Teaching Cultural Content Schemata." *LL* 37 (March 1987): 89–108.

Finds that reading comprehension of ESL students can be improved by first giving them background cultural information and experiences related to the reading content.

1639. Chamot, Anna Uhl, and J. Michael O'Malley. "The Cognitive Academic Language Learning Approach: A Bridge to the Mainstream." *TESOLQ* 21 (June 1987): 227–249.

Presents the theory behind and a description of the Cognitive Academic Language Learning Approach (CALLA), offered as a transition to the mainstream for ESL learners. Distinguishes non-CALLA and CALLA writing activities.

1640. Chenoweth, N. Ann. "The Need to Teach Rewriting." *ELT* 41 (January 1987): 25–29.

Promotes a process approach emphasizing the value of content-based rewriting. Urges teachers to postpone correcting editing errors until the final draft stage.

1641. Crew, Louie. "A Comment on 'Contrastive Rhetoric: An American Writing Teacher in China' [*CE* 47 (December 1985)." *CE* 49 (November 1987): 827–830.

Argues that Matalene ignores much of the rhetoric of revolution in China and the discourse that has shaped its culture.

1642. Diaz, Diana M. "The Adult ESL Writer: The Process and the Context." Paper presented at the NCTE Convention, San Antonio, November 1986. ERIC ED 281 235. 18 pages

An ethnographic study of a New York community college's process curriculum. Finds that process techniques are valuable for ESL students.

1643. Dicker, Susan J. "Abstracting in Writing: A Study of Four ESL College Students." *DAI* 47 (May 1987): 4007A.

Hypothesizes that certain abstracting traits may represent a general communicative tendency. Abstracting traits may also be determined by both individual and cultural factors.

1644. Dominguez, Ramon. "Influencing the Academic Achievement of English as a Second Language at El Paso Community College." *DAI* 48 (July 1987): 31A.

Analysis indicates that the final regression model is capable of predicting cumulative grade point averages for ESL students.

1645. Frey, Kathleen Graham. "An Investigation of Second Language Learning Strategies." *DAI* 48 (October 1987): 856A.

Examines what students report about their own strategies for learning French. Provides a typography and description of 30 strategies.

1646. Hadaway, Nancy L., and Viola Florez Tishe. "Encouraging Process over Product: Writing with Second Language Learners." *ET* 18 (Spring 1987): 18–20.

Teachers who use current writing pedagogy can provide valuable language learning opportunities for students with limited English proficiency.

1647. Hamp-Lyons, Liz. "Raters Respond to Rhetoric in Writing." *TECFORS* 10 (May–September 1987): 16–32.

A study of the "processes of the essay raters as they respond to" ESL papers. Reveals the influence of cross-cultural rhetorical transfer in readers.

1648. Hartel, Jo Anne, Judy Hikes, Kim Gerould, and Stuart Gedal. *A Guide to ESL Literacy*. Boston: Massachusetts State Department of Education, 1986. ERIC ED 274 875. 187 pages

Covers recruitment, assessment, and teaching techniques for adult ESL learners who lack formal schooling in their native languages.

1649. Harvey, T. Edward. "Second Language Composition Instruction, Computers, and First Language Pedagogy: A Descriptive Survey." *FLA* 20 (April 1987): 171–180.

A survey of Spanish faculty members indicates a shift toward process-oriented, student-centered, computer-assisted writing courses.

1650. Herrmann, Andrea W. "Word Processing in the ESL Class: Integrating Reading, Writing, Listening, and Speaking Skills." Paper presented at the MLA Meeting, Chicago, December 1985. ERIC ED 274 980. 12 pages

Advocates the use of computers in a writing workshop for promoting the learning of all skills by ESL students.

1651. Hirsch, Linda M. "The Use of Expressive Function Talk and Writing as a Learning Tool with Adult ESL Students across the Curriculum." *DAI* 47 (February 1987): 2927A.

Community college students used expressive talk and writing to increase significantly their comprehension of course material.

1652. Ho, David. "Intralingual and Interlingual Factors in Language Learning Difficulty." *JPsyR* 16 (September 1987): 399–416.

Concludes that learning a second language is more difficult than learning a first language. There is evidence that interlingual distance is a determinant of learning difficulty.

1653. *Japan Association of Language Teachers Journal* 8 (1986–1987).

Makes available, as ERIC ED 283 398, the November 1986 and July 1987 issues of this journal, which contain 10 articles on ESL instruction.

1654. Johns, Ann M. "On Assigning Summaries: Some Suggestions and Cautions." *TECFORS* 10 (March 1987): 1–5.

Reports research on the variety of summary types, the importance of identifying an audience for the summary in choosing a type, and ways of teaching summarizing.

1655. Johnson, LaVerne B. " 'Gifted' Low Achievers." *ET* 18 (Spring 1987): 33–34.

In a Christmas card to each of her ESL students, this teacher gave the etymology of each student's name.

1656. Kowal, Kristopher H. "Embracing the Tao: Peter Elbow Re-Contextualized—A Review Essay." *TECFORS* 10 (May–September 1987): 6–13.

Reviews Elbow's *Embracing Contraries,* relating Elbow's philosophy to Eastern ideas and his methodology to Asian students.

1657. Kumpf, Lorraine Edith. "Structuring Narratives in a Second Language: Descriptions of Rhetoric and Grammar." *DAI* 47 (April 1987): 3749A.

Studies three Japanese and three Spanish speakers to learn how they structure narratives and what relationship grammatical form has to this structure.

1658. Lapp, Ron. "Using Quickwriting to Facilitate the Writing Process of Intermediate and Advanced ESL Students: Part I of a Two-Part Series." *TECFORS* 10 (January 1987): 1–5.

Defines "quickwriting," explaining how to train ESL writers to quickwrite and to use quickwriting for prewriting and classroom management.

1659. Lapp, Ron. "Using Quickwriting to Facilitate the Writing Process of Intermediate and Advanced ESL Students: Part II." *TECFORS* 10 (March 1987): 9–13.

Discusses how to use quickwriting in ESL courses to aid drafting, revisions, and the evaluation or appreciation of writing.

1660. Liebman-Kleine, JoAnne. "Teaching and Researching Invention: Using Ethnography in ESL Writing Classes." *ELT* 41 (April 1987): 104–111.

This ethnographic study of freshman composition compares hierarchical treeing, open-ended exploratory writing, and systematic heuristics as invention techniques.

1661. Malcolm, Lois. "What Rules Govern Tense Usage in Scientific Articles?" *ESP* 6 (1987): 31–43.

Analyzes discourse in 20 scientific articles, suggesting hierarchical relationships that determine tense choices. Outlines ways to help writers choose tense.

1662. Mangelsdorf, Kate, and Vicki Taylor. "Using Heuristics to Respond to Advanced ESL Composition Students." Paper presented at the CCCC Convention, Atlanta, March 1987. ERIC ED 283 377. 18 pages

Reports on the use of a revision heuristic with six ESL students, finding it successful only for better writers.

1663. Martin-Betancourt, Mary Ellen. "The Composing Processes of Puerto Rican College Students of English as a Second Language." *DAI* 47 (January 1987): 2577A.

Finds similarities in composing processes between ESL and Spanish.

1664. Matalene, Carolyn. "Carolyn Matalene Responds [to Crew, *CE* 49 (November 1987)]." *CE* 49 (November 1987): 830–831.

Clarifies the point of her study, the cultural impact of Chinese rhetoric.

1665. NCTE Task Force on Racism and Bias in the Teaching of English. *Expanding Opportunities: Academic Success for Culturally and Linguistically Diverse Students*. Urbana, Ill.: NCTE, 1986. 2 pages

Provides suggestions for teaching writing and reading to culturally and linguistically diverse students. Offers guidelines for choosing materials.

1666. Obiedat, Hussein Ali. "An Investigation of Syntactic and Semantic Errors in the Writ-

ten Composition of Arab EFL Learners." *DAI* 47 (March 1987): 3415A.

Identifies several linguistic and nonlinguistic factors that affect subjects' writing. Suggests more varied approaches to error analysis.

1667. Olivier, George Alexander, Jr. "Increasing the Syntactic Fluency of Foreign Language Students in Reading through Sentence Combining." *DAI* 48 (July 1987): 38A.

A study to assess the value of sentence combining with sentence reduction in elementary stages of second language learning.

1668. Osburne, Andrea G., and Janice L. Dowd. "Teaching Chinese Students to Write Essay Examinations and Papers." *TECFORS* 10 (May–September 1987): 1–5.

Describes some reasons behind negative features of Chinese students' writing on examinations. Suggests ways to teach Chinese graduate students how to write effective examinations.

1669. Ouaouicha, Driss. "Contrastive Rhetoric and the Structure of Learner-Produced Argumentative Texts in Arabic and English." *DAI* 47 (March 1987): 3339A.

Identifies several similarities in subjects' argumentative texts and recommends further analysis in target areas.

1670. Piper, Alison. "Helping Learners to Write: A Role for the Word Processor." *ELT* 41 (1987): 119–125.

Describes activities and products in an ESL writing class that uses word processing. Explains 12 reasons for using word processing in teaching ESL composition.

1671. Radin, Barbara Sue. "The Effects of Two Communicative Approaches on the Communicative Competence of Adult Hispanic College ESL Students." *DAI* 48 (October 1987): 798A.

Explores the effectiveness of strategic interaction and counseling-learning methodologies in enhancing competence, self-esteem, and self-assessment abilities.

1672. Raimes, Ann. "Language Proficiency, Writing Ability, and Composing Strategies: A Study of ESL College Student Writers." *LL* 37 (September 1987): 439–468.

Think-aloud composing protocols show similarities in the composing strategies of L2 and basic L1 writers. Finds little correspondence among proficiency, writing ability, and composing strategies.

1673. Reid, Joy M. "The Writer's Workbench and ESL Composition." *CC* 4 (August 1987): 53–63.

Describes an adaptation of Writer's Workbench for ESL students. Concludes that its limitations may also be strengths for these students.

1674. Robinson, Peter. "Projection into Dialogue as a Composition Strategy." *ELT* 41 (January 1987): 30–36.

Using business letters, outlines ways to help students develop decision-making processes in original compositions and in revision.

1675. Rooholamini, Simin Dokht. "A Cultural Manual in English as a Foreign Language for Advanced Students from Iran." *DAI* 47 (March 1987): 3343A.

Combines cultural awareness with writing exercises to facilitate EFL training.

1676. Rorschach, Elizabeth Gayle. "The Effects of Reader Awareness: A Case Study of Three ESL Writers." *DAI* 47 (June 1987): 4311A.

Focuses on how L2 writers construe their audience and how that awareness affects their choices when composing.

1677. Sanborn, Jean. "Obstacles and Opportunities: Sentence Combining in Advanced ESL." *JBW* 6 (Fall 1987): 60–71.

Reports on the advantages and disadvantages of teaching sentence combining, emphasizing the usefulness of sentence com-

bining to international advanced ESL students.

1678. Schlumberger, Ann, and Diane Clymer. "What to Do in Composition Classes When You Have ESL Students and No ESL Expertise." Paper presented at the CCCC Convention, Atlanta, March 1987. ERIC ED 283 382. 13 pages

Offers three suggestions for ESL classes: have thematic unity, limit formal themes, and use reading, listening, and speaking tasks.

1679. Silva, Tony. "ESL Composition: An Historical Perspective." Paper presented at the CCCC Convention, Atlanta, March 1987. ERIC ED 282 442. 13 pages

Reviews developments in ESL composition theory since 1945, exploring the dimensions of an adequate model of ESL composition.

1680. Sivall, John. "Inter-School Correspondence: A Rationale and an Invitation." *TECFORS* 10 (May–September 1987): 14–15.

Describes a newsletter exchange among three Canadian ESL programs. Provides address for participating.

1681. Skelton, John, and Makaya Pindi. "Acquiring a New Context: Zairean Students Struggle with the Academic Mode." *ESP* 6 (1987): 121–131.

Studies the interlanguage in the writing of Zairean economics students. Identifies a high tolerance for transfer and errors. Distinguishes types of transfer.

1682. Storla, Steven Redding. "The Role of Reading Materials in University Composition Courses for Native Users of English and for ESL Students." *DAI* 48 (November 1987): 1138A.

Explores the convergence of reading and writing processes and its significance for a literacy-based curriculum.

1683. Swales, John. "Utilizing the Literatures in Teaching the Research Paper." *TESOLQ* 21 (March 1987): 41–68.

Uses the sociology of science, citation analysis, technical writing, and English for academic purposes to teach a research writing class to ESL graduate students and staff.

1684. Taki El Din, Shaker Rizk. "The Effectiveness of Sentence-Combining Practice on Arab Students' Overall Writing Quality and Syntactic Maturity." *DAI* 47 (February 1987): 3022A.

Tentatively concludes that sentence combining is beneficial to EFL Arab students.

1685. Thompson, Mertel E. "Literacy in a Creole Context: Teaching Freshman English in Jamaica." Paper presented at the CCCC Convention, New Orleans, March 1986. ERIC ED 276 054. 19 pages

Recommends that Creole speakers learning academic literacy conceptualize in the native language, switch codes, and practice reading and writing extensively.

1686. Tushyeh, Hanna Y. "Transfer and Related Strategies in the Acquisition of English Relativization by Adult Arab ESL Learners." Paper presented at the Japanese Association of Language Teachers, Kyoto, Japan, September 1985. ERIC ED 276 290. 34 pages

Analyzes written responses to a variety of tests to examine the significance of types of transfer and other psycholinguistic strategies.

1687. Uljin, Jan M., and Jan B. Strother. "Interlanguage and EST Writing: Some Syntactic Evidence." *ESP* 6 (1987): 99–112.

Results of testing Dutch and American students indicate that technical writers tend to prefer the scientific register over common language.

1688. Wallace, David L. *Dialogue Journals: A Tool for ESL Teaching.* Urbana, Ill.: ERIC/RCS, 1987. ERIC ED 380 316. 14 pages

Describes how dialogue journal writing can be used effectively in the ESL classroom to increase fluency.

1689. Wallace, Ray. "Teaching Audience to Advanced ESL Technical Writers." *ExEx* 33 (Fall 1987): 19–21.

Presents a six-step exercise in which students write instructions for making paper airplanes. Classmates must be able to construct the airplanes from the written directions.

1690. Walsh, Catherine. "Language, Meaning, and Voice: Puerto Rican Students' Struggle for a Speaking Consciousness." *LArts* 64 (February 1987): 196–206.

Examines strategies developed by Puerto Rican students to deal with competing tensions between school and community discourses. Bibliography included.

1691. Wang, Moxi. "An Unconventional Approach to Composition Teaching." *TECFORS* 10 (March 1987): 6–8.

Describes a successful writing course based on extensive writing, fast writing, and intensive writing. Teacher grades only the intensive pieces.

1692. Webster, Maree T. "The Relationship between Metalinguistic Ability and Second Language Learning." *DAI* 47 (May 1987): 4008A.

Results show that not all aspects of metalinguistic ability are related to second language proficiency.

1693. Zuckermann, Gertrude. "The Impact of Writing Activities on the Teaching of Reading to Students of English as a Foreign Language." *DAI* 48 (August 1987): 326A.

Sentence writing improved comprehension.

See also 6, 30, 111, 523, 686, 738, 765, 808, 1113, 1245, 1354, 1571, 1620

4.5 RESEARCH AND STUDY SKILLS

1694. Allison, Barbara. "Beginning at the Beginning: Synthesis and the Research Paper." *Leaflet* 86 (Winter 1987): 17–24.

Describes a series of exercises to guide students in the writing of research papers.

1695. Basham, Charlotte Schilling. "Summary Writing: A Study in Textual and Contextual Constraints." *DAI* 47 (March 1987): 3409A.

Studies the summary writing skills of three groups: native Alaskan students, English remedial students, and experienced writers. Suggests that cultural values influence a student's "approach to academic tasks."

1696. Bolt, Janice A. H. "A Study of the Effects of a Bibliographic Instruction Course on Achievement and Retention of College Students." *DAI* 47 (June 1987): 4219A.

The study shows small gains for the group given library instruction.

1697. Cornelius, Dale. "Scientific Research Demands Proficient Prose." *CalE* 23 (January–February 1987): 12.

Reports on biology students who wrote research projects [see also Heaston and Phillips, "Students Research and Write," *CalE* 23 (January–February 1987)].

1698. Croft, W. Bruce. "Approaches to Intelligent Information Retrieval." *IPM* 23 (1987): 249–254.

Explains computerized information retrieval, summarizes current approaches, and relates the retrieval process to artificial intelligence research. Other articles in this issue of *IPM* describe specific models.

1699. Demerley, Ed. "Putting the Past into the Present through Research Papers." Paper presented at the Midwest Regional Conference on English in Two-Year College, St. Louis, February 1986. ERIC ED 276 015. 15 pages

Offers a way of teaching the research paper to community college freshmen.

1700. Dick, Florence, and John R. Dick. "Darwin, Freud, Keynes *et al.*: Theory as Topic for Student Term Papers." *WI* 6 (Winter 1987): 72–79.

Describes courses in which theories in the students' major fields or important figures

in those fields became topics for research papers.

1701. Dubois, Nelson F. "A Review of the Research on Note Taking from Lecture: Some New Directions to Investigate." Paper presented at the American Psychological Association, Washington, D.C., August 1986. ERIC ED 274 896. 19 pages

Concludes that extant research has failed to investigate instructionally relevant variables in ecologically valid contexts.

1702. Galles, Gary M. "Professors Are Woefully Ignorant of a Well-Organized Market Inimical to Learning: The Big Business in Research Papers." *CHE* 34 (28 October 1987): B1, B3.

Universities cannot stop the sale of research papers because proof is difficult and litigation is expensive; yet, teachers can help by requiring drafts and notecards.

1703. Head, Martha Holcomb. "Factors Affecting Summary Writing and Their Impact on Reading Comprehension Assessment." *DAI* 47 (March 1987): 3381A.

Findings show that written summaries can adequately test aspects of reading comprehension. Identifies influences on written recall.

1704. Heaston, Sharon, and Monica Phillips. "Students Research and Write." *CalE* 23 (January–February 1987): 13, 30.

A research report written in Dale Cornelius's class [see "Scientific Research Demands Proficient Prose," *CalE* 23 (January–February 1987)].

1705. Heller, Scott. "Ineffective Teaching and Fuzzy Assignments Can Thwart 'Critical Thinking' by College Students, Scholars Argue." *CHE* 34 (2 December 1987): A13, A20.

Participants at an institute on teaching critical thinking argued that this skill is discipline specific and that professors fail to explain different methods of thinking critically.

1706. Hoffert, Sylvia D. "Toward Solving the Term Paper Dilemma." *HT* 20 (May 1987): 343–348.

Discusses ways to help students implement the goals of term paper assignments, such as hypothesis testing.

1707. Hoffman, Abraham. "Going for the Green: Contests as Motivation for Research Papers." *HT* 20 (February 1987): 195–206.

Contests act as an incentive for students to learn to write good research papers.

1708. Jeske, Jeff. "Borrowing from the Sciences: A Model for the Freshman Research Paper." *WI* 6 (Winter 1987): 62–67.

Advocates a revised structure for the research paper modeled on that used in the hard sciences, including sections on "Materials and Methods," "Results," and "Discussion."

1709. Larsen, Richard B. "Updating the Term Paper Assignment." *CAC* 1 (Winter 1987): 99–101.

Suggests that employing a word processor encourages students to think more critically about research projects.

1710. Malena, Richard F., and Karen J. Atwood Coker. "Reading *O*prehension: The Missing Element." *JDEd* 10 (January 1987): 24–25, 35.

Discusses a reading-learning-study strategy that involves systematic and deliberate instruction in cognitive and metacognitive skills.

1711. Mandel, Miriam B. "On the Value of Secondary Sources as Teaching Materials." *Leaflet* 86 (Winter 1987): 8–13.

Suggests that critical materials form a separate unit for instruction in writing, reading, and research skills.

1712. Polanski, Virginia G. "Real-World Research for Freshmen." Paper presented at the CCCC Convention, New York, March 1984. ERIC ED 283 172. 8 pages

Offers examples of research topics in the real world.

1713. Schmersahl, Carmen B. "Teaching Library Research: Process, Not Product." *JTW* 6 (Fall–Winter 1987): 231–238.

A sequence of assignments that provides a rhetorical context for research, introduces technical skill gradually, and gives repeated practice.

1714. Schmidt, Elizabeth G. "A Quasi-Experimental Study of the Effects of Teacher Bibliographic Instruction on the Library Skills of College Bound High School Students." *DAI* 48 (November 1987): 1046A.

Although teachers' library skills improved, their students' did not.

1715. Sheer, Steven C. "The Fictitious Term Paper." *JTW* 6 (Fall–Winter 1987): 223–229.

Presents a playful but serious use for scholarly writing. The form must be correct, but the content can be imaginative.

1716. Sosville, Jerri. "*Daughter of Time:* Outside Reading for a Research Writing Course." *ExEx* 33 (Fall 1987): 23–26.

Describes an approach to teaching Josephine Tey's *Daughter of Time* (1951), a mystery about the problems confronting researchers.

1717. Spieglehalder, Glenn. *From Darkness into Light: A Group Process Approach to the Research Paper*. Urbana, Ill.: ERIC/RCS, 1983. ERIC ED 280 542. 24 pages

Describes the use of peer groups in writing research papers at El Paso Community College.

1718. Sullivan, Patricia Ann. "Rhetoric and the Search for Extended Stored Knowledge: Toward a Computer Age Art of Research." *DAI* 47 (April 1987): 3601A.

An exploratory study examining how six expert and six novice searchers used the electronic library to find external sources of argument for a college research paper.

1719. Vickery, A., and H. M. Brooks. "PLEXUS—The Expert System for Referral." *IPM* 23 (1987): 99–117.

Describes PLEXUS, a British system prototype that can guide a novice user to appropriate library sources.

See also 148, 855, 1092, 1164, 1373, 1374, 1555, 1562, 1586, 1683

4.6   OTHER

1720. Hirschorn, Michael. "Buddhist College Steers Path from '60s Energy' to Accreditation." *CHE* 33 (29 July 1987): 3.

An experimental two-year upper-division college in Boulder, Colorado, informed by a 1960s *zeitgeist*, has become less zany, more academically rigorous, and accredited.

1721. Kanning, Jimmie McGraw. "Students with Learning Difficulties in the English Classroom." *ET* 18 (Spring 1987): 7–12.

Relating personal teaching experiences, the author describes how to recognize and help students with learning difficulties.

1722. Koenke, Karl. "Keyboarding: Prelude to Composing at the Computer." *EEd* 19 (December 1987): 244–249.

Examines trends in teaching keyboarding prior to college.

1723. Malachowski, Ann Marie. "Composing and Computing by the Writer with Head Trauma." *CC* 5 (November 1987): 52–62.

In describing how she worked with a student disabled by head trauma, the author points the way to working with other disabled students.

1724. Manoff, Robert Karl, and Michael Schudson, eds. *Reading the News*. New York: Pantheon, 1987. 256 pages

A collection of seven essays to help the public read and understand the news in newspapers.

1725. O'Weary, Timothy [pseud.]. "Confession of a Tenure-Track Professor: I Was Addicted to Speed." *TETYC* 14 (May 1987): 150–151.

A humorous essay on breaking the addiction to speedy word processing by using Slo-Write.

5
Testing, Measurement, and Evaluation

5.1 EVALUATION OF STUDENTS

1726. Allina, Amy. *Beyond Standardized Tests: Admissions Alternatives That Work.* Cambridge, Mass.: FairTest, 1987.

Reports on the success of seven colleges and graduate schools that recently dropped or deemphasized standardized admissions tests.

1727. Applebee, Arthur N., Judith A. Langer, and Ina S. Mullis. *Grammar, Punctuation, and Spelling: Controlling the Conventions of Written English at Ages 9, 13, and 17.* Princeton, N.J.: NAEP, ETS, 1987. ERIC ED 282 928. 49 pages

Supplements earlier analyses of the 1984 NAEP Writing Assessment (ERIC ED 273 680 and ERIC ED 273 994) with error counts, finding that errors decrease with age.

1728. Aristides. "Student Evaluation." *ASch* 56 (Spring 1987): 177–184.

A former "B student" and "C original thinker" talks about "good" and "bad" students and about being a teacher.

1729. Baumlin, James S., and Tita French Baumlin. "Belletrism, Cultural Literacy, and the Dialectic of Critical Response." *FEN* 16 (Fall 1987): 2–4, 6–8.

Explains that evaluations of student papers must represent a dialectic between the literary, the political, the psychological, and the sociological.

1730. Berman, Isabel N. "Towards a New Reading Comprehension Test Based on Cognitive Theory." *DAI* 47 (May 1987): 3959A.

Results indicate that an experimental test based on cognitive theories of reading provided more accurate placement data than traditional measures of reading comprehension.

1731. Bizzell, Patricia. "What Can We Know, What Must We Do, What May We Hope?: Writing Assessment." *CE* 49 (September 1987): 575–584.

An essay review of three books on writing assessment. Concludes that practice exceeds theory in writing assessment.

1732. Boonsathorn, Somsak. "C-Tests, Proficiency, and Reading Strategies in ESL." *DAI* 48 (November 1987): 1111A.

Results indicate that the MC-Test "discriminated better, had a greater reliability, and was more valid with regard to factor structures, than the C-Test."

1733. Bracey, Gerald W. "Texts, Tests Don't Match—But Does It Matter?" *PhiDK* 68 (January 1987): 397.

Examines issues in matching curricula with tests. Concludes that teachers manage to teach what students need instead of teaching to a test.

1734. Breland, Hunter M., Roberta Camp, Robert J. Jones, Margaret M. Morris, and Donald A. Rock. *Assessing Writing Skill.* New York: College Board Publications, 1987. 128 pages

Reports on a study of 270 students who each wrote six essays. Examines the reliability of multiple-choice versus writing sample assessments, their cost, the amount of time they take, and their effect on classroom writing instruction.

1735. Brody, Celeste. *A Guide to Published Tests of Writing Proficiency.* Portland, Ore.: Northwest Regional Educational Laboratory, 1986. ERIC ED 278 714. 70 pages

Profiles 49 standard English usage tests for the assessment of writing. Serves as a directory of available test options.

1736. Brossell, Gordon. "Essay Test Topic Development." Paper presented at the Conference on Writing Assessment, Cleveland, April 1986. ERIC ED 279 002. 23 pages

Calls for refining writing assessment variables and investigating ways to bridge the gap between assessment and writing pedagogy.

1737. Carney, Nyla Gilkerson. "Levels of Composition: A Case Grammar and Style Complexity Perspective." *DAI* 47 (June 1987): 4375A.

Evaluates English placement essays of 20 native and 10 nonnative college students to determine if linguistically identifiable syntactic and semantic differences correlate with student placements.

1738. Coffman, William E. *Recommendations on Writing Assessments for Future NAEPs.* Cambridge, Mass.: National Academy of Education, September 1986. ERIC ED 279 669. 7 pages

Expands the recommendations of the NAEP Writing Subcommittee in three areas: stating assessment objectives in writing, reviewing criteria for selecting exercises, and reporting results.

1739. Cook, Thomas H., Steven E. Dyche, and Samuel J. Hubbard. "Bonus Homework, Study Group, Pair Test, and Test Retake." *JCST* 16 (May 1987): 520–523.

A 10-year study shows that these methods are effective, nontraditional means of evaluation that promote study skills and collaborative learning.

1740. Culhane, Terry, Christine Klein Braly, and Douglas J. Stevenson, eds. *Practice and Problems in Language Testing: Papers from the International Symposium on Language Testing.* Occasional Papers, no. 29. Colchester, England: Department of Language and Linguistics, 1984. ERIC ED 275 162. 198 pages

Reprints 13 papers on testing English as a second or foreign language.

1741. Cullen, Roxanne, and Committee on Research and Assessment in Writing. "Research Findings of the Committee on Research and Assessment in Writing, Department of Languages and Literature, Ferris State College." Paper presented at the CCCC Convention, Atlanta, March 1987. ERIC ED 281 417. 41 pages

Reports on the Fall 1985 and Spring 1986 writing assessment of students at Ferris State College. Includes writing samples and a 15-point assessment instrument.

1742. Danis, M. Francine. "The Voice in the Margins: Paper Marking as Conversation." *FEN* 15 (Winter 1987): 18–20.

A philosophical approach to paper marking that describes it as a rhetorical act and discusses values in that approach.

1743. Drain, Susan, and Kenna Manos. "Testing the Test: Mount Saint Vincent University's English Writing Competency Test." *EQ* 19 (Winter 1986): 267–281.

Reports on the results, validity, and reliability of a writing competency test given at Mount Saint Vincent University.

1744. Ellis, P. M., G. W. Mellsop, K. A. Peace, and J. M. Wilson. "Peer Review as an Aid to Improving the Completeness of Psychiatric Case Notes." *MEd* 21 (November 1987): 493–487.

Peer review may work when adequate discussion leads to changed protocols and when those changes are frequently reinforced.

1745. Ferland, J. J., J. Dorval, and L. Levasseur. "Measuring Higher Cognitive Levels by Multiple-Choice Questions: A Myth?" *MEd* 21 (March 1987): 109–113.

A study failed to show that multiple-choice items on examinations can measure cognitive traits other than simple memorization. Suggests further research.

1746. *Foundations of Literacy: A Description of the Assessment of a Basic Knowledge of U.S. History and Literature.* Princeton, N.J.: NAEP, ETS, 1986. ERIC ED 274 684. 23 pages

Assesses what 17-year-olds know about topics in 6 periods of American history and about major authors, themes, and characters in literature.

1747. Freedman, Sarah Warshauer, Cynthia Greenleaf, and Melanie Sperling. *Response to Critical Writing.* NCTE Research Report, no. 23. Urbana, Ill.: NCTE, 1987. 224 pages

Presents the results of a national survey of teachers' response practices and a local ethnographic study of two successful ninth-grade teachers. Argues that ethnographic observations are important in analyzing teachers' responses to "academic argumentation" writing and that the best responses use "collaborative problem solving."

1748. Fuller, David C. "Teacher Commentary That Communicates: Practicing What We Preach in the Writing Class." *JTW* 6 (Fall–Winter 1987): 305–317.

Teacher's comments should focus on the context of the assignment, appreciate the student's subject, assume a single evaluation role, and provide a personal response.

1749. Galbraith, F. Lynn. "The Use of Multiple-Choice Items and Holistically Scored Writing Samples to Assess Student Writing Ability." *DAI* 47 (February 1987): 2927A.

Shows a positive correlation between students' scores on the multiple-choice and the holistically scored essay portions of the New Jersey College Basic Skills Placement Test.

1750. Gentile, Nicholas, comp. *High School Proficiency Test Skill Array: Writing.* Urbana, Ill.: ERIC/RCS, 1985. ERIC ED 281 222. 42 pages

Acquaints teachers with the New Jersey High School Proficiency Test in Writing and suggests ways to prepare students for the exam.

1751. Glenberg, Arthur M., Thomas Sanocki, William Epstein, and Craig Morris. "Enhancing Calibration of Comprehension." *JEPG* 116 (June 1987): 119–136.

Demonstrates the difficulty of tracing knowledge to particular texts. Discusses the implications in pre- and posttesting.

Preparation should mimic the testing method.

1752. Gordon, Barbara L. "Another Look: Standardized Tests for Placement in College Composition Courses." *WPA* 10 (Spring 1987): 29–38.

Considers the validity and reliability of standardized tests and writing samples. Argues for the greater accuracy of standardized tests but notes pedagogical reasons for using writing samples.

1753. Grant-Davie, Keith, and Nancy Shapiro. "Curing the Nervous Tic: Reader-Based Response to Student Writing." Paper presented at the CCCC Convention, Atlanta, March 1987. ERIC ED 282 196. 16 pages

Finds difficulties in teachers' written responses and makes suggestions drawn from research findings.

1754. Grigsby, John L. "Adventures in Admissions Testing: How I Fought ETS and Lost." *CHE* 33 (14 January 1987): 48–49.

Grigsby took the GRE twice; first without preparation, then with. ETS destroyed his second score because it exceeded ethical probability.

1755. Hanger, Nancy Welch. "A Comparison of the Cloze Procedure and the Silent IRI as Predictors of Instructional Reading Level." *DAI* 48 (October 1987): 820A.

Compares Informal Reading Inventory scores with cloze procedures across age, grade, and gender boundaries.

1756. Hayhoe, Mike. "What Are the English Doing to English? Current Issues in Assessment." *EQ* 20 (Summer 1987): 137–144.

Outlines issues in standardized testing. Questions the use of the same test for all ability levels and the adequacy of the curriculum.

1757. Holzman, Michael. "Evaluation in Adult Literacy Programs." *WI* 7 (Fall 1987): 8–20.

Examines several methods of measuring literacy in the U.S. and Great Britain and

concludes that they are inhumane. Proposes instead "direct methods of assessment."

1758. Hult, Christine A. "Assessment Topics: The Importance of the Rhetorical Frame." *WPA* 10 (Spring 1987): 19–28.

Analyzes topics used in writing assessment by the English Composition Board at the University of Michigan. Argues that the rhetorical frame (subject, purpose, audience, and voice) may affect student performance and should be designed carefully.

1759. Huntington, Mary Lee. "Making the Grade at 50: Evaluating Student Writing." *CalE* 23 (November–December 1987): 15.

Attributes her own conflicts about grading to "our compulsive need to rank and rate" teachers.

1760. Jacobs, Suzanne E. "Writing Assessment Reexamined." Paper presented at the International Conference on the Teaching of English, Ottowa, May 1986. ERIC ED 278 014. 16 pages

Critiques teach-and-test models of standardized writing assessment, arguing that such testing should conform to the new logic of process-product relationships.

1761. Johnson, Patricia. "Testing Skills in Expository Writing through Reading Comprehension." Paper presented at the TESOL Conference, New York, April 1985. ERIC ED 281 391. 9 pages

Describes multiple-choice proficiency examinations for placing nonnative English speakers in writing courses.

1762. Jonz, Jon. "Using Pooled Judgements to Develop Tests of Basic Writing." *JBW* 6 (Fall 1987): 16–25.

Explains a procedure followed at East Texas State University "to create, administer, and monitor valid and reliable measures of the writing skills of [basic writing] students."

1763. Kinzer, Charles K. "Effects of Topic and Response Variables on Holistic Scores." *EQ* 20 (Summer 1987): 106–120.

Finds that the topic affects student writing and consequently scores on that writing.

1764. Kramer, Jack J. "On the Question of Professional Standards for Computer-Based Test Interpretation." *AmP* 42 (September 1987): 889–890.

Reviews the controversy over this method of interpretation and suggests questions that might be used to develop professional standards for its use.

1765. Krampen, Gunter. "Different Effects of Teacher Comments." *JEdP* 79 (September 1987): 137–146.

Finds that comments on student work should be content specific and should take into account the student's performance level as well as a concept of the teacher's own competence.

1766. Krape, Morris. "Pennsylvania's Honors Test." *PCTEB* 54 (November 1986): 7–11.

Offers a historical perspective on the development of a statewide honors test for high school seniors.

1767. Lamar, Alexander, H. Thomas James, and Robert Glaser. *The Nation's Report Card: Improving the Assessment of Student Achievement*. Cambridge, Mass.: National Academy of Education, 1987. ERIC ED 279 662. 82 pages

Summarizes seven recommendations of the NAEP Study Group.

1768. Land, Robert E., Jr., and Sandra Evans. "What Our Students Taught Us about Paper Writing." *EJ* 76 (February 1987): 113–116.

Focuses on research that asks students to suggest effective ways for teachers to respond to student writing.

1769. Lee, Valerie E. "Proficiency: 1983–1984 Catholic School Results and National Averages." *National Assessment of Educational* *Progress Writing*. Urbana, Ill.: ERIC/RCS, 1987. ERIC ED 280 068. 30 pages

Reports on the writing achievement of Catholic students in grades 4, 8, and 11.

1770. Lutkus, Alan. "Problems in Measuring Syntactic Development: T-Units Versus Sentence Weight." *JTW* 6 (Spring 1987): 49–68.

"The T-unit approach—despite its occasional problems—continues to be the most useful method of analyzing syntactic complexity and early maturity."

1771. McClelland, Kathleen Anne. "A Case Study of Teachers Marking and/or Commenting While Reading Drafts of Student Papers." *DAI* 47 (June 1987): 4310A.

Focuses on teachers' responses, observed and recalled, while grading students' texts.

1772. McLeod, P. J. "Faculty Assessment of Case Reports of Medical Students." *JMEd* 62 (August 1987): 673–677.

Poor interrater reliability for evaluating written student reports led to the development of a 10-item list of criteria for this task.

1773. Mitchell, Karen J., and Judith A. Anderson. "Estimation of Interrator and Parallel Forms Reliability for the MCAT Essay." Paper presented at the American Educational Research Association, Washington, D.C., April 1987. ERIC ED 283 837 10 pages

Tests of the Medical College Admission Test (MCAT) show that 45-minute essays are more reliable measures than 30-minute essays.

1774. Motley, Jilda Dean. "A National Comparison of Community/Junior Colleges Communication Instructors' Attitudes toward Mandatory Testing and Placement in the Area of Freshman Composition I." *DAI* 48 (July 1987): 32A.

A national study comparing instructors' attitudes concludes that every community or junior college have placement testing for freshmen.

1775. Norman, G. R., E. K. M. Smith, A. C. P. Powles, P. J. Rooney, N. L. Henry, and P. E. Dodd. "Factors Underlying Performance on Written Tests of Knowledge." *MEd* 21 (July 1987): 297–304.

Both multiple-choice and modified essay questions have demonstrated construct validity. Undirected modified essay questions elicit more information but require context information and are less easily scored.

1776. O'Shea, Judith. "Writing Apprehension and University Tests of Writing Competence." *EQ* 20 (Winter 1987): 285–293.

Discusses elements triggering writing apprehension in timed writing competence tests. Suggests ways of providing less threatening writing conditions for students.

1777. Peckham, Irvin. "Statewide Direct Writing Assessment." *EJ* 76 (November 1987): 30–33.

Examines the California Assessment Program, which is "positively influencing classroom writing instruction" since it moves away from "multiple choice competency and toward real writing."

1778. Peckham, Irvin. "Statewide Direct Writing Assessment in California." Paper presented at the CCCC Convention, Atlanta, March 1987. ERIC ED 281 230. 13 pages

Describes the California Assessment Program, discussing the theory behind the writing test, the formulation of the test, the training of readers, and the contents of the test.

1779. Posner, Richard. "Life without Scan-Tron: Tests as Thinking." *EJ* 76 (February 1987): 35–38.

Discusses replacing objective tests with written tests in literature, composition, and vocabulary to help students think and write.

1780. Powers, Donald E. "Who Benefits Most from Preparing for a 'Coachable' Admissions Test?" *JEdM* 24 (Fall 1987): 247–262.

Finds little difference among subgroups of examinees after they study the material on the GRE analytical ability measure.

1781. Quellmalz, Edys. *Recommendations for the Design of NAEP Writing Tasks*. Cambridge, Mass.: National Academy of Education, 1986. ERIC ED 279 692. 9 pages

Argues that the NAEP assessment should stress students' oral and written discourse on social topics. Discusses subjects suitable for such an evaluation.

1782. Rabinowitz, Howard K. "The Modified Essay Question: An Evaluation of Its Use in a Family Medicine Clerkship." *MEd* 21 (March 1987): 114–118.

Describes 12 years of experience using modified essay questions. Lists five "distinct theoretical advantages" for using such questions rather than multiple-choice questions.

1783. Roy, Alice M. "When Discussing Students' Writing. . . Sit on Your Hands." *CalE* 23 (November–December 1987): 18–19, 27.

Traces changes in her response to student writing through the years, from the "Find Every Error" era to sharing responsibility with students and other instructors.

1784. Rudman, Herbert C. "The Future of Testing Is Now." *EdM* 6 (Fall 1987): 5–11.

Discusses forces, both internal and external to the testing industry, that are affecting the future of testing.

1785. Ruth, Leo, and Sandra Murphy. *Designing Writing Tasks for the Assessment of Writing*. Writing Research. Norwood, N.J.: Ablex, 1987. 368 pages

Intended to guide evaluators in designing writing tasks. Reports results of the Bay Area Writing Project's investigations into the properties of writing tasks, their author's intentions, and the differing responses evoked by student writers and teacher raters.

1786. Scenters-Zapico, John T. "Rhetorician's Guide to Correction Symbols." *ExEx* 32 (Spring 1987): 15–18.

Presents a list of numbered comments for marking students' papers. Comments address *ethos, logos, pathos,* purpose, stance, context, and organization.

1787. Schreyer, Catherine Foy. "Evaluation as Dialogical Praxis." Paper presented at the CCCC Convention, Atlanta, March 1987. ERIC ED 280 072. 14 pages

Studies how evaluation can be viewed as a transactional event between students and teachers.

1788. Shea, Renee Hausmann. "The Influence of Writing Prompt on Process and Product: An Exploratory Study Using the LSAT Writing Sample." *DAI* 48 (October 1987): 858A.

Examines the influence of writing prompts on mechanics, style, organization, development, advocacy, creativity, and the use of Toulmin's approach to argument.

1789. Sneed, Don. "Tenuous Faculty Rights." *CollT* 35 (Winter 1987): 28–29.

Discusses judicial actions affecting academic freedom in cases of student litigation. Suggests that "writing teachers whose grading is highly subjective" are "especially vulnerable."

1790. Sperling, Melanie, and Sarah Warshauer Freedman. "A Good Girl Writes like a Good Girl: Written Responses to Student Writing." *WC* 4 (October 1987): 343–369.

The information, skills, and values the teacher and student bring to a written response affect how the student misunderstands the teacher's comments.

1791. Stansfield, Charles W. "A History of the Test of Written English: The Developmental Years." Paper presented at the International Invitational Conference on Research in Language Testing, Kiryat Anavim, Israel, 1986. ERIC ED 275 199. 20 pages

Describes the development of the new 30-minute essay test for TOEFL.

1792. Stiggins, Richard J. "NCME Instructional Module on Design and Development of Performance Assessments." *EdM* 6 (Fall 1987): 33–42.

Presents a strategy and guidelines for maximizing the reliability, validity, and economy of performance assessments of communication skills.

1793. Stowers, Robert Howard. "The Relationship of School Characteristics to Student Writing Performance on an English Placement Test." *DAI* 47 (April 1987): 3689A.

Focuses on the institutional characteristics of schools and their potential contribution to developing writing ability. Findings suggest a need for further investigation.

1794. Sullivan, Frances J. "Negotiating Expectations: Writing and Reading Placement Tests." Paper presented at the CCCC Convention, Atlanta, March 1987. ERIC ED 279 022. 17 pages

Acknowledges contradictions in placement test writing. Describes a taxonomy of new, inferable, and old information used to evaluate the essays of 99 freshmen at Temple University.

1795. Tuman, Myron, and Thomas H. Miles. "Cloze Testing and the Evaluation of Writing: Some Preliminary Findings." *TETYC* 14 (February 1987): 10–17.

Cloze tests may have potential as placement instruments for writing courses, though skills tested and course requirements frequently differ. Predictive instruments may be inaccurate in individual cases.

1796. Valentino, Marilyn J. "Assessing the Writing Competence of High School Students: Lorain's EECAP, Its History and Implementation." Paper presented at the Annual Conference on Writing Assessment, Cleveland, April 1986. ERIC ED 275 005. 9 pages

Describes one community college's response to the Early English Composition

Assessment Program, established by the Ohio State Board of Education in 1983.

1797. Venezky, Richard L. *Literacy and the NAEP Reading Assessment.* Cambridge, Mass.: National Academy of Education, 1986. ERIC ED 279 702. 22 pages

Surveys literacy and literacy assessment, discusses the NAEP Young Adult Literacy Assessment, and makes four recommendations for the NAEP Reading Assessment.

1798. Venezky, Richard L., Carl F. Kaestle, and Andrew M. Sum. *The Subtle Danger: Reflections on the Literacy Abilities of America's Young Adults.* Princeton, N.J.: Center for the Assessment of Educational Progress, ETS, 1987. ERIC ED 284 164. 67 pages

Summarizes the findings of the NAEP Young Adult Literacy Assessment, drawing social and instructional conclusions. The complete report is available as ERIC ED 275 701.

See also 98, 1131, 1162, 1345, 1359, 1647

5.2 EVALUATION OF TEACHERS

1799. Baggott, James. "Reactions of Lecturers to Analysis Results of Student Ratings of Their Lecture Skills." *JMEd* 62 (June 1987): 491–496.

Multivariate analysis of student evaluations can yield specific feedback for teachers if they understand the analysis and its interpretation.

1800. Buckman, Lois, Teri Lesesne, and Bob Seney. "Just When You Thought It Was Safe to Go Back into the Classroom." *ET* 18 (Winter 1987): 39–40.

Concludes that the Texas teachers' appraisal system has destroyed the morale of teachers and has rewarded them on their "showmanship," not their performance.

1801. Irby, David M., Gerald M. Gillmore, and Paul G. Ramsey. "Factors Affecting Ratings

of Clinical Teachers by Medical Students and Residents." *JMEd* 62 (January 1987): 1–7.

Instructors who had extensive involvement with students received higher evaluations than those who only lectured. Academic rank did not affect the evaluation.

1802. Jones, Gregory R. "A Rhetorical Analysis of Teaching in the College Classroom." *DAI* 47 (March 1987): 3239A.

Four case studies suggest that rhetorical criticism has value in understanding observations and a possible use in improving teaching.

1803. Keeler, Carolyn Jane. "Observation of Classroom Climate: The Development of an Observational Tool." *DAI* 48 (October 1987): 792A.

Describes an assessment instrument that focuses on the teacher as a "climate setter" and is based on four areas of behavior: esprit, disengagement, hindrance, and intimacy.

1804. Kirby, W. N. "Getting There Together." *ET* 18 (Winter 1987): 30–33.

Discusses the Texas statewide teacher appraisal system and the challenges that face administrators.

1805. Norcini, John J. "The Answer Key as a Source of Error in Examinations of Professionals." *JEdM* 24 (Winter 1987): 321–331.

Studies variability in keys for written examinations of physicians and teachers. Recommends the aggregate method of key construction.

1806. Piazza, Carolyn L., and Cynthia Wallat. "Performance-Based Teacher Education: Steps toward Identifying Excellence in the Teaching of Writing." *EEd* 19 (February 1987): 44–50.

Provides guidelines for evaluating the teaching of writing.

1807. Schlessinger, June H. "Teacher Accountability and Educational Product Orientation:

Sweatshops in the 20s and Education in the 80s." *ET* 18 (Winter 1987): 18–23.

> Expresses concern that the education "industry" is changing schools into factories and teachers into sweatshop workers.

1808. Shafer, Robert E. "State Competency Testing for Teachers: Problems with Testing Grammar." Paper presented at the American Educational Research Association, San Francisco, April 1986. ERIC ED 277 724. 21 pages

> Describes interviews with examinees who expressed concern about the validity of questions concerning conventions of usage and grammar.

1809. Turner, Judith Axler. "Software for Teaching Given Little Credit in Tenure Reviews." *CHE* 33 (18 March 1987): 1, 20.

> While some schools approve of faculty members' designing software, most tenure committees interpret such work not as research but rather as service or teaching.

See also 992, 1759

5.3   EVALUATION OF PROGRAMS

1810. Battle, Mary Vroman. "Professional Evaluators' Insights Applied to Assisting Freshman English Programs." Paper pre-

sented at the CCCC Convention, Minneapolis, March 1985. ERIC ED 284 224. 17 pages

> Discusses the steps in and requirements for program evaluation.

1811. Davis, Barbara Gross, Michael Scriven, and Thomas Scriven. *The Evaluation of Composition Instruction.* New York: Teachers College Press, 1987. 256 pages

> An outgrowth of the Bay Area Writing Project, this guide provides an overview of the process of evaluating writing programs.

1812. Scharton, Maurice. "Establishing a Composition Testing Program: A Feasibility Report." *BADE* 86 (Spring 1986): 38–42.

> Favors testing programs. Explains their functions, costs, and benefits and examines an effective program at Illinois State University.

See also 901

5.4   OTHER

1813. McPhee, Robert D., and Austin Babrow. "Causal Modeling in Communication Research: Use, Disuse, Misuse." *ComM* 54 (December 1987): 344–366.

> Offers a set of standards for conducting and reporting causal modeling and a format for executing and evaluating path analyses.

Subject Index
Name Index

Subject Index

Numbers in the righthand column refer to sections and subsections (see Contents). For example, entries containing information on achievement tests appear in Section 5, Subsection 5.1 (Evaluation of Students). When the righthand column contains only a section number, information on the subject appears in several subsections. Entries addressing assignments in the classroom, for example, appear in several subsections of Section 4, depending on the kind of course for which the assignments are appropriate.

Name Index

This index lists authors for anthologized essays as well as authors and editors for main entries.